AF600385

APOSTOLIC ADMINISTRATORS

THE CATHOLIC UNIVERSITY OF AMERICA
CANON LAW STUDIES
No. 139

APOSTOLIC ADMINISTRATORS

AN HISTORICAL SYNOPSIS AND COMMENTARY

A DISSERTATION

Submitted to the Faculty of Canon Law of the Catholic University of America in Partial Fulfillment of the Requirements for the Degree of

DOCTOR OF CANON LAW

BY

REV. THOMAS JOSEPH McDONOUGH, A.B., J.C.L.
Priest of the Archdiocese of Philadelphia

THE CATHOLIC UNIVERSITY OF AMERICA PRESS
WASHINGTON, D. C.
1941

NIHIL OBSTAT:

EDUARDUS J. ROELKER, S.T.D., J.C.D.,
Censor Deputatus.

Washingtonii, D. C., die XVI Maii, 1940.

IMPRIMATUR:

D. CARD. DOUGHERTY,
Archiepiscopus Philadelphiensis.

Philadelphiae, Pa., XVIII Maii, 1941.

COPYRIGHT 1941, BY
THE CATHOLIC UNIVERSITY OF AMERICA

PRINTED IN THE UNITED STATES OF AMERICA
BY THE WATKINS PRINTING CO., BALTIMORE

TO MY MOTHER AND FATHER

TABLE OF CONTENTS

PART II—CANONICAL COMMENTARY

FOREWORD

The present dissertation is divided into two parts: 1) the historical synopsis, and 2) the canonical commentary. The historical synopsis endeavors to show that the office of "Apostolic Administrator", as mentioned in the Code of Canon Law, is of comparatively recent origin, receiving its first official recognition in the Constitution *Sapienti Consilio,* promulgated by Pope Pius X (1903-1914) on June 28, 1908. The modernity of the name, however, is no indication that the office itself does not antedate the year 1908. In reality, the office dates back to the fourth century of the Church when the present day Apostolic Administrator was exemplified and identified in the offices of the Interventor in Africa, the Visitator in Italy and France, and the Commendator in Spain. It is of paramount importance, therefore, to state at the outset that throughout this study particular emphasis will be placed on the office rather than on the name of the Apostolic Administrator.

With the appearance of the Decretal Law and the subsequent ancestors of the Cathedral Chapter and the Vicar Capitular the juridical ancestors of the Apostolic Administrator passed into desuetude. From the time of the Decretals until the time of the *Sapienti Consilio,* a number of different names are found all of which refer to the official who is at present designated by the title *Apostolic Administrator.* In comparing these different titles and the offices indicated by them it was necessary to examine the Decretal Laws of Pope Boniface VIII (1294-1303); the post-Tridentine Constitution *Immensa Dei* of Pope Sixtus V (1585-1590); and the Bull *Inscrutabili* of Pope Gregory XV (1621-1623). From these sources come the names *Administrator* and *Vicar Apostolic.* A comparison was then made between the present Apostolic Administrator and these two offices. More attention was given to the Vicar Apostolic, because this office had greater affinity to that of the present Apostolic Administrator. Examples are resorted to very often, both in the historical synopsis and the canonical commentary, because they provide the best means of ascertaining the various duties, rights, and privileges of the Apostolic Administrator.

The second part of the dissertation, the canonical commentary, is devoted to an analysis of the principles enunciated in canons 312-318. Throughout the canonical discussion repeated reference is made to the necessity of differentiating between a permanent and a temporary Apostolic administrator, and between a see that is *vacans* and one that is *plena*. It is believed that with this distinction clearly in mind many potential difficulties will be avoided.

Canon 315, in so far as it enumerates the rights, duties, and privileges of the permanent and temporary Apostolic Administrator, is the most important canon in this section; consequently it has demanded the most consideration.

There have not been many commentaries written on this particular office; from this, however, it must not be inferred that the office lacks importance. Furthermore, that a study of it is of practical value is evident from the fact that, even in the present times, owing to troubled conditions in various countries, the Sovereign Pontiff has on several occasions appointed men to this office.

The writer takes this occasion to express his sincere gratitude to His Eminence, Dennis Cardinal Doughtery, D.D., Archbishop of Philadelphia, for the opportunity he has given him to pursue graduate studies at the Catholic University of America. He wishes to acknowledge his indebtedness to the members of the Faculty of the School of Canon Law of the Catholic University for invaluable assistance and suggestions in the preparation of this manuscript.

PART I

HISTORICAL SYNOPSIS

CHAPTER I

PRELIMINARY NOTIONS

Residential bishops, as a rule, administer canonically erected dioceses. Upon the vacancy of an episcopal see, however, which may be due to the death, resignation, deprivation or transfer of the incumbent bishop,[1] the diocese is provisionally ruled by the cathedral chapter.[2] But in accordance with the legislation formulated by the Council of Trent,[3] and retained by the Code of Canon Law,[4] the cathedral chapter is commanded to elect a vicar capitular within eight days after the vacancy occurs. This vicar capitular possesses full administration of the vacant diocese until the Holy See rules otherwise.

In extraordinary circumstances, however, regardless of whether the bishop is in possession of his see, the Sovereign Pontiff is accustomed to commit the government of a diocese to an apostolic administrator.

According to the definition of the Code, an apostolic administrator is one to whom the Sovereign Pontiff, induced by grave and special reasons, entrusts the government of a canonically erected diocese *sede plena* or *sede vacante*. Such an appointment may be of temporary or permanent duration, depending on the stipulations expressed in the letter of appointment.[4a]

The reasons for appointing an apostolic administrator, as out-

[1] Canon 430.

[2] Canon 431.

[3] Sess. XXIV *de ref.*, c. 16—*Canones et Decreta Sacrosancti Oecumenici Concilii Tridentini* (Lipsiae: Bernhard Tauchnitz, 1863), pp. 166-167.

[4] Canon 432.

[4a] Canon 312; Cicognani, *Canon Law* (2. ed., Philadelphia: Dolphin Press, 1935), pp. 113-114; Ayrinhac, *Constitution of the Church in the New Code of Canon Law* (New York: Blase Benzinger & Co., Inc., 1925), p. 133; (Bachofen) Augustine, *A Commentary on Canon Law,* (Vol. II, 4. ed., St. Louis: B. Herder Book Co., 1923), II, 326; Woywod, *A Practical Commentary on the Code of Canon Law* (5. ed., 2 vol., New York: Joseph F. Wagner, 1939), I, p. 114, n. 233.

lined by Bouix, are as follows: misgovernment, old age, suspension from jurisdiction, summons to trial or to the Holy See, nonresidence, failure of the Chapter to elect a successor, lack of capacity on the part of the vicar capitular, a summons to Rome for the vicar capitular and, finally, the long vacancy of the see without prospect of any immediate election of an apostolic administrator. This list, however, is not exhaustive and other reasons may be deemed sufficient to warrant the appointment of an apostolic administrator.[5]

Vermeersch, following the definition contained in canon 312, divides the reasons for deputizing an apostolic administrator into two classes. The first division deals with the cases wherein the diocese is not actually deprived of its bishop, but in which the circumstances are such as to make him incapable of administering the affairs of the see. Such a see, technically known as *sedes plena,* can be supplied with an apostolic administrator when the bishop rules badly, when he is mentally ill, or when he is prevented from ruling by the civil authorities. The second division pertains to the cases wherein the see is vacant. Such a see is referred to as *sedes vacans,* and may be supplied with an apostolic administrator when there exist grave dissensions in the Chapter, when the vicar capitular elected by the Chapter is unworthy, or when political discord warrants the appointment of a temporary Administrator.[6]

The office of apostolic administrator under its present terminology does not date back to the early centuries of the Church. It received its title and form only a short time prior to the promulgation of the Code. It is indebted to the Code for its present stability. But in spite of the comparatively recent origin of the name and the consequent impossibility of tracing the present title back many centuries, this is not an apodictic argument for the total non-existence of the office indicated by the terminology of

[5] *Tractatus de Curia Romana* (Parisiis: Bourguet-Calas & Cie., 1895), p. 674.

[6] *Epitome Iuris Canonici* (6. ed., 3 vols., Romae: H. Dessain, 1936-1939), I, 331.

the Code. Certainly, the early centuries are not devoid of this office under similar terminology, for specific mention of *administrator* is found in the Decretals of Pope Boniface VIII (1294-1303).[7]

The first Pontiff to have recourse to the employment of the office of Administrator, as such, was Innocent IV (1243-1254), who in 1243 committed to Aegidius, the former Bishop of Foligno, the administration of the diocese of Nocera in Umbria which had been deprived of its bishop.[8]

From the time of the Christian era up to the time of Innocent IV there is no reference made to the name of Administrator. Nevertheless, some vestiges of this office existed prior to the thirteenth century. It is true that the name may not have antedated the year 1243, but the office itself existed, under various names, before that time. It is of paramount importance, therefore, to trace the development of these early offices which contain the elements of the office now held by an apostolic administrator.

Hence, Coronata says that, although the present name of apostolic administrator receives its greatest stability from the Code, there are vestiges of this office in the earlier days of the Church. In proof of this view he specifically cites the visitator as being a predecessor of the apostolic administrator.[9]

Maroto, lending support to this opinion, refers to the Admin-

[7] ". . . visitatorem seu administratorem eidem Ecclesiae licite poterit deputare."—c. 4, *de supplenda negligentia praelatorum* I, 8, in VI°.

[8] ". . . Aegidio Episcopo quondam Fulginati administrationem Ecclesiae Nucerinae pastore vacantis committit."—Berger, *Les Registres D'Innocent IV* (4 vols., Parisiis: E. Thorin, 1884-1897), I, n. 338; Potthast. *Regesta Pontificum Romanorum* (2 vols., Berolini: R. De Becker, 1874-1875), I, n. 11201.

[9] ". . . officium antiquum et iam occurrit in Decretalibus Bonifacii VIII, correspondetque officio Visitatorum. Etiam ante Bonifacium VIII officium Administratoris existebat, at non vocabatur Apostolicus Administrator quia non eligebatur a R. Pontifice."—*Institutiones Iuris Canonici ad Usum Utriusque Cleri et Scholarum* (5 vols., Taurini: Marietti, vols. I and II (2. ed., 1939), vol. III (1933), vol. IV (1935), vol. VI (1936)), I, 457, n. 379.

istrator in the early Church under various names depending on the various countries. The Administrator in Africa was called interventor or intercessor; in Spain, he was referred to as the commendator; and in Italy and France he was known as the visitator.[10]

In like manner, Thomassinus refers to the interventor, the intercessor, the commendator, and the visitator.[11]

Cance, in his treatment of apostolic administrator, refers to the fact that from the year 1298 the Sovereign Pontiff became the only person possessing the power to appoint apostolic administrators. Up to that time, he says, the administrators could also be created by episcopal authority; and were known as intercessors in Africa, visitators in France, and commendators in Spain.[12]

Thus, under the term *Administrateur Apostolique,* in the dictionary edited by Villien and Magnin, the historical ancestors of this office are outlined. The article traces the history of the apostolic administrator back to the commendator in Spain, the intercessor in Africa, and the visitator in Italy and France. One statement from it will illustrate this point:

> En Espagne, au VI siecle, l'episcopus commendator devait jour le même role que l'intercessor Africain ou

[10] "Qui administratores in Africa solebant vocari Interventores aut Intercessores, in Hispania Commendatores, In Italia Visitatores, et similiter in Gallia."—*Institutiones Iuris Canonici* (2 vols., vol. I (2. ed., Romae: Apud Commentarium Pro Religiosis 1921), vol. II (1. ed., Madrid: Editorial Del Corazion De Maria, 1919)), II, p. 80, n. 759.

[11] *Vetus et Nova Ecclesiae Disciplina circa Beneficia, et Beneficiarios* (3 vols., Lucae: L. Venturini, 1728), Part. III, Book II, c. 51, n. 2; II, III, c. 10, nn. 2-3. This manner of quoting Thomassinus will be observed throughout the work. The first figure refers to the part, the second to the book.

[12] "Jusqu'à l'epoque du Sexte (1298), on ne voit pas les papes intervenïr habituellement pour nommer des Administrateurs Apostoliques; il n'y avait jusqu'alors que des administrateurs creés par auctorité episcopale, appelés intercessores en Afrique, visitatores en Gaule, commendatores en Espagne. Boniface VIII reserva au Souverain Pontife ce genre de delegation.—*Le Code de Droit Canonique* (4. ed., 3 vols., Parisiis: J. Gabalda, 1930), I, 304.

> le visitator Gaulois (ce nom fut donné par le Concile de Riez à l'evêque charge d'administrer un diocese vacant).[13]

From these sources it can be readily ascertained that the office of apostolic administrator antedated the time of Pope Innocent IV by many centuries. Consequently, the task of demonstrating the development of each of these offices, decidedly similar to that of the apostolic administrator in effect, and differing only nominally, will be undertaken in the following pages.

[13] *Dictionnaire de Droit Canonique* (Paris, 1924), s.v. "Administrator Apostolique."

Chapter II

LEGISLATION TO THE TWELFTH CENTURY

Art. 1—Legislation of the First Four Centuries

With the exception of St. Ambrose's appointment of Constantinus as visitator to the Church of Imola, with the express command that he visit this diocese frequently, the first four centuries contain no reference to the office of administrator.[1] At first glance, this appointment effected by St. Ambrose resembles that of a person sent to perform merely the canonical visitation of the diocese. However, Nicolai is certain that this visitation was not for such a purpose, but connoted an appointment corresponding to the visitator whose office comprised the administration of the diocese until a new bishop was sent.[2]

Prescinding from this incident related in the letter of St. Ambrose, the first four centuries of the Church offer no example of the use of the visitator, the commendator, or the intercessor. In fine, there can be found no office which would correspond to the apostolic administrator. The transition from the early centuries to the period wherein may be observed the beginning of ecclesiastical offices, varying in name but agreeing in almost every other detail with the apostolic administrator, will be sketched in outline fashion by narrating the method of administering dioceses which had become vacant due either to the death or incapacity of its bishop. Such a background study is necessary, since it was as a result of abuses in the administration of vacant dioceses during the first four centuries that the offices of visitator, intercessor, and commendator were inaugurated.

[1] ". . . commendo tibi, fili, Ecclesiam quae est ad Forum Cornelii, quo eam de proximo intervisas frequentius, donec ei ordinetur episcopus."—*Ep. II*—Migne, *Patrologiae Cursus Completus,* Series Latina (221 vols., Parisiis, 1844-1864), XVI, 886-887; (hereafter this collection will be referred to as *MPL*).

[2] "Que certe visitationem regimen, et jurisdictionem importasse nemo dubitabit." — *Dissertatio Historico-Canonica de Episcopo Visitatore* (Romae: Franciscus Gonzaga, 1710), p. 55.

The Presbyterium

Priests from the earliest days of the Church acted in an auxiliary capacity to the bishops in the governing of the Church.[3] Hence, the priests and deacons possessed much power and gradually were formed into a group known as the presbyterium whose duties included aiding the bishop in the administration of the Church, as well as actually taking over the office of the bishop in the event of his death, absence, or excommunication. Besides this actual ruling in the absence of the bishop, Bingham says that the priests

> were considered as a sort of ecclesiastical senate, or council to the bishop, who scarce did anything of great weight and moment without asking their advice, and taking their consent, to give the greater force and authority to all public acts done in the Church.[4]

Indeed, many actions of the bishop were nullified if this body was not present to confirm them.[5]

Consequently, with the progress of time, the office of the *presbyterium* became stronger. This is very realistically portrayed in the second century when Marcion, the Bishop of Pontus, was excommunicated. After Marcion had made many futile attempts at reconciliation and failed, he finally appealed to the *presbyterium* in Rome. But Rome was in sympathy with the decision of the *presbyterium* at Pontus.[6]

[3] "Let the priests that rule well, be especially worthy of double honor: especially they that labor in the word and doctrine."—1 Tim., V, 17; Acts, XV.

[4] *The Antiquities of the Christian Church* (2 vols., London: Henry G. Bohn, 1850), I, 77.

[5] "Episcopus nullius causam audiat absque praesentia clericorum, alioquin irrita erit sententia Episcopi, nisi clericorum praesentia firmetur."—St. Ambrose, *De officio,—MPL,* III, 139; Thomassinus, *Vetus et Nova Ecclesiae Disciplina,* I, III, C. 7, nn. 2, 4.

[6] Jaeger, *The Administration of Vacant and Quasi-Vacant Dioceses in the United States,* The Catholic University of America, Canon Law Studies, n. 81 (Washington, D. C.: The Catholic University of America, 1931), p. 4; St. Epiphanius, *Adversus Haereses,* XLII, 2—*MPG,* XLI, 695.

Two events related by Jaeger are worthy of note. The first occurred during the Decian persecution in which Pope St. Fabian was martyred. Rome was in consequence without a Pope. The election of a successor to Fabian being untimely, the care and administration of Rome was submitted to the *presbyterium.*[7] The second case demonstrates the power of the *presbyterium* in the absence of a bishop. For when St. Cyprian, Bishop of Carthage (249-258), elected exile in preference to death, he wrote letters informing the *presbyterium* of Carthage about their duty during his absence.[8]

From the cases quoted above one can recognize the great extent of power accorded to the *presbyterium.* But quite naturally, too, such power ultimately served to effect the downfall and subsequent elimination of the *presbyterium.* This was due to the fact that often, when this power of administering and ruling the diocese was committed to the *presbyterium,* great abuses followed. The possessions of the absent bishop were frequently plundered by members of the *presbyterium.* Eventually, these abuses became so rampant that some form of new discipline was imperative to extirpate them. The outcome of the legislation to curtail these scandalous plunderings resulted in the origin of the new offices of interventor, visitator, and commendator. These new offices are historical ancestors of the apostolic administrator. In substantiation of this assertion, each one of these offices will be analyzed and compared with the apostolic administrator to show their absolute agreement.

Art. 2—The Interventor or Intercessor in Africa

The advent of Donatism in the African Church occasioned the vacancy of many episcopal sees. Very often the resident bishops

[7] ". . . post excessum nobilissimae memoriae viri Fabiani, nondum est episcopus propter rerum et temporum difficultates constitutus."—Baronius, *Annales Ecclesiastici* (37 vols., Barri-Ducis, 1864-1883), III, 4-5; "Et cum incumbat nobis, qui videmur praepositi esse, et vice pastoris, custodire gregem. . . ."—*MPL,* IV, 224.

[8] *Ep. IV—MPL,* IV, 230-232.

were forced to flee from their respective dioceses in order to escape the barbaric treatment inflicted by the adherents of the schism. In addition to this situation, it sometimes happened that when a bishop died the priests and people were either thwarted in the election of a successor, or else neglected this important duty. The Donatists took every opportunity to fill these vacant dioceses with one of their own men, and even threatened with death those who were instrumental in choosing a Catholic bishop. Such conditions continued until at one time the number of vacant Catholic sees reached the well nigh incredible number of sixty.[9] These crises called for a remedy, and one was eventually found by the creation of the office of interventor or intercessor.

Du Cange defines an "Interventor" as one who administers a vacant episcopal see until a proper bishop has been elected.[10] Bingham says,

> There is one appellation more given to some Bishops in the African Councils which must here be taken notice of . . . which is the name of intercessor and interventor: a title given to some bishops upon the account of a pro-tempore office which was sometimes committed to them.[11]

In designating these interventors, it was the practice either of the Metropolitan or of the Provincial Council to appoint persons whom they believed capable of undertaking the responsibility. The person designated was, in most instances, one of the neighboring bishops who came into the vacant diocese first to conduct the

[9] ". . . for in Africa, at the time of the collation of Carthage, there were no less than threescore bishoprics void at one time, which was above an eighth part of the whole . . ."—Bingham, *The Antiquities of the Christian Church, Tom.* I, lib. II, ch. XI, par. 3.

[10] "Interventores, dicti, qui Sede Vacante episcopatum administrabant, donec proprius aliquis electus esset."—*Glossarium ad Scriptores Mediae et Infimae Latinitatis* (6 vols., Parisiis: C. Osmont, 1733-1736), s.v. "Interventor."

[11] *The Antiquities of the Christian Church,* Tom. I, Lib. II, ch. XV; Since the names interventor and intercessor are synonymous it is superfluous to mention the two simultaneously. Hereafter, only the name interventor will be used.

funeral of the deceased bishop, then to administer the affairs of the diocese, and finally to effect a hasty election of the new bishop.[12] Bingham, therefore, in reference to the office of interventor, states that in the African Church upon the vacancy of a bishopric, it was usual for the primate to appoint one of the provincial bishops to be a quasi-procurator of the diocese: partly to take care of the vacant see, and partly to promote and effect the speedy election of a new bishop.[13] Saint Augustine was one of the initial exponents of this means of administering a vacant diocese.[14]

The purposes of this office was manifestly and primarily to promote the good of the Church and to prevent Catholic sees from being administered by bishops consecrated and appointed by the Donatists. However, the office of interventor, like the *presbyterium* it supplanted, was subjected to abuses. The interventors had many opportunities to ingratiate themselves with the people, and were, therefore, able to promote their own personal interests. This was usually accomplished by deliberately postponing the appointment of a bishop to the see longer than was necessary, or, if the diocese happened to be a wealthier and better one than their own, by having themselves elected to it. Most remarkably,

[12] V Council of Carthage (401), c. 8—Mansi, *Sacrorum Conciliorum Nova et Amplissima Collectio* (53 vols., Parisiis, 1901-1927), III, 970; (hereafter this collection will be referred to as Mansi); Harduin, *Acta Conciliorum et Epistolae Decretales ac Constitutiones Summorum Pontificum* (12 vols., Parisiis, 1715), I, 987; (hereafter this collection will be referred to as Harduin).

[13] *The Antiquities of the Christian Church,* Tom. I, lib. II, ch. XV.

[14] "Narravit etiam in ipsa schismatica novitate majores suos, cum cogitarent culpam Caeciliani, ne schisma fieret, . . . dedisse quemdam interventorem populo suae communionis apud Carthaginem constituto, antequam Majorinus adversus Caecilianum ordinaretur."—Ep. XLIV—*MPL* XXXIII, 177; ". . . contra quam paucissimis Afris partis suae primo Interventores adventitios furtim longeque mittebant . . . donec deceptae plebeculae quasi proprios Episcopos ordinarent."—*De Unico Baptismo contra Petilianum*—*MPL* XLIII, 610. In each of these instances a footnote was cited after the words "*interventorem*" and *Interventores*" explaining that such persons administered a diocese "*sede vacante.*"

then, the office which had been established to eliminate the seizure of Catholic sees by the Donatists became itself the object of many abuses.[15] Obviously, it became imperative once again to curtail such abuses, and the following measures, briefly summarized by Bingham, were adopted:

> To obviate any such designs the African fathers in the fifth Council of Carthage made a decree, that no intercessor should continue in his office for above a year; but if he did not procure a new bishop to be chosen in that time, another intercessor should be sent in his room; and the more effectually to cut off all abuses and prevent corruption, they enacted it also by law, that no intercessor should be capable of succeeding himself in the vacant see, whatever motions or solicitations were made by the people in his behalf.[16]

Yet, notwithstanding all the care and diligence exercised by the Church in filling vacant sees, it sometimes happened that the election of a bishop was deferred for a much longer time than stipulated by the V Council of Carthage (401). Oftentimes the fault was with the people who were either negligent, or else quite satisfied with the interventors and would not admit a new bishop. That is why the Council of Macriana (c. 419) took notice of this

[15] "Dans l'Eglise d'afrique, pendant le quartrieme et le cinquieme siecle, ce nom fut donné aux evêque administrateurs d'un eveche vacant. C'etait le primat qui le nommait pour gouverner le diocese et pour procurer l'election d'un nouvel evêque. Mais cette commission donna lieu a deux abus; le premier fut que ces intercesseurs profitaient de l'occasion pour gagner la faveur du peuple et du clerge, . . .; le second, qu'ils faisaient quelquefois durer longtemps la vacance, pour leur profit particulier."—Andre, *Cours Alphabetique et Methodique de Droit Canon* (Paris, 1844), s.v. "Intercesseur."

[16] *The Antiquities of the Christian Church,* Tom. I, lib. II, ch. XV; c. 8, "Item constitutum est, ut nulli intercessori licitum sit Cathedram cui intercessor datus est, quibuslibet populorum studiis vel seditionibus retinere, sed dare operam, ut inter annum eisdem episcopum provideat. Quod si neglexerit, anno exempto, intercessor aliud tribuatur."—Mansi, III, 970; Harduin, I, 987; Bruns, *Canones Apostolorum et Conciliorum Saeculorum IV, V, VI, VII* (2 vols., Berolini: G. Reimeri, 1839), I, 174, n. 74.

dilatory practice in some of the African Provinces and condemned it in a canon ordering the interventors to be removed, and the negligent Churches to continue without them until they sought a bishop of their own.[17]

The conclusions to be drawn from this analysis of the office of interventor, who was deputized by the Metropolitan or by the Provincial Council to administer vacant dioceses in the African Church and effect the election of a new bishop, will serve to illustrate the similarity of this office with the present day apostolic administrators. This similarity may be more clearly apprehended by a parallel comparison of the offices.

First, the object of the appointment; in both the offices the appointee is sent to a canonically erected diocese.

Second, the consideration of the terms of the two offices: the apostolic administrator may be sent *ad tempus* or *in perpetuum;* while at first there was no definite time attached to the office of interventor, it became necessary, through the growth of abuses, to limit the term of this office to one year.[18]

Third, the causes which demand the installation of an interventor or of an apostolic administrator: the usual causes necessitating the sending of an interventor were the death of the bishop, his absence, or finally, the capture of the bishop by enemies of the Church. The causes requiring the deputizing of an apostolic administrator are more numerous, but include the usual three that applied to an interventor.

Fourth, the faculties and duties attached to the offices of interventor and apostolic administrator: usually the letter of appointment outlined what the particular interventor was permitted to do. The primary duties were to establish peace and harmony in the vacant diocese and to preside over the election of a new bishop. From the canons of the Council of Macriana previously referred to, it appears that this assignment was given for the

[17] "Ut ad eligendum Episcopum sufficiat matricis arbitrium. Ut Interventores Episcopi conveniant plebes quae Episcopum non habent, ut Episcopum accipiant. Quod si accipere neglexerint remoto Interventore sic remaneant quamdiu sibi Episcopum quaerant."—Harduin, I, 1251.

[18] *V Council of Carthage* (401), c. 8—Mansi, III, 970.

purpose of having the appointee rule the diocese in the same capacity as the former bishop. At the same time, it must be remembered that these interventors were neighboring bishops; and this makes the assumption that they possessed the same power in the diocese where they substituted as they did in their own respective diocese all the more plausible. Although the apostolic administrator received his powers, duties, and privileges from the letter of appointment, he now obtains his faculties from the Code. However, any restriction or extension of these faculties is mentioned in the letter of appointment.

Fifth, by reason of the appointer: in this detail of comparison, the two offices seem to be at variance; for the interventor was appointed by the Metropolitan or by the Provincial Council,[19] while, on the other hand, the apostolic administrator is commissioned solely by the Sovereign Pontiff.[20] However, Maroto states that the Sovereign Pontiff very frequently sent visitators to the Italian and Frankish Provinces.[21]

From these texts it may be concluded that outside the Italian and Frankish Provinces it was the usual procedure for the Metropolitan to appoint the interventors. Nevertheless, even though this deputation appeared to be a special prerogative of the Metropolitans, such was not the case. Unquestionably the Sovereign Pontiff had the power to send interventors to vacant sees, but he refrained from using it. For it often happened, in the early centuries of the Church, that although bishops generally acknowledged the primacy of Peter in jurisdiction as well as honor, they were, nevertheless, loath to have Rome intervene in the ruling

[19] "Designatio administratorum solebat fieri maxime in Africa a Metropolitano vel ab eiusdem provinciae Episcopis: . . ."—Maroto. *Institutiones Iuris Canonici,* II, p. 81, n. 759: Bingham, *The Antiquities of the Christian Church,* Tom. I, lib. II, ch. XV: Cance, *Le Code de Droit Canonique,* I, 304: Andre, *Cours Alphabetique et Methodique de Droit Canon,* s.v. "Intercesseur."

[20] Canon 312.

[21] ". . . at in Italia saepius est facta ab Ipso Romano Pontifice qui et aliquando ad Galliae quoque dioceses misit Visitatores."—*Institutiones Iuris Canonici,* II, 81, n. 759.

and affairs of their diocese. One example of this is St. Cyprian's well known resistance to the Sovereign Pontiff's intervention in the affairs of his diocese.[22]

Hence, this difference; namely, that one received his appointment from the Metropolitan and the other from the Sovereign Pontiff, is not so important when the different periods of time are taken into consideration. Often in the early centuries of the Church, and even up to the time of Pope Boniface VIII-(1294-1303), the practice of permitting bishops to appoint administrators was prevalent outside the Italian Province. This practice was curtailed only by the pronouncement of Pope Boniface VIII.[23]

In conclusion, although the office of Interventor does not coincide so well as that of the Visitator with the office of apostolic administrator, there is, however, a remarkable similarity between these two offices. The interventor, then is quiet evidently an ancestor of the Apostolic Administrator.

Art. 3—The Visitator In Italy

Almost simultaneously with the appearance of the interventor in Africa the office of the visitator was inaugurated in Europe. A visitator, according to Du Cange, was a bishop sent by the Metropolitan or the Sovereign Pontiff to perform the episcopal duties upon the death, suspension or removal of the resident bishop. This appointment was to last until a new bishop

[22] "Qua in re, nec nos vim cuiquam facimus aut legem damus, cum habeat in Ecclesiae administratione voluntatis suae arbitrium liberum unusquisque praepositus, rationem actus sui Domino redditurus."—*Ep. 72* —*MPL,* III, 1050.

[23] C. 42, *de electione et electi potestate,* I, 6, in VI°; c. 4, de supplenda *negligentia praelatorum,* I, 8, in VI°; "Avant l'époque du Sexte (1298) nous ne voyons pas les papes intervenir d'une façon habituelle pour deleguer un évêque chargé d'administrer temporariment un diocese dont il n'est pas le titularie: au contraire avec Boniface VIII ce genre de delegation est reservé exclusivement au souverain pontife et soustrait au metropolitan ou à l'episcopat provincial auxquels il appartenait auparavant en regle generale."—Villien-Magnin, *Dictionnaire de Droit Canonique,* s.v. "Administrateur Apostolique."

had been elected under the supervision of the visitator.[24]

From the definition alone the striking resemblance of this office to that of the apostolic administrator can be seen. Yet, to appreciate this affinity, it is necessary to examine the development of this office, which for many centuries constituted the ordinary way of administering a see that had become vacant through the absence, death, or exile of the resident bishop. For this office did not reach the zenith of its development until the Pontificate of Gregory the Great (590-604). This Pope frequently appointed men to this office throughout the Roman and Sicilian dioceses, as well as in the Province of Gaul.

The first record of this office appears in the Council of Riez held in Gaul in 439.[25] But even though this office evidently existed prior to the time of Pope Gregory, it is to this Pontiff that we are indebted for many examples illustrating the practical use, extension, and purpose of the visitator.

Pope St. Gregory the Great, who ruled in the chair of St. Peter during the last decade of the sixth century and for the first four years of the seventh, had many occasions for sending visitators to administer both the spiritual and temporal welfare of dioceses. These appointments were not restricted to those dioceses where the resident bishop had died, but were frequently utilized in those sees where the bishop, though resident, had been deemed incapable or unworthy of administering the affairs of the diocese, and also where, because of ill health, absence, capture by an enemy, summons to Rome, or obligation to perform penance, the bishops were actually unable to exercise their jurisdiction.

The letters of Pope Gregory are replete with incidents portray-

[24] "Visitator est episcopus qui in locum alterius episcopi demortui, vel propter crimen a communione suspensi, aut remoti, a metropolitano, vel Summo Pontifice, mittebatur ad obeunda in ea diocesi Episcopalia munera, donec alius Episcopus ordinaretur, cujus electioni intererat."—*Glossarium,* s.v. "Visitator."

[25] C. 6—Bruns, *Canones Apostolorum et Conciliorum,* II, 120; Harduin, I, 1750; Hefele-Leclercq, *Histore des Conciles* (10 vols., in 19, Parisiis, 1907-1938), II, part I, 429.

ing the above mentioned situations, and the remedy in each case was invariably the commissioning of a visitator to administer the welfare of the see in question until other adjustments could be effected. Consequently, the next part of this work will be devoted to the examination of the most pertinent letters of Pope Gregory in an effort to show the remarkable similarity of the Gregorian Visitator to the apostolic administrator. The conclusions drawn from these letters will manifest the similarities existing between the two offices, even in minute details.

A) *Through The Death of a Bishop*

Under this heading letters containing the appointment of a visitator to a diocese left vacant by the death of its bishop will be grouped. Usually this deputation was made when it was feared that a long interval would occur before the election of a new bishop.

1) Pope Gregory in a letter addressed to the clergy and people of Bevagna mourned the loss of their bishop. Then he enjoined them to come to a prompt and conscientious election of a successor. In the interim, however, he entrusted the care of the see to Honoratius, a visitator.[26]

2) Leo, a Bishop of Corsica, was sent by Pope Gregory as visitator to the Church of Sagone. The letter of appointment gave Leo permission to ordain priests and deacons of this diocese—a concession made in view of the fact that the see had been vacant for several years and the immediate need of priests was urgent.[27]

3) Barbarus, the Bishop of Benevento, was appointed by Pope Gregory to administer the affairs of the diocese of Orte. This letter, likewise, contained permission to ordain clerics, provided the good of the diocese warranted it.[28]

[26] Quod non providentes ne hoc vestrae contingere possit Ecclesiae, ejus curam utilitatemque Honorato presbytero ad praesens elegimus quatenus res utilitatesque ecclesiae per eum et procurari valeant, et modis omnibus custodiri."—*Lib. I, Ep. LXXXI—MPL,* LXXVII, 532.

[27] *Lib. I, Ep. LXXVIII—MPL,* LXXVII, 532.

[28] "Hoc tamen scitote, quia ei ordinandi presbyteros ac diaconos, si

4) Agnellus, the Bishop of Terracina, was appointed visitator to the Church of Formia.[29]

5) The above mentioned Barbarus, the Bishop of Benevento, was sent later as visitator to the diocese of Palermo left vacant by the death of Bishop Victor. Afterwards the Pontiff sent a letter to the people of Palermo reminding them of the obedience and allegiance they owed Barbarus.[30]

This group of letters, indicating administration by visitators, pertains to dioceses vacated by death of the bishop. But from this it is not to be deduced that this was the only occasion for deputizing a visitator. On the contrary, the letters reveal that other circumstances also prompted him to send visitators to administer vacant or quasi-vacant dioceses. However, it must be admitted that the death of the resident bishop did furnish more opportunities and occasions for such actions, since Gregory insisted upon such appointments for vacant dioceses which might otherwise suffer harm through a long delay in the election of a successor.

B) *Through Inability Because of Sickness*

Among the letters of Gregory is one addressed to Anatolius, a Deacon at Constantinople, informing him that even though John, the Bishop of Achrida, was severely ill and desirous of having someone put in his place, yet such a procedure would be contrary to the Canons which forbade removal of John. Gregory, however, proposes that John, while retaining his office, select some reliable person and entrust to him the administration of the see.[31]

C) *Through Absence Occasioned By Illness*

A letter addressed to Leontius, Bishop of Urbino, an Archdiocese of Italy, relates how Castor, the Bishop of Rimini, was sick and therefore prevented from returning to his own see and

necesse fuerit, quos dignos ad hoc officium invenire potuerit, dedimus licentiam . . ."—*Lib. IV, Ep. XLI—MPL,* LXXVII, 716-717.

29 *Lib. VII, Ep. XVI—MPL,* LXXVII, 870.

30 *Lib. XIII, Eps. XII, XIV—MPL,* LXXVII, 1268-1269.

31 "Aegrotanti invito non succeditur, accedere potest alius, qui loco ipsius regat."—*Lib. XI, Ep. XLVII—MPL,* LXXVII, 1167.

handling its active administration. Pope Gregory, in consideration of this fact, deemed it imperative to send a visitator to the diocese of Rimini to take active charge of the spiritual and temporal welfare of the Church and thus prevent any harm befalling it through the prolonged absence of Castor. The visitator designated by Gregory was Leontius.[32] The following letter (book III, letter XXV) is addressed to the people of Rimini wherein Gregory orders them to be obedient to Leontius, the visitator, in all things, ". . . *vos ergo ita ei in omnibus obedite.*"

D) *Through Deposition of a Bishop*

Writing to the clergy, nobles, and people of Naples, Pope Gregory related in great detail how Demetrius, the Bishop of Naples, being involved in certain crimes and scandals was eventually deposed. Therefore, lest the Church should suffer, the Pope admonished the people and clergy that neither delay nor discord should prevent the prompt election of a new bishop.[33] Writing shortly afterwards to Paul, the Bishop of Nepi, he commissioned him to administer the vacant see of Naples. This quick change of mind can be attributed to the partisan feeling then existing in Naples which made it practically impossible to elect a successor to Demetrius without prejudices intervening. In this letter the Pope disregarded the former letter wherein he had instructed the clergy and people of Naples to effect a prompt election of a new bishop, and instead deputized Paul to be visitator. This appointment of Paul's was a temporary one.[34]

Many more letters could be quoted which contain references to the appointing of visitators, but it seems more advisable to indicate the letters of Gregory wherein they can be found rather than to discuss each one individually.[35]

[32] "Et quia nunc ad suam Ecclesiam non valet remeare, . . . quidquid autem tibi visum fuerit pro utilitatibus ejusdem Ecclesiae ordinare, habebis modis omnibus ex nostra permissione licentiam."—*Lib. III, Ep. XXIV--MPL,* LXXVII, 622.

[33] *Lib. II, Ep. VI—MPL,* LXXVII, 542.

[34] *Lib. II, Ep. X—MPL,* LXXVII, 546-547; *Lib. II, Ep. XV—MPL,* LXXVII, 550-551.

[35] *Lib. I, Eps. XV, XIX, LI, LXXVI, LXXXVIII; Lib. II, Eps.*

Summarily, then, it may be concluded that although the vacancy of a diocese through the death of the resident bishop furnished the reason for the vast majority of appointments of the visitators by Pope Gregory, it was not the only motive for their deputation. On the contrary, the adaptability of this office to a variety of circumstances was clearly shown when this Pontiff sent visitators to administer sees where the bishop was deposed, suspended, or in any other way rendered incapable of administering the affairs of his diocese.

In comparing the office of visitator, as used by Pope Gregory, with the apostolic administartor, a striking parallel is found, and it can be claimed with assurance that the visitator is indubitably an ancestor of the apostolic administrator.

First, canon 312 states that the apostolic administrator is appointed by the Sovereign Pontiff. Quite obviously this requisite is identified in the visitator of Pope Gregory, since in all the incidents cited the Pontiff himself indicated the visitator by name.

Second, the canon specifies that the appointment is made to a canonically erected diocese. Likewise this requisite is verified in the appointments of St. Gregory.

Third, the canon stipulates that the appointment may be made to a diocese *sede plena* or *sede vacante.* The appointments of Pope Gregory were made both to dioceses in which the bishop was ill and unable to administer and which thus existed ***sede plena,*** and to dioceses in which bishop had died and which thus existed ***sede vacante.***

Fourth, the appointment of an apostolic administrator stipulates that the duration of the office is either permanent or temporary. In most of the deputations of visitators commissioned by Pope Gregory the Great the time was usually expressed by the terms, *ad praesens,* or *ad beneplacitum nostrum.* But usually the time alloted by Gregory was expressed in the words—"Until a new bishop is chosen."

Fifth, the causes for sending an apostolic administrator mostly

XXXVI, XXXVIII; Lib. IV, Ep. XX; Lib. V, Ep. XXI; Lib. VII, Ep. XCI.

concern the good of the Church and the welfare of the souls in a particular diocese. These causes also prompted the sending of a visitator in the early centuries of the Church. The causes for the appointment of a visitator in those days corresponds beyond doubt to those usually present now for the appointment of an apostolic administrator.

Conclusively, then, these two offices possess a great similarity, easily ascertained by a comparative analysis, and, since in all the essentials they are so nearly identical, the terms apostolic administrator and visitator practically refer to the same institute.

Art. 4—The Visitator in France

The same discipline which was in force in Italy, particularly during the Pontificate of Gregory the Great (590-604), was utilized in France in those dioceses where episcopal sees were vacant. Although the visitator in France possessed less power and stability than the Gregorian visitator, nevertheless, this office existed there from the time of the Council of Riez (439). From this time it became the rather common practice throughout the whole of Gaul to send visitators to sees left vacant by the death of their resident bishops. Such a custom resulted from the frequent plunderings of the deceased bishop's posessions made by both the priests and the laity.[36]

At the Council of Reiz (439) legislation was enacted in an effort to eliminate such abuses. Canons 6 and 7 are particularly relevant. These two canons decree that no one, except the bishop of the neighboring Church, could enter the vacant see and attend to the funeral arrangements or any other matter that demanded consideration. His stay in the deceased bishop's see was limited to seven days, after which he was to return to his own diocese, and no one else was to enter the vacant see without the permission of the Metropolitan.[37]

[36] Villien-Magnin, *Dictionnaire de Droit Canonique*, s.v. "Administrateur Apostolique."

[37] C. 6: "Nequis ad eam Ecclesiae, quae Episcopum perdidisset, nisi vicinae Ecclesiae Episcopus exequiarum tempore accederet, qui Visitatoris

Even though the office of the visitator as it existed in France does not exactly coincide with that of the Gregorian visitator, it does, nevertheless, illustrate that France in the fifth century was acquainted with such an ecclesiastical official whose primary duty it was to direct the funerals of the deceased bishop of the neighboring diocese. The office of the visitator was obviously of short duration. In most instances the neighboring bishop acted under the direction and guidance of the Metropolitan.[38]

Despite this early conception of the visitator in France as appointed by the Metropolitan, there are found visitators commissioned by different Pontiffs who possessed all the powers and duties formerly accorded by Pope Gregory. Though most of the incidents connected with the mission of a visitator in fifth century France are concerned only with the sees that were vacant through the death of their resident bishops, some, however, were commissioned by Sovereign Pontiffs for such reasons as the following: apostasy of the resident bishop, his recall to Rome or unjust removal from office.

Pope John II (532-535) deputized Caesarius the Archbishop of Arles, to appoint a visitator to the see of Riez. The diocese of Riez had been made vacant through the deposition of Bishop Contumeliosus. The Pontiff in a letter to the bishops of France related how Contumeliosus, having been deposed on account of his crime, was committed to a monastery to perform penance. In the meantime John does not wish to expose Riez to any harm, and so commands Caesar to appoint a visitator.[39] Finally, the Pope reminds the priests of their obligation to obey the visitator until

vice . . ."—Bruns, *Canones Apostolorum et Concilorum,* II, 120; Harduin, I, 1750; C. 7: "Haec autem omnia exequiarum tempore usque ad septimum defuncti diem agat . . ."—Bruns, *op. cit.,* II, 120; Harduin, I, 1750; Mansi, V, 1003-1004; Villien-Magnin, *Dictionnaire de Droit Canonique,* s.v. "Administrateur Apostolique."

[38] Thomassinus, *Vetus et Nova Ecclesiae Disciplina,* II, II, c. 3, n. 6.

[39] "In cujus locum visitatorem constituite, donec proprium Ecclesia, quae evacuata est ejus sacerdotio merere valeat."—*Mansi,* VIII, 807.

a proper bishop was appointed.[40] This visitator, however, was not given the permission to ordain clerics.[41]

This same Pontiff, in a letter addressed to the Bishops of Gaul, orders them to fill any vacant Church through the appointment of visitators, but likewise denied these the permission to ordain clerics.[42]

Pope Zachary (741-752) appointed St. Boniface, a legate of the Holy See, to administer the see of Rheims. This appointment was occasioned when Rigobertus, the Bishop of Rheims, was unjustly deprived of his see through the machinations of Milo.[43]

Pope Adrian II (867-872) appointed Hincmar, the Archbishop of Rheims, as visitator to the diocese of Lyons. In his letter the Pope told Hincmar, the Archbishop of Rheims, that he had summoned his nephew, Hincmar, the Bishop of Lyons, to Rome. After these introductory remarks he informed the Archbishop that he was to administer the diocese of Lyons while his nephew was in Rome. This administration, however, was temporary, commencing when the nephew left for Rome and terminating with his return to his diocese. This letter contained certain directions which Hincmar, the Archbishop of Rheims, was to follow in the care and administration of the diocese of Lyons.[44]

40 "Omnem hanc vero sollicitudinem Caesario Fratri et coepiscopo nostro injungimus, ad cujus curam cuncta quae necesse sint pertinere censuimus." —Baronius, *Annales Ecclesiastici*, IX, 456.

41 "ut nihil de ordinibus clericorum . . . presumat."—*loc. cit.*

42 "Ne ejus Ecclesia destituta videatur, in ejus locum Visitatorem dari praesenti auctoritate decernimus, qui a se ita noverit, omnia exhibenda, ut nihil de ordinibus clericorum, nihil de Ecclesiastica facultate praesumat; sed ea quae ad sacrosancta mysteria pertinent exequatur . . ."—Baronius, *Annales Ecclesiastici*, VII, 690.

43 "Quamdiu ejecto sine ullo crimine ab ea suo Pontifice Rigoberto, violentia tyranni Milonis, tempore Caroli Principis, Pastore vacans, Bonifacio Apostolicae Sedis legato aliquandiu, sicut & Ecclesia Trivirensis, commissa fuit."—Thomassinus, *Vetus et Nova Ecclesiae Disciplina*, II, III, c. 13, n. 14; Hermes, *Dissertatio Historico-Canonica de Capitulo Sede Vacante vel Impedita et de Vicario Capitulari* (Lovanii, 1873), p. 33.

44 "Quicunque igitur a tempore quo Roman venire coeperit usque in id quo, Christo duce, ad propria remeaverit, in quibuslibet rebus illius

The transfer of Actardus from the Bishopric of Nantes to the Archbishopric of Tours by Pope Adrian II provides another example of direct Papal intervention in the appointment of a visitator. The letter of appointment contained the stipulation that he was to retain the administration of the See of Nantes until the election of its own proper bishop. During this administration he still retained all the rights and powers which he enjoyed as the Bishop of Nantes.[45]

Pope JohnVIII (872-882), in a letter addressed to the clergy and the people of the Church of Bourges, informs them that he had appointed Frotärius, the Archbishop of Bordeaux, to administer their see. This appointment was not a permanent one, for the letter stated that Frotarius had been forced to abandon his own see when the pagans overran his territory. As soon as the pagans left the territory of Bordeaux, Bishop Frotarius was to return there to resume his duties. The Pontiff states that the appointment of Frotarius to Bourges was made primarily to keep the Bishop of Bordeaux active.[46]

The preceding examples of the appointment of a visitator to attend to the spiritual and temporal welfare of a canonically erected diocese present convincing evidence of the similarity between this office and that of the present day apostolic administrator. It is true that the restrictions of the Council of Riez (439)

Eccclesiae quodlibet operatus fuerit detrimentum, quoniam episcopatum ejus sanctitati tuae specialiter post regem servandu committimus tandiu se noverit sacramento corporis et sanguinis Domini fore privandum, quamdiu sanctae Lugdunensi Ecclesiae . . ."—*MPL, CXXII,* 1280-1281.

[45] "Adrianus II Actardo in Metropolin Turonensem translato, Nannetensem ei episcopatum commendatum reliquit, donec proprius ibi eligi posset episcopus."—Thomassinus, *Vetus et Nova Ecclesiae Disciplina,* II, III, c. 13, n. 14; "Ita tamen hoc permittentes, ut Nanneticae Ecclesiae, cui fuerat ordinatus, in eo quod remansit, quod destructa habetur, jura potestatemve nullo modo subtrahamus."—*Ep.* 38—*MPL, CXXII,* 1311-1312.

[46] ". . . idoneum esse comperimus, ne talis tantusque vir otio, quo prodesse aliis valeat, minime vacat, ejusdem sanctae Bituricensis Ecclesiae cui subestis, ei pastoralem curam apostolica auctoritate committimus . . ." —*Ep. XXXVI—MPL,* CXXII, 690.

on the powers of the visitator diminish somewhat the resemblance between these officials and the visitator appointed by Pope Gregory the Great; nevertheless, the examples contained in the letters of the Pontiffs John II, Zachary, Adrian II and John VIII undoubtedly bear an identity in every detail to the visitor of Gregory, and, consequently, in great part also, to the apostolic administrator.

First, the appointment of the apostolic administrator is effected by the Sovereign Pontiff. This requisite is precisely realized in those visitators sent to France by the Roman Pontiffs.

Second, the appointment of both is made to a canonically erected diocese.

Third, the apostolic administrator is sent to a diocese either *in perpetuum* or *ad tempus.* In most of the instances in which a Pontiff sent a visitator to France the arrangement was *ad tempus.*

Fourth, the appointment of an Apostolic administrator to a diocese requires a grave cause. So, too, only serious reasons prompted the commissioning of the visitator to France, such as: the deposition of a bishop, his recall to Rome, the temporary appointment to another diocese of a bishop who has been constrained to leave his own see due to invasion of the infidels.

Fifth, the faculties of the apostolic administrator are obtained from the Code of Canon Law and from the letter of appointment. However, the faculties, duties, and privileges of the visitator sent to France were usually stipulated in the letter of appointment.

It may be inferred, then, that these appointments made in France by the Pontiffs may be placed in the same category as the appointment of visitators made by Gregory the Great, and ultimately these visitators may be referred to as being the historical ancestors of the apostolic administrator.

Art. 5—The Commendator in Spain

As Italy and France had employed the visitator to administer vacant dioceses, so Spain had a similar office termed the *commendator.* Although this official does not possess so clear a resemblance to the apostolic administrator as the visitator, he does nevertheless, represent in the Spanish Church the one who ordinarily was designated to rule over a vacant diocese.

Du Cange defines a commendator as one to whom was committed the care and administration of a vacant episcopal see. This appointee was usually the neighboring bishop.[47] According to Maroto, he was the recipient of an ecclesiastical benefice over which he was to exercise care and administration.[48]

The origin of this office dates back to the Council of Valencia (524) which refers to the bishop "Commendator" as the administrator of a vacant diocese.[49] Though in the beginning the office of commendator was occupied exclusively by the neighboring bishops whose sole duty was simply to arrange and supervise the funeral services of the deceased bishops, the passing years, however, witnessed a great change, and the original title began to assume new meanings.

In time the term commendator came to designate one who administered either two dioceses simultaneously, or one diocese and an abbey. Such a radical change had its foundation in the existing dangers of the time. The invasion of Spain by the Saracens had left many dioceses without a bishop. In these circumstances, the administration of the vacant sees was not committed to a new bishop, but invariably another bishop was assigned as commendator. Naturally the bishop so appointed already possessed his own see. Consequently, he became known as titular of his own see and commendator to the other diocese.[50]

[47] "Cum Ecclesia vacans erat sede Episcopali; illius administrator & cura fere Episcopo viciniori secundum jus antiquum."—*Glossarium* s.v. "Commendatarius."

[48] *Institutiones Iuris Canonici,* II, n. 755.

[49] C. 2—"Le corps d'un evêque defunt ne doit pas rester trop longtemps sans etre enseveli, à cause de l'absence de l'Episcopus Commendator."—Hefele-Leclercq, *Histoire des Conciles,* II, (2), 1068; Bruns, *Canones Apostolorum et Conciliorum,* II, 25; Harduin, III, 622.

[50] "Posterioribus saeculis vero regnante abusu Commendarum, Commendatatius dictus est episcopus, qui plures simul Ecclesias obtinebat, unum cujus erat titularis, alteram aliasve quas Commendatarius administrabat . . . "—Du Cange, *Glossarium,* s.v. "Commendatarius."

Many authors, therefore, do not hesitate to affirm that the commendator is a historical ancestor of the present apostolic administrator.[51]

The following analysis of the two offices show that their assertions are based on logical reasons. First, the apostolic administrator is appointed by the Roman Pontiff; the commendator, though usually deputized by the Metropolitan, was nevertheless occasionally appointed by the Pope, as history proves. Pope Paschal I (817-824), for instance, selected a commendator in Spain when Bernard, the Archbishop of Toledo, was appointed administrator both of the Abbey vacated by the monks during the Saracen invasion, and of the diocese of Segovia. The appointment to Segovia was temporary, lasting until the election of a new bishop by the priests and people.[52] Though the commendator usually received his appointment from the Metropolitan and the apostolic administrator from the Sovereign Pontiff, the following passage from Toso, however, indicates that this contrast must not be exaggerated:

> Praxis autem Administratores Ap. mittendi exordia sumpsisse videtur labente saec. XIII, ita ut iam Bonifacius VIII aperte declararet Administratorem dioceseon constitutionem soli Ap. Sedi competere, nec ab alio quam a R. Pontifice deputari posse. Contra, ante id tempus et Metropolitae et quandoque etiam episcopi viciniores, sede vacante, Administratorem constituebant.[53]

Second, both Commendator and apostolic administrator are appointed to a canonically erected diocese.

[51] Coronata, Institutiones Iuris Canonici, I, 441; Maroto, *Institutiones Iuris Canonici,* II, n. 755; Toso, *Ad Codicem Iuris Canonici Commentaria* (Romae, 1921), II, 134; Villien-Magnin, *Dictionnaire de Droit Canonique,* s.v. "Adminisrateur Apostolique"; Cance, *Le Code de Droit Canonique,* I, 304.

[52] "Non monasterium ipsum sollicitudini tuae restaurandum dispondendumque committimus. Sed Episcopatum etiam Segoviensem, dum ne Segoviensis cives proprium sibi suum habere Episcopum decrevissent."—Thomassinus, *Vetus et Nova Ecclesiae Disciplina,* II, III, c. 19, n. 4.

[53] *Ad Codicem Iuris Canonici Commentaria Minora,* II, 134.

Third, an apostolic administrator may be sent to a diocese either *sede plena* or *sede vacante*. This is also true of a Commendator. Oftentimes the commendator administered a diocese whose bishop had been forced to flee from the persecutions of the Saracens.

Fourth, in both cases serious reasons have to be present before such an appointment is made.

Fifth, an apostolic administrator is sent to a diocese either *ad tempus* or *in perpetuum*. The commendator's appointment, on the other hand, though not always stated definitely in years and months, generally lasted until a specified circumstance was effected, e. g., until the proper bishop returned from exile, until a new bishop been elected, etc.

The similarity in important details between the two offices, then, leads to the valid conclusion that the commendator is a historical ancestor of the apostolic administrator.

Art. 6—The Duties, Faculties, and Prerogatives of the Interventor, Visitator, and Commendator

A) *The Duties*

This section will treat of the most important duties of the visitator. This title will be used throughout in a comprehensive fashion as referring also to the interventor and commendator.

Generally considered, these duties varied according to the country and the particular needs of the diocese. A strict rule cannot be formulated, for a visitator sent to Italy did not necessarily possess the same duties and faculties as one sent to France, although he might if the same situation were present. In short, all exigencies were provided for in the letters of appointment. Since most of the examples of visitators quoted in the earlier part of this work were taken from the letters of Gregory the Great, it will be to these letters that reference will be made in ascertaining the duties and faculties of the visitator. The selection is justified insofar as they contain distinctive characteristics of this office.

It was the usual procedure for the visitator in the Spanish Church to carry out the funeral service of the deceased bishop.

This assignment was obligatory in view of the fact that the visitator in this Church was, in most instances, the neighboring bishop. This duty was specifically mentioned in the Council of Valencia (524),[54] in the VII Provincial Council of Toledo (646)[55] and the II Council of Orleans.[56]

Pope Gregory, however, in none of his letters makes reference to this duty. This, no doubt, is attributable to the fact that in most of the instances in which he sent a visitator to rule a vacant see the former resident bishop had been dead for quite some time and the need of a visitator arose from either the neglect of the people in electing a bishop, or their inability to arrive at an agreeable selection.[57]

The visitator was frequently required to take inventory of the see he occupied as administrator. The Council of Valencia stated this duty in canon 2,[58] and Gregory makes a reference to it in the case of Maximianus who had been sent as visitator to the Churches of Italy; "If anyone of the bishops should depart life, or should be removed for his transgressions, the hierarchy and all the chiefs of the clergy being assembled, and in thy presence making an inventory of the property of the Church."[59]

The customary and by far the most important duty of the visitator was the administration of the vacant diocese. This obligation entailed the promotion of both the temporal and spiritual welfare of the diocese by endeavoring to check the prevalent vices among the people and making the changes he perceived were required for the good of the Church. This duty is very well exemplified in the letter sent by Pope Gregory to Leo, the Bishop of Urbino,

[54] C. 4—Bruns, *Canones Apostolorum et Conciliorum,* I, 26; Hefele-*Leclercq,* Histoire des Conciles, II, par. II, 1068.

[55] C. 4—Bruns, *op. cit.,* II, 263.

[56] Cans. 5-6—Bruns, *op. cit.,* II, 185; *Harduin,* II, 1175.

[57] "Gregorius Passivo Episcopo Firmano: bene novit fraternitas vestra quam longo sit tempore Aprutium pastorali sollicitudine destitutum."—*Lib. XII, Ep. XII—MPL,* LXXVII, 1226.

[58] Bruns, *Canones Apostolorum et Conciliorum,* II, 25.

[59] *Lib II, Ep. VII—MPL,* LXXVII, 593; *Lib. IV, Ep. XI—MPL,* LXXVII, 679.

when he sent him as visitator to the diocese of Bevagna, "Quidquid autem tibi, visum fuerit pro utilitatibus ejusdem Ecclesiae ordinare, habebis modis omnibus ex nostra promissione licentiam. Et praeter ordinationes clericorum cetera omnia in praedicta Ecclesia . . . te volumus agere."[60]

The final duty to be considered is the election of a new bishop. The visitator had to make the necessary preparations for this function, and order its fulfillment as quickly as possible. This office was common to both the European and African church, and its importance in the latter can be gauged from the V Council of Carthage (401) when it declared that if an interventor or intercessor did not procure a new bishop within a year the said interventor or intercessor was to be removed and another sent in his place.[61] Although this duty was not imposed *ex officio* on the visitator of Gregory the Great, nevertheless there are many letters wherein he definitely stated that the visitor was to take charge of the election of a new bishop.[62]

Though the duties mentioned are not assigned to every visitator, they illustrate the variations of this office in different countries. There are indeed many other duties which are imposed on the visitator and inserted in the letter of appointment. To enumerate them all, however, would not only be an arduous, but also a quite unnecessary task. The duties chosen, being the important ones, are sufficient to show the nature and characteristics of the office.

B) *The Faculties and Prerogatives*

Ordinarily the visitator possessed the same faculties in administration as the deceased bishop. These faculties are similar in every detail, save that the visitator was not granted the permission to ordain clerics.[63]

Denial of this permission to ordain clerics was explicitly stated

[60] *Lib. III, Ep. XXIV—MPL,* LXXVII, 622.

[61] C. 8—*Mansi,* III, 970; Bingham, *The Antiquities of the Christian Church,* Tom. I, Lib. II, ch XV.

[62] *Lib. I, Ep. XIX—MPL,* LXXVII, 464-465.

[63] *St. Gregory, Lib. III, Ep. XXV—MPL,* LXXVII, 732.

in canon 8 of the V Council of Orleans (549),[64] in the II Council of Auvergne (549)[65] and in a letter of Pope John II, (532-536).[66]

From these sources it is easily discernible that the denial of this faculty to ordain was contained in the ordinary appointment of visitators. The following quotation from a letter of Pope Gregory to Chrysanthus, visitator to the Church of Vienne, proves that it was not customary for him to grant this faculty. " . . . in quo de more scrinii nostri nihil vos de provectionibus facere voluimus clericorum." [67] With the exception of this one faculty, then, the visitator and his predecessor enjoyed the same faculties.

In extraordinary circumstances, however, the discipline was relaxed and the visitor was granted the faculty even to ordain. The need of clerics, for example, induced Pope Gregory to grant Balbinus, Bishop of Rosello, this permission when he was appointed administrator to the diocese of Piombino.[68]

The same faculty was granted to Felix, bishop of Manfredonia, when he was sent as visitator to Conusina,[69] and to a Bishop in Corsica when he was appointed visitator to Sagone[70]

When the see of Naples had been vacant for a long time the clergy of that city requested the ordination of certain clerics. This request was granted, and Gregory appointed Paul, the Bishop of

[64] "Ut in civitate, ubi Pontifex jure humanae conditionis obierit nullus episcopus ante substitutionem reparati per ordinem successoris aut in civitate aut per parochias ordinare clericos . . ."—Bruns, *Canones Apostolorum et Conciliorum,* II, 210; *Harduin,* II, 1445.

[65] C. 8—Bruns, *op. cit.,* II, 216; *Harduin,* II, 1452.

[66] "Ne ejus Ecclesia destituta videatur, in ejus locum Visitatorem dari, . . . ut nihil de ordinibus clericorum, nihil de Ecclesiastica facultate presumat . . ."—Baronius, *Annales Ecclesiastici,* VII, 690.

[67] *Lib. III, Ep. LXIV—MPL,* LXXVII, 661-662.

[68] "Visitator accedas ut unum presbyterum et duos diaconos ordinare." —*Lib. I, Ep. XV, MPL,* LXXVII, 515.

[69] ". . . duos parochiales presbyteros debeas ordinare."—*Lib. I, Ep. LIII—MPL,* LXXVII, 515.

[70] "In qua etiam Ecclesia vel ejus parochiis diaconos atque presbyteros tibi concedimus ordinandi licentiam."—*Lib. I, Ep. LXXVII—MPL, LXXVII,* 532-533.

Nepi and visitator to the Church of Naples, to ordain these clerics.[71]

Quite naturally the visitator's faculties might be curtailed or extended as the case demanded. Each situation was judged in the light of its accompanying circumstances. One letter gave the visitator full power to do whatever the former bishop could do; in another case this power was reduced to a minimum. Evidently, then, in order to ascertain the exact faculties and prerogatives granted to each visitator the letter of appointment had to be carefully read and examined in regard to each detail. All faculties granted were therein mentioned.[72]

[72] Nicolai, *De Episcopo Visitatore* (Romae: Franciscus Gonzaga, 1710), p. 62.

[71] *Lib. II, Ep. VII—MPL,* LXXVII, 516.

Chapter III

DISCIPLINE FROM THE THIRTEENTH CENTURY TO THE COUNCIL OF TRENT

Art. 1—The Decline of the Visitator and the Commencement of the Cathedral Chapter

In Italy, then, from the fifth to the eighth century vacant dioceses were administered by visitators. These officials attended to the spiritual and temporal welfare of vacant sees in the interim between the death of one bishop and the election of a new one, or until the return of the duly appointed bishop to his episcopal see. It must not be inferred, however, that every time a diocese was vacant a visitator was commissioned to administer the see. On the contrary, this deputizing of the Gregorian visitator occurred only in those dioceses where the election of a successor was unduly delayed, or where there existed a fear either of dissension arising among the people, or an invasion by the barbaric or pagan nations who would install their own bishop. Attention has already been directed to such situations.[1]

The situation was somewhat different in France. Here, according to the canons of the Council of Riez (439) the neighboring bishop entered the deceased bishop's diocese and administered it for seven days.[2] Strictly taken, then, the office of visitator in Gaul did not possess the same degree of development as that of the Italian or Gregorian visitator. Nevertheless, as was indicated already, some visitators sent to France by the Pontiffs enjoyed the same privileges and prerogatives as those in Italy. Corresponding to the visitator in France and Italy was the commendator in Spain, a dignitary who was also occasionally appointed by the Sovereign Pontiff. In Africa vacant sees were ruled by interventors, whose office was similar to the two mentioned above.

[1] *St. Gregory Lib. II, Ep. X*—*MPL,* LXXVII, 546-547; *Lib. II, Ep. XV*—*MPL,* LXXVII, 550-551.

[2] *Cans. 6-7*—Bruns, *Canones Apostolorum et Conciliorum,* II, 120.

Although the office of interventor in the African Church existed for only a short time, that of the visitator and commendator lasted for many centuries. In Italy the highly developed office of visitator in as far as it enjoyed a plentitude of spiritual and temporal power, was particularly potent from the time of Pope Gregory I (590-604) to the eighth century. From the end of the eighth century, however, this office began to decline gradually and by the thirteenth century it had passed into desuetude.[3] The reason of this decline can be traced to the gradual limitation of the powers of the visitator and the subsequent and early formation of the cathedral chapter.

The cathedral chapter developed from the practice of community life by the bishop and the priests of the cathedral chapter.[4] This community life was introduced in Africa as early as the time of St. Augustine and consisted in this that the clerics of the episcopal city lived in the same establishment with the bishop.[5] Spain, France, and Italy were quick to adopt this form of common life of the cathedral clergy.[6] St. Chrodegang, the

[3] ". . . a saeculo octavo usque ad duodecimum, cum instituerentur iam capitula apud ecclesias cathedrales, ac eorum auctoritas paulatim, evolveretur, factum est ut Administratores (Visitatores) sedium vacantium minus frequenter designarentur, et tandem cessaret eorum usus aut fuerit duntaxat servatus in quibusdam extraordinariis rerum adiunctis."—Maroto, *Institutiones Iuris Canonici,* II, n. 759; "Cum inde ex saeculo octavo magis magisque cresceret auctoritas Capitulorum Cathedralium, paulatim exclusis Visitatoribus circiter ex saeculo duodecimo unice Capitula Cathedralia administrationem diocesis vacantis consecuta sunt."—Wernz, *Ius Decretalium* (6 vols., Romae: Ex Typographia Polyglotta, 1906-1913), II, 605, n. 785; Thomassinus, *Vetus et Nova Ecclesiae Disciplina,* I, III, c. 51, n. 11.

[4] Hermes, *De Capitulo Sede Vacante vel Impedita et de Vicario Capitulari* (Lovanii: Valinthout Fratres, 1873), p. 27.

[5] Brueck, *History of the Catholic Church* (2 vols., New York, 1885), I, 272; St. Augustine, *Confessions,* VIII, c. VI, n. 15—*MPL,* XXXII, 755; Thomassinus, *Vetus et Nova Ecclesiae Disciplina,* I, III, c. 4, nn. 1-2; St. Augustine, *Sermon,* n. 353, c. IV—*MPL,* XXXIX, 1572-1573.

[6] II Provincial Council of Toledo (531), c. 1—Mansi, VIII, 785; Bruns, *Canones Apostolorum et Conciliorum,* I, 207; *Harduin,* II, 1139; IV Provincial Council of Toledo (633), c. 23—Mansi, I, 628; Bruns, *op. cit.,* I,

Bishop of Metz, around the year 750, took the initial steps to encourage the spread of community life. Through his impetus the community life of the cathedral clerics spread rapidly throughout the Frankish Kingdom.[7] This movement was heartily endorsed by several kings of France, particularly by Pepin, Charlemagne, and Louis the Pious.[8] Quite naturally with the strong stimulus given by the various bishops and kings, the spread of communal organization among the episcopal or cathedral clergy was phenomenal.

So, just as formerly the visitator had replaced the presbytery as the ordinary means of ruling a vacant diocese, now is witnessed the transmission of this power to the cathedral chapter in the various countries. In the words of Jaeger:

> It was this institution of the Church, therefore, which grew more and more influential in the administration of vacant episcopal sees, gradually supplying entirely the office of the visitator.[9]

Yet despite this strong and rapid growth and spread of the cathedral chapter the office of visitator was not abolished immediately, but continued for three more centuries in a lesser capacity than it originally enjoyed.[10] The visitators of the ninth, tenth, and eleventh centuries were sent, in most instances, to supervise the election of a new bishop.[11]

230; Harduin, III, 586; III Council of Orleans (538), c. IX, Mansi IX, 15.

[7] Wernz, *Ius Decretalium,* II, p. 569, n. 767; Castillo, *Disertacion Historico-Canonica Sobre La Potestad Del Cabildo en Sede Vacante O Impedida Del Vicario Capitular,* The Catholic University of America, Canon Law Studies, n. 4 (Washington: The Catholic University of America, 1918), pp. 20-21; Hermes, *De Capitulo Sede Vacante,* pp. 26-27.

[8] Wernz, *Ius Decretalium,* II, p. 569, n. 767; Castillo, *Del Vicario Capitular,* p. 21; Jaeger, *The Administration of Vacant and Quasi-Vacant Dioceses in the United States,* p. 22.

[9] *The Administration of Vacant and Quasi-Vacant Dioceses in the United States,* p. 22.

[10] Hermes, *De Vicario Capitulari,* pp. 27-30.

[11] Jaeger, *The Administration of Vacant and Quasi-Vacant Dioceses in the United States,* p. 25.

The Roman Council (1080) held under Pope Gregory VII (1073-1085) made special efforts to curb the interference of lay princes in canonical elections, and, in particular, sought to outlaw this royal right. Formerly, this had been necessary for every visitator appointed in the Frankish Kingdom.[12]

The close of the eleventh century, however, witnessed the termination of the office of visitator and the gradual appearance of the cathedral chapter. From this time on the visitator became the extraordinary way of administering the affairs of a vacant diocese. Several Councils allude to the cathedral chapter and recognize it as the proper administrator of such a see. The Council of Nîmes (1096) directed the cathedral clergy to choose two of the more capable persons of the see to administer the temporal affairs of the deceased bishop, and to guard all that pertained to the safety of the diocese.[13] The II General Lateran Council of 1139 granted the cathedral chapter the right to hold episcopal elections.[14]

Art. 2—The Authentic Recognition of the Cathedral Chapter and Vicar Capitular

Pope Gregory IX (1227-1241) in 1227 selected and commissioned St. Raymond of Penyafort to undertake the enormous task of assembling and compiling all the extant ecclesiastical laws into one complete work. Upon the completion of this work it was published and promulgated with the authentic approval of the Pontiff by his bull *Rex Pacificus* of September 5, 1234.[15]

[12] " . . . quoties defuncto Pastore alicujus Ecclesiae, alius est ei canonice subrogandus instantis Visitatoris Episcopi, qui ab Apostolica, vel Metropolitana Sede directus est."—c. 6—Mansi, XX, 533; Harduin. VI, 1585. Reference to this consent of the lay princes is witnessed when Hincmar, the Archbishop of Rheims (845-882) appointed Hadebertus, Visitator to the Church of Bois-le-Duc, ". . . Consensu domini nostri Ludovici."—Labbeaus-Cossartius, *Sacrosancta Concilia ad Regiam Editionem Exacta* (15 vols., in 16, Lutetiae-Parisiorum, 1671-1672), VIII, 1866.

[13] C. 4—*Mansi*, XX, 235.

[14] C. 4—*Mansi,* XXI, 533; Council of Rheims (1131), c. 7—Mansi, XXI, 465.

[15] *Bullarium Diplomatum et Privilegiorum Sanctorum Romanorum*

The Gregorian Collection was followed by the *Liber Sextus Decretalium* of Pope Boniface VIII (1299-1303), which was promulgated and authenticated by the bull *Sacrosanctae* of March 3, 1298.[16] These authentic collections laid down a definite course of procedure for the cathedral chapter during the episcopal vacancy of a diocese.

Gregory IX in a decree [17] declared it to be the right of the cathedral chapter during the vacancy of a see, to confirm the elections held in monasteries. Since the power to confirm such an election constituted part and parcel of the ordinary jurisdiction of the bishop, it was acknowledged that the chapter possessed the same jurisdiction as the bishop during a vacancy.[18] Boniface VIII likewise acknowledged the power of the cathedral chapter to administer a diocese during an episcopal vacancy.[19]

In view of the fact that no specific norm was given whereby the cathedral chapter was to exercise this power upon the vacancy of an episcopal see, several methods were followed. According to Wernz, the chapter either administered the diocese collectively, or else different groups of members ruled for successive periods.[20] Experience, however, having proved that both these arrangements were inconvenient and open to abuse, the Council of Trent decreed that the chapter could not retain the administration of the vacant diocese indefinitely, but must commit it to a vicar capitular

Pontificum (25 vols., Augustae Taurinorum: Seb. Franco et Henrico Dalmazzo, 1847-1872), III, 485; Jaeger, *The Administration of Vacant and Quasi-Vacant Dioceses in the United States,* p. 27; Van Hove, *Commentarium Lovaniense in Codicem Iuris Canonici* (I vol. in 5 toms., 1928-1939, Tom. I, *Prolegomena,* Mechliniae,-Romae: H. Dessain, 1928), Tom. I, p. 174. (Hereafter this first tome of this commentary will be designated simply as *Prolegomena*).

[16] Van Hove, *Prolegomena,* pp. 177-178.

[17] C. 14, X, *De maioritate et obedientia,* I, 33.

[18] Hermes, *De Vicario Capitulari,* p. 36; Jaeger, *The Administration of Vacant and Quasi-Vacant Dioceses,* p. 28; Castillo, *Del Vicario Capitular,* p. 21.

[19] C. 3, *de supplenda negligentia,* I, 8, in VI.°

[20] *Ius Decretalium,* II, 605; n. 795; Hermes, *De Vicario Capitulari,* p. 38.

after eight days.[21] By this decree the Council of Trent placed no restriction on the jurisdiction of the chapter but merely limited the time of its actual administration of vacant dioceses.[22]

Thomassinus states that, in his opinion, this office of vicar capitular was not instituted by the Council of Trent, but owes its origin to the Council of Toledo held in 1347. This Council ruled that when the episcopal see was vacant the Chapter could commit it to either the suffragan bishop or the Vicar.[23] Whether or not this opinion offered by Thomassinus concerning the origin of the vicar capitular is tenable, is of no great import at this time. The important thing is that the Council of Trent did definitely establish a *modus agendi* obligatory on the cathedral chapter. The legislation here initiated lasted until the Code of Canon Law.[24]

From this brief treatment of the decline of the visitor and the subsequent rise of the vicar capitular it can be concluded that:

1) The office of visitator declined after the eighth century.

2) This decline of the office of visitator is attributable partly to the restriction of the powers and faculties previously given to visitators, and partly to the rise of the cathedral chapter.

3) After the Decretals promulgated by Gregory IX and Boniface VIII the visitator ceased to exist as the ordinary administrator of a vacant diocese. From this time on his power was transferred to the cathedral chapter.

4) No definite *modus agendi* was imposed on the chapter until the Council of Trent legislated that a vicar capitular be selected by the chapter within eight days of the vacancy.

5) This legislation laid down by the Council of Trent has been adopted by the Code of Canon Law.

21 "Item officialem, seu vicarium infra octo dies post mortem episcopi constituere, . . . "—*Sess. XXIV,* de ref., c. 16.—*Canones et Decreta Sacrosancti Oecumenici Concilii Tridentini* (Romae: Bernhard Tauchnitz, 1863), p. 166.

22 Hermes, *De Vicario Capitulari,* p. 85; Jaeger, *The Administration of Vacant and Quasi-Vacant Dioceses in the United States,* p. 44.

23 "Episcopi suffraganei nostri, vel sede vacante Vicarii per capitulum deputati."—c. 3—Mansi, XXVI, 126; Thomassinus, *Vetus et Nova Ecclesiae Disciplina,* I, III, c. 10, n. 13; Castillo, *Del Vicario Capitular,* p. 23.

24 Canon 432.

6) Since that time of the Decretals the appointment of visitators (now called administrators) became the extraordinary way of administering a vacant diocese.

ART. 3—THE EXTRAORDINARY ADMINISTRATION OF VACANT AND QUASI-VACANT DIOCESES

The cathedral chapters introduced by universal law in the Decretals of Popes Gregory IX and Boniface VIII and their subsequent duty to elect a vicar capitular furnish the ordinary means of administering vacant dioceses. This law introduced in the thirteenth century has been incorporated into the Code of Canon Law.[25] Nevertheless, occasionally the Holy See intervenes in dioceses where the vicar capitular is incapable of administering the affairs of the diocese, or when the chapter has delayed unduly in the selection of a vicar capitular, and the Metropolitan has neglected to fulfill his duty by appointing one. Under these circumstances the Sovereign Pontiff usually appoints an administrator to rule the vacant diocese. This administration is extraordinary, and the person is always appointed by the Holy See. Pope Boniface VIII mentions this administrator in his *Liber Sextus*:

> Ecclesiae Cathedrali vacanti visitator ab alio quam a Romano Pontifice deputari non potest, nisi forte Capitulum in spiritualibus et temporalibus negligenter aut perperam administret. Tunc enim Archiepiscopus ob negligentiam vel malitian capituli, eo vocato causaeque super hoc cognitione praemissa, visitatorem seu administratorem eidem Ecclesiae licite poterit deputare. Huiusmodi quoque visitator, quanquam spiritualium et temporalium administrationem legitimam censeatur habere, beneficia tamen, quae ad collationem pertinent episcopi, conferre non potest, si ab alio quam a Romano Pontifice fuerit deputatus.[26]

From these words of Pope Boniface it can easily be ascertained that the appointment of this administrator or visitator connotes something over and above the ordinary mode of acting. Quite

[25] Canon 429.

[26] C. 4, *de supplenda negligentia praelatorum,* I, 8, in VI°.

obviously, too, this office was inaugurated in order to eliminate abuse among the members of the cathedral chapter. The Metropolitan could effect the deputation of a visitator only when he discovered that the chapter was negligent in expediting its administration. Even in this instance the power of the Metropolitan was limited insofar as he could not grant the visitator the faculty to confer benefices, whereas the visitator appointed by the Sovereign Pontiff had full and complete power of administration.[27]

In another part of the *Liber Sextus*[28] Boniface VIII outlines the power of the administrator:

> Is cui procuratio seu administratio cathedralis ecclesiae plena et libera in spiritualibus et temporalibus a Sede Apostolica cui hoc soli competit, est commissa, potest, alienatione bonorum immobilium duntaxat excepta, omnia, quae iurisdictionis episcopalis exsistunt, et quae potest electus exsequi confirmatus, libere exercere. Illa quippe, quae ministerium consecrationis exposcunt, nisi fuerit episcopus, per alios faciat episcopos expedire.

From these two texts of Boniface VIII can be recognized the resemblance between this visitator or administrator and the apostolic administrator of canon 312. Like the apostolic administrator he is appointed by the Sovereign Pontiff and possesses unrestricted freedom in the administration of the spiritual and temporal welfare of the vacant diocese. Jaeger agrees that the administrator mentioned in the Decretals of Boniface VIII is the forerunner of the present apostolic administrator.[29] In substantiation of this assertion he makes reference to Maroto who says that the visitator

[27] "Ratio est: –quia ad Capitulum Cathedrale, Sede Vacante, pertinet jus administrationis in spiritualibus et temporalibus, et ipsum potest administratorem circa spiritualia, & temporalia constituere. Quod ius non potest Archiepiscopus illi, sine causa necessaria auferre. At vero S. Pontifex, ex plenitudine suae potestatis, libere potest administratorem constituere; etsi non soleat dare, nisi capitulum deliquerit."—Pirhing, *Jus Canonicum in Quinque Libros Decretalium* (5 vols., in 4, Dilingae: John Bencard, 1674), p. 390.

[28] C. 42, *de electione et electi potestate,* I, 6, in VI°.

[29] *The Administration of Vacant and Quasi-Vacant Dioceses in the United States,* p. 29, footnote 1.

mentioned in the Decretals of Boniface VIII were not usually, at that time, called apostolic administrators, but were known rather as vicars apostolic. Then he proceeds to say that since those clerics who were sent to mission countries were called by the name of vicar apostolic it became imperative to divide vicars apostolic into two classes; namely, those sent to regions where no constituted hierarchy existed, and those sent to rule canonically erected dioceses either *sede plena* or *sede vacante.*[30] With the promulgation of the Code of Canon Law this twofold use of the name vicar apostolic was discontinued. The Code designates those persons sent to missionary countries as vicars apostolic;[31] and those sent to canonically erected dioceses as apostolic administrators.[32]

Around the year 1298 the office of administrator was officially recognized as the extraordinary way of administering a vacant diocese. Prior to this time there are found several instances of Pontiffs deputizing *Administrators.* These are worthy of note for they indicate that this office existed before the canons of Pope Boniface VIII. In every respect they resembled the *Administrator* mentioned by Boniface; they were appointed by the Roman Pontiff, and the reasons prompting such an appointment were usually the ineffectiveness of the chapter to rule well, the incompetence of the resident bishop, or the undesirability of a long vacancy of the see.

The office of *Administrator* was first resorted to by Pope In-

30 "Attamen II, quibus praefata administratio committebatur, non vocabantur communiter Administratores Apostolicos, sed potius Vicarii Apostolici; cum vero solerent quoque eo nomine nuncupari illi qui charactere episcopali insigniti regerent Missiones, hinc recentiores Auctores (Wernz, Bouix, Sebastianelli) solebant dividere Vicarios Apostolicos in eos qui mittebantur ad regiones ubi nondum erat constituta hierarchia ecclesiastica, et in eos qui ad dioecesim, sive sede plena sive sede vacante, regendam deputabantur."—*Institutiones Iuris Canonici,* II, p. 63, n. 765.

31 Canon 293.

32 Canon 312. The twofold use of the name vicar apostolic from the year 1622 to the Constitution "*Sapienti Consilio*" will be treated at length later in this work.

nocent IV (1243-1254) who in 1243 assigned to Aegidius, the former Bishop of Foligno, the administration of the Church of Nocera in Umbria which had been deprived of its bishop.[33] The same Pontiff made Henry, the Archdeacon of Chartres, administrator of the Church of Nevers for one year. This Archdeacon had been unanimously elected to the bishopric of Nevers by the chapter and had received the approval of the Holy See. Notwithstanding this Henry had not yet given his assent to be consecrated the Bishop of Nevers. Then the Holy Father, fearful lest a long delay in filling the see might be harmful to the diocese, appointed Henry, administrator for one year.[34] In another instance this same Pope, Innocent IV, was obliged to intervene and impose his will when his appointment of the Bishop of Brixen as administrator of the Church of Trent met with expressed disapproval from the cathedral chapter of that diocese. Innocent granted the Bishop administrator the power to excommunicate publicly the Archdeacon and the members of the cathedral chapter if they persisted in their refusal to obey.[35]

Pope Clement IV (1264-1268) transferred to William of Viguzzolo, the Canon of Piacenza, the administration of Piacenza.[36]

Boniface VIII (1294-1303) in his *Liber Sextus Decretalium,*[37] as already indicated, laid down the definite rule that an *Admin-*

33 " . . . Aegidio Episcopo quondam Fulginati administrationem Ecclesiae Nucerinae pastore vacantis committit."—Berger, *Les Registres D'Innocent IV* (4 vols., Parisiis: E. Thorin, 1884-1897), I, n. 388; Potthast, *Regesta Pontificum Romanorum* (Berolini: R. De Decker, 1874-1875), I, n. 11201.

34 "Cum igitur electioni idem de se nondum assensum praebuerit . . . curam et administrationem Ecclesiae antedictae in spiritualibus et temporalibus a festo purificationis Beatae Mariae Virginis proximo usque ad annum eidem archdiacono auctoritate apostolica duximus committendam . . . "—Berger, *Les Registres D'Innocent IV,* III, n. 6594.

35 Berger, *op. cit.,* II, nn. 3896 and 3942.

36 Potthast, *Regesta Pontificum Romanorum,* II, n. 19183.

37 This collection was compiled by William of Mandagato, the Archbishop of Embrun, Berengarius Fredoli, Bishop of Vezieres, and by Richard Petronius, Vice-Chancellor of the Roman Curia.—Van Hove, *Prolegomena,* pp. 177-178.

istrator was to be elected by the Pope alone, the only exception to this law being made for cases in which it came to the notice of the Metropolitan that the cathedral chapter was negligent in its duties. Even before the *Liber* Sextus was promulgated, Pope Boniface VIII had occasion to send an administrator. Pandulphus, the Bishop of Patti, was appointed by him in 1296 to administer the diocese of Ancona which was at this time without a bishop.[38] After the Bull *Sacrosanctae* of March 3, 1298, Boniface VIII made greater use of this office of *Administrator.* In 1299, John was transferred from the diocese of Padua to the Archdiocese of Bologna, retaining, however, the administration of his former see, in both spiritual and temporal affairs.[39]

Pope John XXII (1316-1334) in 1318 made Aemilius the administrator of the Church of Fermo in both spiritual and temporal affairs.[40] In 1320 Pope John again had recourse to this office of administrator. The See of Pavia was vacant because of the perpetual sentence of deposition pronounced on Isnardus, the former Bishop of Antioch and administrator of Pavia. In order to prevent harm to the Church through a long delay in filling the episcopal see, he conferred on John of Beccaria the administration of the see of Pavia.[41]

The appointment of administrators to rule vacant dioceses continues till the twentieth century. The cases referred to prove sufficiently the similarity that exists between the office of *Administrator* and that of the *Apostolic Administrator.*

[38] Digard-Faucon-Thomas, *Les Registres de Boniface VIII* (Paris, 1884-1909), I, n. 1055; Potthast, *Regesta Pontificum Romanorum,* II, n. 24330.

[39] Digard-Faucon-Thomas, *Les Registres de Boniface VIII,* I, n. 2837; Potthast, *Regesta Pontificum Romanorum,* II, n. 24763. Other examples may be found in nn. 3080, 3622, 4324, 4590.

[40] Mollat, *Jean XXIII Lettres Communes* (15 vols., Parisiis: Albert Fontemoing, 1904-1933), II, n. 9065.

[41] ". . . commissio administrationis in spiritualibus et temporalibus Ecclesiae Papiensis, vac. per sententiam perpetuae depositionis latam contra Isnardum quondam Patriarchum Antiochensum tunc dictae Eccl. Papien. Administratorem, et jam per Bertrandum S. Marcelli Card. Presb. ex potestate a Papa sibi collata commissae fratri Joanni de Beccaria, O. M. . . ." Mollat, *Jean XXII Lettres Communes,* III, n. 14191.

First, the apostolic administrator is sent solely by the Roman Pontiff. This requisite is found verified in every appointment of the administrator.

Second, the apostolic administrator and the administrator are both sent to a canonically erected diocese.

Third, both the administrator and the apostolic administrator are appointed to a diocese either *sede plena* or *sede vacante.*

Fourth, the same reasons justified the mission of both the administrator and the apostolic administrator.

Fifth, the apostolic administrator receives his faculties and duties from the Code of Canon Law and the letter of appointment. The administrator received his from the letter of appointment.

The very marked similarity that exists between these two offices, then, offers convincing evidence that the present office of apostolic administrator has developed from that of the administrator.

Chapter 4

DISCIPLINE FROM THE COUNCIL OF TRENT TO THE PROMULGATION OF THE CODE OF CANON LAW

Art. 1. The Constitution *Immensa Dei*

Sixtus V (1585-1590) on January 22, 1588, published his Constitution *Immensa Dei.*[1] In this Constitution the Pontiff instituted and outlined the duties, faculties, and jurisdiction of fifteen Roman Congregations. The twelfth of these was entitled the Congregation of Bishops and Regulars. In addition to outlining the duties and faculties imposed on this Congregation he added the phrase, "that whenever necessity demanded it they were to choose men of good qualities, and endowed with knowledge to rule Churches as vicars apostolic."[2] It is important to note that the words *"Vicarii Apostolici"* are interpreted by the "Dictionnaire de Droit Canonique" as "apostolic administrators."[3]

Hilling, in considering the duties of the Congregation of Bishops and Regulars, says: "The *Negotia Episcoporum* include the administration of a diocese in case the bishop is hindered in the efficient discharge of his duties, either by illness, mental incapacity, suspension, or other causes. In such a case the Congregation delegates an administrator (*Vicarius*) *Apostolicus.*"[4]

[1] *Bullarium Diplomatum et Privilegiorum Sanctorum Romanorum Pontificum,* VIII, 994-995.

[2] "Insuper, ubi necessitas exergerit, viros usu et doctrina idoneos, rectos et timentes Deum deligant, qui nostrarum litterarum auctoritate suffulti, Ecclesias ut Vicarii Aposolici regant."—*Loc. cit.*

[3] "Sixte V par sa constitution *Immensa Dei* du 22 Janvier 1588, confia le soin de nommer les administrateur apostoliques à la Congregation de evêques appellee alors: Congregatio duodecima pro consultationibus episcoporum et aliorum praelatorum. Les Administrateur Apostoliques y sont designes, coma cela avait lieu generalement dans l'ancien droit, par le terme de vicaires apostoliques."—Villien-Magnin, *Dictionnaire de Droit Canonique,* s.v. "Administrateur Apostoliques."

[4] *Procedure at the Roman Curia* (New York: Joseph F. Wagner, 1907), p. 74, n. 4.

Maroto, moreover, states in his treatment of vicars and prefects apostolic that Pope Gregory XIII (1572-1585) in 1583 appointed Wosmer vicar apostolic to Holland, but that, in reality, this vicar apostolic was an apostolic administrator.[5]

From this time on the names administrator and vicar apostolic were interchangeable. One Pontiff would use the title administrator while the next would seem to prefer vicar apostolic.

Art. 2. The Vicar Apostolic

In addition to the offices of interventor, intercessor, visitator, commendator, and administrator, which have been treated as steps in the gradual development of the present apostolic administrator, there is still another: namely, the vicar apostolic.

The vicar apostolic, as known today, is a person nominated by the Apostolic See to rule a territory which has not yet been canonically erected into a diocese.[6]

Before the Code the term "vicar apostolic" was used in a much wider sense. An analysis of the appointment of a vicar apostolic as it occurred from the sixteenth century to the year 1908 will reveal little resemblance between the office as it existed then and as it exists today. One will become aware, however, of a similarity between the vicar apostolic and the present apostolic administrator. An example will clarify this. In 1662 Pope Alexander VII (1655-1667) sent John Dorivallius, the Archdeacon of the Church of Luxeiul and Canon of Besançon, as vicar apostolic to the Church of Besançon. The occasion for this appointment was the election by the cathedral chapter, contrary to the Pontiff's command, of William Humber as vicar capitular of the vacant see. The Pope immediately annulled this election of William and sent John as vicar apostolic. In this letter of appointment John was given all the faculties and privileges which the former Archbishop John had enjoyed, except the power to confer benefices and the right to grant dimissorial letters for sacred orders. This appointment was to last until a new bishop was elected to the see of

[5] *Institutiones Iuris Canonici,* II, n. 757.

[6] Canon 293.

Besançon.[7] In no way is this appointment correlated to the vicar apostolic as now defined by the Code.[8] But it does agree with the requirements of a present day apostolic administrator in the following very important details. The appointment was made by the Holy Father; it was to a canonically erected diocese; the diocese was vacant though the death of its former archbishop; the cause for nominating this vicar was one now listed among those which may call for the deputizing of an apostolic administrator, that is, the failure of the cathedral chapter to follow the commands of the Sovereign Pontiff; and lastly, the duration of this appointment was until a new bishop was appointed for Besançon. This is sufficient evidence to prove that the vicar apostolic is the historical ancestor of the apostolic administrator. An examination of some authors who treat of this question will serve to render this conclusion still more convincing.[9]

According to Pellegrinus, who lived in the late seventeenth century, a vicar apostolic is one sent by the Holy Father, or by the Sacred Congregation of Bishops and Regulars, when a grave cause justified it to administer a diocese with full episcopal jurisdiction. The appointment could occur either *sede plena* or *sede vacante*.[10]

[7] "Joannes Dorivallius Archdiaconus Luxoviensis et Canonicus Ecclesiae Bisuntinae hujus Ecclesiae Vicarius Apostolicus deputatur."—*Bullarium Diplomatum et Privilegiorum Sanctorum Romanorum Pontificum Taurinensis Editio,* XV, 782.

[8] Canon 293.

[9] Augustine asserts: "There is a material difference between the vicars apostolic formerly appointed for, e.g., Thessalonica or Arles, and the vicars apostolic now (since the Code) appointed for missionary countries. The former were *quasi legati nati,* whereas the vicars of whom the present canon (293) treats are really vicars of the Apostolic See. . . "—*A Commentary on the New Code of Canon Law,* II, 310; Andreucci makes a distinction between the vicar apostolic previous to his time and the vicars apostolic of his time—the former "qui habebat Romani Pontificis vices sibi commissas in certas quasdam provincias, earumque Metropolitas; . . ." and the latter "qui mittitur vel a Pontifice immediate vel a Sacra Congregatione Episcoporum . . . ad regendam aliquam diocesim sive sede plena, sive vacante . . ."—*Hierarchia Ecclesiastica in Varias Partes Distributa* (2 vols., Romae: Generosus Salomonus, 1766) I, 325.

[10] " . . . nos loqui intendimus de illo Vicario Apostolico qui mittitur

Andreas Andreucci († 1771),[11] and Lucius Ferraris (†c.1763) [12] have the same definition as Pellegrinus for a vicar apostolic.

The definition given by these three commentators for a vicar apostolic could not be applied to the vicar apostolic as understood by the Code. Consequently, then, it is proposed here that this definition is identical with that of the apostolic administrator of the Code. This can be best ascertained by testing whether it meets the demands or requisites necessary for deputizing an apostolic administrator. Four essential requisites are demanded for constituting an apostolic administrator: 1) the appointment must be made by the Sovereign Pontiff; 2) the appointee must be assigned to a canonically erected diocese; 3) the appointment must be made *sede plena* or *sede vacante*; 4) the reason for deputizing the apostolic administrator must be a grave one.[13]

A) Appointment By the Sovereign Pontiff

Analyzing these elements singly, it will be observed that Pellegrinus states that a vicar apostolic is sent by the Sovereign Pontiff or by the Congregation of Bishops and Regulars. This concession was granted to this Congregation by the Constitution *Immensa Dei* of Pope Sixtus V on January 22, 1588.[14] By the Constitution *Sapienti Consilio* Pope Pius X discontinued this Conregation,[15] and granted to the Congregation of the Consistory,

a Summo Pontifice cum Brevi vel a Sacra Congregatione Episcoporum et Regularium, ex aliqua legitima causa, cum litteris, ad regendam aliquam Ecclesiam cum facultate administrandi totam iurisdictionem Episcopalem, aliquibus tamen exceptis casibus in particulari. Quod solet fieri aliquando sede Episcopali plena, & aliquando sede vacante."—*Praxis Vicariorum* (Venetiis: Franciscus Groppus, 1696), p. 54.

[11] *Hierarchia Ecclesiastica in Varias Partes Distributa*, I, 235.

[12] *Prompta Bibliotheca Canonica, Juridica, Moralis, Theologica, necnon Ascetica, Polemica, Rubricistica, Historica* (9 vols., Romae: Ex Typographia Polyglotta, 1885-1889), s.v. "Vicarius Apostolicus," n. 1.

[13] Canon 312.

[14] *Bullarium Diplomatum et Privilegiorum Sanctorum Romanorum Pontificum*, VIII, 995.

[15] *Acta Apostolicae Sedis*, Commentarium Officiale, Romae, 1909—I (1909), 27; (hereafter this will be referred to as *AAS*); Leitner, *De Curia Romana* (Ratisbonae: Fr. Pustet, 1909), n. 1.

which he restored, the power to nominate Apostolic Administrators. Today, with the Code, this same Congregation still has the power to propose apostolic administrators for appointment.[16]

B) Appointment To A Canonically Erected Diocese

This requisite is verified in the instance wherein John Dorivallius was sent as vicar apostolic to the see of Bensançon. Many more examples will follow, all of which fulfill the requisite that the appointment be made to a canonically erected diocese.[17]

C) The Appointment To A See *SEDE PLENA* or *SEDE VACANTE*

The definitions given by Pellegrinus, Andreucci, and Ferraris contain the phrase that this appointment may be made to a see that is vacant or to a see that has a resident bishop.[18] The duration of the appointment depended on the time specified in the letter of appointment. For instance, a vicar apostolic could be sent to rule a diocese where the bishop was ill and thereby incapacitated for actual duty, and naturally the term of this office could not be definitely determined. Again it was often stated that the appointment was to last until the Holy See provided otherwise. And finally, the term of office could be very precisely determined as, for instance, for one year, for two years, until the return of the bishop to his see, etc.

D) Causes Necessary For Appointment

Vermeersch in his commentary on canon 312 divides the causes which require the deputizing of an apostolic administrator into two classes: those which exist when the see is vacant, and those which exist when the see is filled.

[16] Canon 248, §2: Ayrinhac, *Constitution of the Church in the New Code of Canon Law* (New York: Blase Benziger & Co., Inc., 1925), p. 58; Augustine, *A Commentary on the Code,* II, 254.

[17] *Bullarium Diplomatum et Privilegiorum Sanctorum Romanorum Pontficum,* XVI, 782.

[18] *Praxis Vicariorum,* p. 54; *Hierarchia Ecclesiastica,* I, 235; *Prompta Bibliotheca,* s.v. "Vicarius Apostolicus," n. 1.

A) *Sede vacante*—sufficient causes are present if grave dissensions exist in the cathedral chapter; if the vicar capitular is incapable of administering the see; if politico-ecclesiastical situations make it necessary.

B) *Sede plena*—if the bishop governs badly; if the bishop is not *sui compos;* if the bishop is prevented from ruling by the existing civil government.[19]

Pellegrinus enumerates twenty cases in which a vicar apostolic could be appointed by the Holy See, the more important of which are:

1) The bishop rules the Church badly;

2) The bishop is avaricious and extorts money unjustly from his subjects;

3) The bishop is old and therefore impeded from actively administering his diocese;

4) The bishop has been called to Rome;

5) The bishop violates the law of residence;

6) The see is vacant and the cathedral chapter disagrees on the choice of a vicar capitular;

7) The cathedral chapter elects an unworthy or incapable vicar capitular;

8) The see has been vacant for a long time.[20]

Ferraris states three reasons why a vicar apostolic could be sent to rule a diocese: 1) the fear of a long delay in appointing a new bishop to the vacant see; 2) the resident bishop is old or else suffering from poor health; 3) the resident bishop has been suspended or removed from the administration of the see.[21] Strictly

[21] *Prompta Bibliotheca,* s.v. "Vicarius Apostolicus," n. 52; cf. also Andreucci, *Hierarchia Ecclesiastica,* I, 236.

considered the twenty cases enumerated by Pellegrinus can very easily be brought within the scope and range of the categories of reasons advanced by Vermeersch. The list of Pellegrinus, like the categories of Vermeersch, is not exhaustive in its enumeration of possible cases and therefore does not preclude other cases

[19] *Epitome Iuris Canonici,* I, 331.

[20] *Praxis Vicariorum,* p. 54.

which perhaps reflect even additional causes for the appointment of an apostolic administrator.

From this analysis and comparison of the offices of vicar apostolic and apostolic administrator it is concluded that these two are identical even in minute details and that the definition given by Pellegrinus for the former could very easily be substituted for the Code's definition of the apostolic administrator.

Very often, says Ferraris,[22] in addition to the ordinary power accorded to him, the vicar apostolic was given powers either on accounts of his dignity or because of the needs of the particular diocese to which he had been assigned. Ferraris insists, therefore, that it is imperative to examine carefully the letter of appointment wherein was stated in detail the power of each vicar apostolic. Quite naturally, too, the power varied according to whether the see was vacant or filled. Therefore, Andreucci divides the power on the basis of this distinction.[23]

A vicar apostolic deputied when the see was vacant could do all that the former bishop was permitted to do, except those things expressly forbidden by the letter of appointment: he could grant dimissorial letters after a year, and even before that time if he had formerly been the vicar capitular; he could confer benefices; he could execute letters or bulls or matrimonial dispensations directed to the former bishop or vicar general. Briefly he could do all that the former bishop could do except pontificate, and even this was permitted if he was a titular bishop.[24]

A vicar apostolic appointed to a see that is not vacant could: 1) visit the diocese; the bishop, in the event that he accompanied the vicar apostolic on this visitation, could in no way interpose his authority save in the exercise of pontifical functions; and [25] 2)

[22] *Prompta Bibliotheca,* s.v. "Vicarius Apostolicus," n. 3.

[23] *Hierarchia Ecclesiastica,* I, 37.

[24] "Demum, Vicarius Apostolicus, sede vacante omnia facere potest, . . . exceptis Pontificalibus: nisi fuerit Episcopus Titularis, . . . "—Andreucci, *Hierarchia Ecclesiastica,* I, 237-238; Pellegrini, *Praxis Vicariorum,* p. 57; Ferraris, *Prompta Bibliotheca,* s.v. "Vicarius Apostolicus," nn. 25-45.

[25] "Episcopus se ingerere minime potest in regimine Dioecesis cum

hold concourses and synods without the intervention of the bishop.[26]

On the other hand, the vicar apostolic had no power to:

1) grant dimissorial letters, unless this faculty was contained in the letter of appointment;

2) confer benefices; or

3) interfere, in any way, with the juridical affairs of the bishop.[27]

Very briefly the obligation of the vicar apostolic can be stated as including residence, vigilance and judgment. The first, RESIDENCE—the vicar apostolic was held strictly to the law of residence. In the event that he wished to leave his diocese for a long period of time it was necessary for him to obtain permission from the Congregation of Bishops and Regulars.[28] The second, VIGILANCE—the vicar apostolic was held responsible for the integrity of morals and the enforcement of the canons.[29] The third, JUDGMENT—the vicar apostolic had the right to examine and hear any action taking place in his diocese. Likewise he had the power to impose penalities on those who violated ecclesiastical laws.[30]

E) Cessation of Office

The vicar apostolic sent by the Sovereign Pontiff does not lose his office when the Pontiff dies.[31] If the bishop for whom the

Vicarius Apostolicus deputatus fuerit."—S.C. Ep. et Reg., *Caputaquen.*, 27 mart. 1580—Bizzari, *Collectanea in Usum Secretariae Sacrae Congregationis Episcoporum et Regularium edita* (Romae: Ex Typographia Polyglotta, 1885), p. 229.

[26] "Cum ad ipsum Vicarium Apostolicum hoc spectet non ad Episcopum, qui non habet, nisi administrationis, nisi sit ipsi interdicta etiam ista administratio."—Pellegrinus, *Praxis Vicariorum*, p. 57.

[27] ". . . quia iudex minor non potest exercere iurisdictionem suam, praesente maiore iudice."—Pellegrinus, *op. cit.*, p. 57; Ferraris, *Prompta Bibliotheca*, s.v. "Vicarius Apostolicus," n. 13.

[28] Andreucci, *Hierarchia Ecclesiastica*, I, 240; Pellegrinus, *Praxis Vicariorum*, p. 57.

[29] Andreucci, *Hierarchia Ecclesiastica*, I, 241.

[30] Andreucci, *op. cit.*, I, 242.

[31] "Vicarius Apostolicus qui datus est a Pontifice non cessat Sede

vicar apostolic is administering dies, the power of the vicar apostolic remains and the cathedral chapter is incapable of electing a vicar capitular to supersede him.[32] Nor can a vicar apostolic be removed from his jurisdiction by the bishop.[33]

The office and jurisdiction of a vicar apostolic could cease in many ways, particularly:

1) by death;
2) by express renunciation;
3) by revocation which generally happened when:
    a) the vacant Church was provided with a new bishop;
    b) the bishop was restored to full jurisdiction of his church;
    c) the vicar apostolic was found to be unfit;
    d) the vicar apostolic neglected to guard the liberty and rights the Church and of ecclesiastical persons;
    e) the vicar apostolic was found involved in crimes;
    f) the vicar apostolic was odious to the clergy and the people;
    g) the vicar apostolic's time for which he was appointed had expired.

In a word, anything that might prove detrimental to the good of

Vacante Apostolica."—S.C. Ep. et Reg., *Lycien.,* 17 nov. 1590—Bizzarri, *Collectanea,* p. 230; Pellegrinus, *Praxis Vicariorum,* p. 58; Ferraris, *Prompta Bibliotheca,* s.v. "Vicarius Apostolicus," n. 23.

[32] ". . . le facolte dei Vicarii Apostolici non spirano colla morte del Vescovo, ma unicamente dopo che il nuovo vescovo avra presa il possesso leggittimo della sua Chiesa, per loche li dovrete ammonire de astenersi di venire a tale elezione."—S.C. et Reg., *Aprutina.,* 24 ian. 1749—Bizzarri, *Collectanea,* p. 31; S.C. Ep. et Reg., *Aquilan.,* 4 aug. 1578—Bizzarri, *op. cit.,* p. 214; S.C. Ep. et Reg., *Lycien.,* 22 dec. 1628—Bizzarri, *op. cit.,* p. 248; "sed est advertendum, quod capitulum non potest devenire ad electionem Vicarii Capitularis, post habitam notitiam mortis vel translationis Episcopi, quando Vicarius Episcopo defuncti, vel translati missus fuerat a Sancta Sede Apostolica vel a Sacra Congregatione."—Pellegrinus, *Praxis Vicariorum,* p. 38.

[33] "Revera tamen, talis vicarius missus ab Urbe talibus modis, est vere Vicarius Apostolicus, nec Episcopus eum removere potest."—Pellegrinus, *op. cit.,* p. 19.

the souls committed to his care was a sufficient reason for his recall.

In concluding this section on the comparison of the vicar apostolic with the apostolic administrator one may safely state that the two offices are similar in definition, powers, duties and privileges.[34]

Art. 3—The Constitution *INSCRUTABILI*

On June 22, 1622, Pope Gregory XV (1621-1623) published his Constitution *Inscrutabili.*[35] This Constitution organized the Congregation of the Propagation of the Faith to which was assigned and entrusted all that pertained to the propagation of the faith throughout the world. At the same time it declared the jurisdiction of this Congregation to extend over all Societies of Clerics and over all Seminaries founded exclusively for missionary work. To supplement its actual jurisdiction over missionary countries, Pope Gregory assigned to this congregation the duty to appoint the persons who were to govern these regions. Today the persons assigned to govern these territories possess the same name as that which was formerly given to them, namely, vicars or prefects apostolic. The term prefect apostolic however, does not enjoy the same antiquity, for first mention of the prefect apostolic was made in the letter of Pope Clement XII (1730-1740) *"Nuper pro Parte"* published on August 23, 1738.[36]

Naturally the use of this title of vicar apostolic to designate one who was sent to rule a missionary territory not yet canonically

[34] Andreucci, *Hierarchia Ecclesiastica,* I, 244-246; Pellegrinus, *Praxis Vicariorum,* p. 58; Ferraris, *Prompta Bibliotheca,* s.v. "Vicarius Apostolicus," n. 52.

[35] *Codicis Iuris Canonici Fontes cura Emi. Petri Card. Gasparri editi* (9 vols., Romae [later Civitate Vaticana]: Typis Polyglottis Vaticanis, 1923-1939, [vols. VII, VIII, IX *ed cura et studio Emi. Justiani Card Serédi*]), n. 200; (hereafter this work will be cited as *Fontes*).

[36] Winslow, *Vicars and Prefects Apostolic,* The Catholic University of America, Canon Law Studies, n. 24 (Washington, D. C., The Catholic University of America, 1924), p. 9; Ayrinhac, *Constitution of the Church in the New Code of Canon Law,* p. 65; De Martinis, *Ius Pontificum de Propaganda Fide* (Pars I) (7 vols., Romae, 1888-1897), I, 493.

erected into a diocese caused confusion in view of the fact that the name already (since January 22, 1588) indicated one who was sent to administer a diocese in extraordinary cases. Winslow alludes to this when he says:

> Besides the vicar apostolic sent to mission countries there were others appointed by the Holy See to govern dioceses where the hierarchy had been canonically established. They were appointed during a vacancy or when the Bishop was prevented from exercising his jurisdiction by some impediment, e.g., infirmity, insanity, or because of excommunication, or suspension. They are known as apostolic administrators.[37]

Later in his work Winslow offers this example—that the Bishop of Belgrade was appointed vicar apostolic to the Church of Hungary, which under the Turks had no residential bishop. He states, however, that this kind of vicar apostolic may be admitted to belong to the old rather than to the new species.[38] This example, quoted by Winslow, according to his own admission refers to the vicar apostolic as indicating the apostolic administrator. From the time of the Constitution *Inscrutabili* until the twentieth century the name of vicar apostolic was used indiscriminately to indicate both the one sent to rule a missionary country, and the one sent to administer a see that was already canonically instituted as a diocese.

Pope Benedict XIV (1740-1758) used the term vicar apostolic as indicative exclusively of an apostolic administrator. This is particularly discernible from the following passage:—

> Atque hujus generis Apostolicos Vicarios frequenter deputari contingit, sive quum metus est, ne diutius Ecclesia aliqua pastore viduata permaneat, sive quum in Vicarii Capitularis electione controversias et turbas excitandas fore prospicitur; vel quando Episcopus adversa valetudine, aut senio affectus, gregi gubernando impar agnos-

[37] *Vicars and Prefects Apostolic*, p. 5.

[38] *Vicars and Prefects Apostolic*, p. 5; *Appendix ad Bullarium Pontificum Sacrae Congregationis de Propaganda Fide* (2 vols., Romae: Typis Collegii Urbani), I, 250.

> citur; aut denique quum illius culpa fit, ut ab Episcopatus administratione suspendi, aut perpetuo removeri debeat.[39]

From this quotation of Pope Benedict XIV can be derived all the necessary requisites which constitute an apostolic administrator as defined by the Code.[40]

Furthermore, such a use of the term *Vicar Apostolic* to indicate the office of the apostolic administrator was exemplified by many appointments of this Pontiff. One case is particularly important in so far as it enumerates the powers, duties, and obligations of the commisioned vicar apostolic.[41] There existed grave and notorius dissensions in that part of the Diocese of Aquileia which was subjected to Austrian rule. These dissensions, Benedict said, could not be eliminated by his predecessors and up to the present time he himself had obtained no results. He was of the opinion, therefore, that nothing could be done or accomplished in that part unless an ecclesiastical superior, in the person of a vicar apostolic, were deputized to rule by and with the authority of the Holy See.[42] The person chosen for this duty was Charles of Basle, and the term of his office was expressed by means of the phrase, "Ad nostrum, et Sedis Apostolicae beneplacitum." This vicar apostolic was given power to visit churches, pious places, and monasteries of exempt nuns in reference to the cloister; to convoke synods; to elect judges and recall them; to impose penalties; to alienate church property; and, in short, to perform many other duties pertinent to his office.[43] Very clearly this example substantiates the claim that the vicar apostolic of Pope Benedict XIV enjoyed the powers of the apostolic administrator as the latter exists today.

[39] *De Synodo Dioecesana* (2 vols., Romae: Ex Typographia Sacrae Congregationis de Propaganda Fide, 1806), Tom. I, lib. II, c. X, n. 9.

[40] Canon 312.

[41] *Bullarium Benedicti* XIV (12 vols., Mechliniae: P. J. Hanico, 1827), IX, 331 sq; De Martinis, *Ius Pontificum de Propaganda Fide* III, p. 405.

[42] " . . . statuimus, atque decernimus ut ea pars Dioecesis Aquilejensis, quae temporali Austriacae Domus ditioni subest, per unum Vicarium nostrum Apostolicum in spiritualibus gubernetur."—*Bullarium Benedicti* XIV, IX, 335.

[43] *Op. cit.*, IX, 368.

Earlier in Chapter X of his *De Synodo Dioecesana* Pope Benedict XIV refers to Constitution 117 of Sixtus V (*Immensa*), wherein that Pontiff had commissioned the Sacred Congregation of Bishops and Regulars to choose men endowed with knowledge and fear of God to rule dioceses as vicars apostolic whenever the situation warranted it. Then the Pope enumerates the reasons for deputizing these vicars apostolic. It has already been shown that these vicars apostolic mentioned by Pope Sixtus V enjoyed an office almost identical with that of the present day apostolic administrators. The vicar apostolic mentioned by Pope Benedict XIV in this section may therefore be regarded practically as an apostolic administrator.[44]

Art. 4—Writers of the Nineteenth and Twentieth Centuries

The two fold use of the term *Vicar Apostolic* lasted until the publication of the Constitution *Sapienti Consilio* (1908) of Pope Pius X (1903-1914).[45] Writers of the nineteenth and twentieth centuries definitely indicated that a vicar apostolic was one who was sent either to a country where no constituted hierarchy existed, or one who was sent to administer canonically erected dioceses. Many eminent canonists of these two centuries have been consulted relevant to this point. It is believed that instead of delineating the tenets of each author individually, which would prove superfluous, the following conclusions will sufficiently indicate them.

1) Vicars apostolic were of two species: those who were sent to missionary regions, and those who were sent to canonically erected dioceses.[46]

[44] *De Synodo Dioecesana,* Tom. I, lib. II, c. X, n. 9.

[45] *AAS,* I (1909), 21.

[46] Devoti, *Institutionum Canonicarum Liber IV* (2 vols., Leodii: H. Dessain, 1860), I, n. 86; Bouix, *Tractatus de Curia Romana* (Parisiis: Bourget Calas & Cie., 1895), p. 646; De Angelis, *Praelectiones Iuris Canonici* (6 vols., Romae: Ex Typographia Della Pace, 1877-1878) Tom. I, pars. II, 111-113; Zitelli, *Apparatus Iuris Ecclesiastici* (Romae: Ex

2) It was the exclusive prerogative of the Sovereign Pontiff to appoint a vicar apostolic to a canonically erected diocese.[47]

3) There was postulated the presence of a grave cause to call for the appointment of a vicar apostolic.

4) Not one of the consulted authors treated the *Apostolic Administrator ex professo.* This naturally induces one to believe that the name was not established. A few of the authors did refer *en passant* to the term *Apostolic Administrator.*[48]

From the reading of the authors of the nineteenth and twentieth centuries it may be concluded that the term *Vicar Apostolic* was used up to the time of the *"Sapienti Consilio"* to indicate a prelate sent to administer a canonically erected diocese. Only gradually did the name *Apostolic Administrator* begin to appear, and in 1908 it was declared the official title to indicate an official sent by the Sovereign Pontiff to rule a vacant or quasi-vacant diocese.

ART. 5—EXAMPLES OF APOSTOLIC ADMINISTRATORS COMMISSIONED DURING THIS PERIOD

Although the name vicar apostolic predominately indicated those prelates who were sent either to a region where no canonically erected dioceses existed or to a diocese which was vacant or occupied, yet there are found instances in the nineteenth and

Typis Soc. Ecit. Rom., 1886), pp. 127-133; De Brabandere, *Iuris Canonici et Iuris Canonico- Civilis Compendium* (2 vols., Brugis, 1866-1867), I 225; Baart, *The Roman Curia* (New York: Fr. Pustet & Co., 1895), p. 317; Lega, *Praelectiones in Textum Iuris Canonici de Iudiciis Ecclesiasticis* (4 vols.,Romae: Typis Vaticanis, 1896-1901), I, 451; Wernz, *Ius Decretalium,* II, 468, n. 698.

[47] *Ibid.*

[48] Lombardi, *Iuris Canonici Privati Institutiones* (Romae: 1906), p. 281; "Interdum sede Episcopali plena, si Episcopus a regenda dioecesi impediatur, a Rom. Pontifice non datur Vicarius Apostolicus, sed ob causas speciales Administrator Apostolicus."—Wernz, *Ius Decretalium,* II, 472, n. 706; "Potestas Vicarii seu Administratoris Apostolici."—Lega, *Praelectiones in Textum Iuris Canonici de Iudiciis Ecclesiasticis,* I, 451; " . . . non semper deputatur Vicarius Apostolicus; sed quandoque ejusmodi dioecesi regimen Administratori Apostolico committitur."—Bouix, *Tractatus de Curia Romana,* p. 662.

twentieth centuries, prior to the Constitution *Sapienti Consilio,* in which some persons who were sent to administer dioceses were called apostolic administrators. In fact, even some of the Pontiffs of these two centuries used the name vicar apostolic and apostolic administrator indiscriminately. For every Pontiff from Pius VII (1800-1823) to Leo XIII (1878-1903) had occasion to commission vicars apostolic (or as some preferred to call them, *Apostolic Administrators*) to dioceses either *sede plena* or *sede vacante.*[49] The existence of vicars apostolic dates back to 1588 when Pope Sixtus V gave them official recognition. They have been pointed out definitively as the prototype of the apostolic administrator. Naturally the question arises, when did the name *Apostolic Administrator* actually come into use. To give a precise answer by indicating a certain year and date is practically impossible. However, it can be asserted with assurance that this name was used during the nineteenth century by various pontiffs. In illustration of this point recourse will be had to several pontificates wherein can be found examples of the commission of *Apostolic Administrators.*

Pope Pius VII (1800-1823) made John Carroll the first apostolic administrator in the United States. During Bishop Carroll's time the United States acquired the territory of Louisiana from the French Government in 1803. Consequently, the territory acquired came under the jurisdiction of the Bishop of Baltimore as apostolic administrator.[50] In view of the magnitude of the task the Bishop of Baltimore was then endeavoring to perform, this new office of apostolic administrator to Louisiana proved too much for him to fulfill. As a result, on April 5, 1808, the Sacred Congregation of the Propagation of the Faith sent a letter to Bishop Carroll instructing him to appoint Charles Nerinckx, or

[49] The Popes included between Pius VII, and Leo XIII are: Leo XII, (1823-1829), Pius VIII (1829-1830), Gregory XVI (1831-1846) and Pius IX, (1846-1878).

[50] Shearer, *Pontificia Americana,* The Catholic University of America, Studies in American Church History, n. 15 (Washington, D. C.: The Catholic University of America, 1933), p. 91.

some other fitting priest, apostolic administrator to the diocese of Louisiana.[51] Charles Nerinckx refused to accept the post and no apostolic administrator was appointed to the diocese until August 12, 1812, when William Du Bourg received the following letter from Archbishop Carroll:

> I, the undersigned Archbishop of Baltimore . . . delegate and send you, very Rev. William DuBourg to the diocese of New Orleans . . . to rule this same diocese in the capacity of apostolic administrator, and with the rights of an Ordinary, for so long as shall be the Sovereign Pontiff's and the Holy See's good pleasure.[52]

Pope Leo XII (1823-1829) used in one instance the name vicar apostolic, and then a few years later in effecting the same type of appointment designated the appointee as an apostolic administrator. On June 3, 1824, Pope Leo appointed Gregory, the titular Bishop of Hippo, vicar apostolic to the united dioceses of Osimo and Cingoli.[53] Gregory was granted permission to exercise full power of orders and of jurisdiction in both dioceses, only the conferring of benefices being reserved to the Holy See.[54] But when on March 20, 1827, Pope Leo XII appointed Joseph

[51] " . . .fraternitati tuae tunc per praesentes committimus et mandamus quatenus, si expedire judicaveris in Domino, ad supradictam Louisiana Provinciam, aut dilectum Carolum Nerinx, de cujus zelo et virtute plurimum in Deo confidimus, aut eo forsan se imparem sentiente, alium idoneum quem noveris cum qualitate Administratoris Apostolici et juribus ordinarii ad tempus."—This document is not contained in the *Bullarium Sacrae Congregationis de Propaganda Fide,* or *Ius Pontificium de Propaganda Fide,* but is found in the *St. Louis Catholic Historical Review,* I (1918), 73; Shearer, *Pontificia Americana,* pp. 95-96.

[52] *St. Louis Catholic Historical Review,* I (1918), 75. Du Bourg was appointed Bishop of New Orleans in 1815.

[53] " . . . te, de cujus fide, doctrina, prudentia rerumque experientia plurimum in Domino confidimus, Vicarium Apostolicum supradictarum vacantium unitarum Episcopalium Ecclesiarum tam in spiritualibus, quam in temporalibus, ad nostrum et Sedis Apostolicae beneplacitum, tenore praesentium eligimus, constituimus et deputamus . . . . "—*Continuatio Bullarii Romani Leonis XII* (Prati: In Typographia Aldina, 1854), p. 72.

[54] *Loc. cit.*

Rosati to the Bishopric of St. Louis, it was with the specification that he also continue to rule the diocese of New Orleans as the APOSTOLIC ADMINISTRATOR.[55] On August 16, 1828, the same Pontiff in a communication to the same Joseph Rosati addresses the letter thus:

> "Venerabili Fratri Josepho Episcopo S. Ludovici, et APOSTOLICO Ecclesiae Neo-Aurelianensi ADMINISTRATORI." [56]

Pope Gregory XVI (1831-1846) on September 9, 1831, induced by very grave causes, deprived Henry Conwell (Bishop of Philadelphia) of all jurisdiction in Philadelphia, and declared that the power and jurisdiction formerly enjoyed by him were transferred to Bishop Kenrick, coadjutor of Philadelphia and Titular Bishop of Arath.[57] Although the appointee is neither referred to as a vicar apostolic nor as an apostolic administrator, this case, nevertheless, presents a true example of our present day apostolic administrator.

During the same Pontificate Bishop Dionysius, the vicar apostolic to Lugano, wrote to the Congregation of Bishops and Regulars to ascertain whether or not he remained in office after the death of the Archbishop of Lugano who was very ill. The Congregation replied that his power would continue even after the death of the Archbishop and that the cathedral chapter possessed no power to elect a vicar capitular. This answer was given on March 21, 1832.[58]

[55] " . . . ac praeterea mandamus ut tu tamquam Administrator Apostolicus dioecesim Novae Aureliae donec aliter haec Apostolica Sede statuerit gubernare prosequaris . . . "—*Ius Pontificum de Propaganda Fide* (Pars I), IV, 682; *Bullarium Pontificum Sacrae Congregationis Propaganda Fide* (5 vols., Romae: Typis Collegii Urbani, 1839-1841), V, 25.

[56] *Jus Pontificum de Propaganda Fide,* Pars I, IV, 705.

[57] " . . . quo idem Episcopus Conwell omni jurisdictione Episcopali in illam Dioecesim destitutus intelligi deberet, et praeterea eam omnem jurisdictionem ipsi episcopo Kenrick ejus Coadjutori confirmare statuit." —*Bullarium Pontificum Sacrae Congregationis dePropaganda Fide,* V, 67.

[58] *Analecta Juris Pontificii* (Romae, 1853; Paris 1860-1890), XIII (1874), 1144.

On another occasion, on June 23, 1844, Pope Gregory appointed Charles Pooten, titular Bishop of Maronana, apostolic administrator to the Archdiocese of Antivari in Montenegro. This appointment was necessitated by the conduct of Vincent Battucci,the Archbishop of Antivari, who was suspended from the exercise of his episcopal jurisdiction. Apostolic Administrator Pooten was given the same faculties Archbishop Battucci had possessed.[59]

Again, when Gregory was informed of the poor health of Cardinal Benevenuti, the Bishop of Cingoli and Osimo, he sent Cardinal Ostini, the Bishop of the Diocese of Jepi, as apostolic administrator to Osimo and Cingoli. This step was taken by the Pontiff to forestall any harm coming to the spiritual welfare of the diocese of Cingoli and Osimo. Cardinal Ostini was given full and free jurisdiction in all things which would prove beneficial and necessary for his administration.[60]

Pope Pius IX (1846-1878) on May 21, 1851, stated that Peter di Benedetto, Archbishop of Reggio, due to old age and infirmity was unable to perform the exercise of his pontifical duties. Therefore, with the good of the Church of Reggio in mind the Pontiff relieved di Benedetto from the worry and care of his office and appointed Raphael Terrigno, Bishop of Bovia, apostolic administrator to Reggio. Bishop Terrigno was given full power over the Church and enjoyed the same faculties as were formerly held by Archbishop di Benedetto. Some of the power accorded to Bishop Terrigno was:—

a) to administer the *"mensa episcopalis;"*
b) to deputize a vicar-general;
c) to exercise pontifical functions;

59 " . . . Administratorem Apostolicum Archdioecesis Antibarensis, suspenso interim ac remoto ab exercitio jurisdictionis episcopalis ven. fratre Vincentio Battucci Archiepiscopo, cum omnibus et singulis facultatibus quibus ipse Vincentius potiebatur, auctoritate Nostra Apostolica, hisce litteris eligimus, constituimus et deputamus."—*Acta Gregorii XVI* (4 vols., Romae: A. M. Bernasconi, Ex Typographia Polyglotta, 1901-1904), III, 321.

60 *Analecta Iuris Pontificii,* XIII (1874), 547-548.

d) to confer benefices;
e) to ordain;
f) to grant commendatory and dimissorial letters for Sacred Ordinations.[61]

During the same Pontificate Archbishop John Sabbioni of Spoleto died. Rather than leave the see vacant Pius IX appointed John Arnaldi apostolic administrator. John was granted the faculties of giving dimissorial letters and of ordaining clerics. However, he was not permitted to confer ecclesiastical benefices.[62]

Pope Leo XIII (1878-1903) appointed Vincent Molo, the Titular Bishop of Calliopolis, apostolic administrator to Lugano, a diocese in Switzerland. In a very lengthy letter the Pontiff outlined the duties, powers, and faculties of this apostolic administrator. These faculties included the power to ordain clerics; to offer public prayers when the good of the Church demanded it; to convene a chapter; to convoke and celebrate synods; to publish the acts of the synods; to pontificate; to possess and use all insignia, prerogatives, and honors pertinent to his episcopal rank.[63]

Art. 6—The Constitution *SAPIENTI CONSILIO*

In 1903 Pope Pius X (1903-1914) succeeded Pope Leo XIII to the throne of St. Peter. This Pontiff through the medium of his Constitution *Sapienti Consilio,* published on June 29, 1908, reorganized the Roman Curia.[64] According to this Constitution the Sacred Congregation of Bishops and Regulars was discontinued and the Sacred Congregation of the Consistory took over part of its work. This Congregation was given the duty of,

> . . . founding new dioceses and chapters both cathedral and collegiate; of dividing dioceses already constituted;

[61] *Analecta Iuris Pontificii,* XXIII (1884), 767-768.

[62] *Analecta Iuris Pontificii,* XXIII (1884) 767-768.

[63] *Leonis XIII Pontificis Maximi Acta* (22 vols., Romae: Ex Typographia Vaticana, 1881-1903), VIII, 301-325.

[64] *AAS,* I (1909), 21; Martin, *the Roman Curia* (New York: Benziger Brothers, 1913), p. 11; Cappello, *De Curia Romana Iuxta Reformationem a Pio X* (2 vols., Romae: Fr. Pustet, 1911), I, 25; Leitner, *De Curia Romana* (Ratisbonae: Fr. Pustet, 1909), p. 1.

> of electing bishops, APOSTOLIC ADMINISTRATORS, coadjutors, and auxiliary bishops . . .[65]

This Constitution, then, marks the first official recognition given to the title *APOSTOLIC ADMINISTRATOR.* Henceforth there is found a sharp distinction between the vicar apostolic and the apostolic administrator. No longer are these two names used interchangeably. Quite definitely this Constitution is responsible for outlining the duties of the various congregations in such a manner as to avoid the concurrent competence of several Congregations in the same affair. It now became the exclusive right of the Sacred Congregation of the Propagation of the Faith to exercise jurisdiction over Prefects and vicars apostolic. Martin says,

> There are some districts over which the Sovereign Pontiff appoints prefects apostolic, districts in which the Gospel having been preached by missionaries, he appoints some priests to carry on the work of teaching the Catholic doctrine and administering the Sacraments. There are other places where the Catholic Church has made greater progress and over which the Sovereign Pontiff has appointed Vicars recommended by the Congregation of the Propaganda. These are usually Bishops; but they differ from ordinary Bishops since the latter exercise jurisdiction in their own name, because they receive it attached to the office conferred upon them by the Pope; the former exercise the jurisdiction immediately delegated to them by the Pope.[66]

The legislation indicated in the Constitution *Sapienti Consilio,* wherein the Sacred Congregation of the Consistory was entrusted with the power of nominating and commissioning *Apostolic Administrators* to dioceses when the good of the Church and the welfare of souls necessitated it, remained unchanged to the time of the promulgation of the Code of Canon Law.

Art. 7—The Promulgation of the Code of Canon Law

With the promulgation of the Code of Canon Law by the

[65] Martin, *The Roman Curia,* p. 31.
[66] Martin, *The Roman Curia,* pp. 63-64.

Constitution *Providentissima Mater* of Pope Benedict XV on May 27, 1917, and its subsequent binding force on the universal Church commencing on May 19, 1918, the office of *Apostolic Administrator,* as outlined in canons 312-318, became permanently established. The Sacred Congregation of the Consistory retained the power to nominate apostolic administrators.[67]

[67] " . . . Episcopos, Administratores Apostolicos, Coadiutores et Auxiliares Episcoporum constituendas proponere, . . . "—Canon 248, § 2.

PART II

CANONICAL COMMENTARY

Chapter V

NOMINATION AND ACCESSION OF THE APOSTOLIC ADMINISTRATOR

Canon 312. Dioecesis canonice erectae regimen, sive plena, sive vacante sede, aliquando Summus Pontifex ob graves et speciales causas Administratori Apostolico vel in perpetuum vel ad tempus committit.

Art. 1. Exclusive Competence of the Sovereign Pontiff to appoint apostolic administrator *in perpetuum* or *ad tempus.*

The Canon states clearly and definitely that the appointment of an apostolic administrator is an exclusive prerogative of the Sovereign Pontiff. This provision was initially stated in the *Liber Sextus* of Pope Boniface VIII (1294-1303) in the following words:

> Ecclesiae Cathedrali vacanti visitator ab alio quam a Romano Pontifice deputari non potest, nisi forte capitulum in spiritualibus et temporalibus negligenter aut perperam administret. Tunc enim Archiepiscopus ob negligentiam vel malitiam capituli; eo vocato, causaeque super hoc cognitione praemissa, visitatorem seu administratorem eidem ecclesiae licite poterit deputare.[1]

The present Code of Canon Law retains this legislation when it inserts the term *Summus Pontifex* in the body of canon 312. Previous to the time of Pope Boniface VIII, however, this faculty of deputizing an extraordinary administrator for a diocese that was vacant or quasi-vacant was committed to the Metropolitan, as well as to those bishops who were contiguous to the diocese in

[1] C. 4, *de supplenda negligentia praelatorum,* I, 8, in VI°.

[2] Villien-Magnin, *Dictionnaire de Droit Canonique* (Paris, 1924), s.v. "Administrateur Apostolique," n. 181; Toso, *Ad Codicem Iuris Canonici Commentaria Minora* (5 vols., Romae: Marietti, 1920-1934), II, 134; Cance, *Le Code de Droit Canonique* (4 ed., 3 vols., J. Gabalda et Fils., 1930), I, p. 304, n. 303.

question.[2] Moreover, this ancient practice, which was in vogue prior to the time of the Decretals, was permitted and retained in the United States until the promulgation of the Code of Canon Law.[3]

It is not to be inferred, however, that this office of apostolic administrator is utilized every time a see is vacant. On the contrary, this is the extraordinary manner of administering a vacant or quasi-vacant diocese. Therefore, the insistence on the word *aliquando* is important for it serves to impress forcibly the whole notion of this office: namely, an extraordinary measure adopted by the Sovereign Pontiff to provide for the government of dioceses which demand special attention. Consequently, then, this administrator, as Coronata says, is termed apostolic because he owes his origin to the Successor of the Apostles, the Supreme Pontiff, who alone is capable of appointing prelates to this office.[4] Another obvious reason for calling this prelate an apostolic administrator is that like the vicar apostolic and the prefect apostolic[5] he receives his power and authority directly from the Supreme Pontiff.[6]

For the Pope personally to select capable men, and attend to the various and minute details necessary for the election of an Apostolic Administrator would be a prodigious task. Necessarily, then, he has imparted the faculty of nominating apostolic administrators to the Sacred Congregation of the Consistory. Occasionally, also, this power is exercised by the Sacred Congregation for Extraordinary Ecclesiastical affairs.[7]

[3] *AAS,* XI (1919), 75-76; Toso, *Ad Commentaria Minora,* II, 134.

[4] CIC, Lib. II, Sec. II, Tit. VII; *Institutiones Iuris Canonici ad Usum Utriusque Cleri et Scholarum* (5 vols., Taurini: Marietti, vols. I and II (2 ed. 1939), vol. III (1933), vol. IV (1935), vol. V (1936), I, p. 457, n. 379.

[5] Canon 293.

[6] "Apostolicus Administrator regit dioecesim loco et auctoritate a R. P. accepta, unde participat R. P. Supremae Potestatis . . . "—Cocchi, *Commentarium in Codicem Iuris Canonici ad usum Scholarum* (5 vols., in 8, Taurinorum Augustae: Marietti, 1922-1930), II, p. 153, n. 229.

[7] Canons 248, § 2; 255; *AAS,* XIV (1922), 598-599.

The duration of the appointment of an apostolic administrator may be permanent (*in perpetuum*) or temporary (*ad tempus*), depending entirely on the stipulations expressly contained in the letters of appointment. The office of an apostolic administrator is termed permanent when no specific limit of time is affixed to the term of the office. Bishop Borghini was made the permanent apostolic administrator of Treja by the following words contained in his letter of appointment.

> . . . qui proinde Episcopus Sancti Severini [Adam Borghini] et Administrator Apostolicus Treiensis perpetuo nominabitur . . . .[8]

A temporary apostolic administrator is one assigned to administer a diocese for a certain period of time usually stipulated in the letter of appointment. One pre-Code appointment is worthy of mention, because it specified when the office of temporary apostolic administrator commenced and when it terminated:

> Cum igitur electioni idem de se nondum assensum praebuerit . . . curam et administrationem Ecclesiae antedictae in spiritualibus et temporalibus a festo purificationis Beatae Mariae Virginis proximo usque ad annum eidem Archdiacono auctoritate apostolica duximus committendam . . . [9]

The present method of indicating the appointment of a temporary apostolic administrator is the use of the words, *ad beneplacitum nostrum,* or in the event the diocese is vacant, *quousque autem haec dioecesis de proprio pastore provideatur,* in the letter of appointment.[10]

A) Resident Bishop Impeded

The apostolic administrator, unlike the vicar capitular who is sent or elected to rule only a vacant diocese,[11] may be sent by the Sovereign Pontiff to rule a see either *sede plena* or *sede vacante.*

[8] *AAS,* XII (1920), 321.

[9] Berger, *Les Registres D'Innocent IV* (4 vols., Parisiis: E. Thorin, 1884-1897), I, n. 388.

[10] *AAS,* XIV (1922), 598; XIII (1921), 250; XIII (1921), 410.

[11] Canon 433.

Naturally, it is of paramount importance, therefore, to discern and ascertain when a diocese is *plena* or *vacans*. A diocese *sede plena* retains its resident bishop. Such an episcopal see, however, becomes impeded when its incumbent, although retaining the title, cannot discharge the functions of the office owing to the presence of physical or canonical impediments.[12] Physical impediments include captivity, relegation, exile, or incapacity or inability on the part of the resident bishop. Captivity does not necessarily and exclusively imply the abduction of a bishop from one place, and the subsequent induction of him into another place, but may likewise refer to instances in which the bishop is deprived of all modes of communication with his priests or people. The obvious outcome of this type of physical impediment is the curtailment of all acts of jurisdiction. Pagans, heretics, and schismatics are most frequently the motivating force in the removal of a bishop.[13] Relegation is the confinement of the bishop to a given place outside his respective diocese. Exile is the expulsion of the bishop from his proper country. Inability or incapacity is the failure to administer a diocese in a capable manner. The impediment of incapacity may attach culpably or inculpably to the resident bishop according as he evinces an absolute indifference to the cares of his diocese or suffers from some mental and rational unbalance.[14]

Unlike physical impediments, which prevent him from exercising his power, canonical impediments forbid the resident bishop not only to exercise his office but also to entrust the

[12] Canon 429, § 1; Ayrinhac, *Constitution of the Church in the New Code of Canon Law* (New York: Blase Benziger & Co., Inc., 1925), p. 268; Coronata, *Institutiones Iuris Canonici*, I, p. 545, n. 456; Blat, *Commentarium Textus Codicis Iuris Canonici* (6 vols., Romae: Ferrari, 1921-1927), II, 462.

[13] Coronata, *Institutiones Iuris Canonici*, I, p. 545, n. 456; Jaeger, *The Administration of Vacant and Quasi-Vacant Dioceses in the United States*, pp. 213-214.

[14] Jaeger, *op. cit.*, p. 214; Ayrinhac, *Constitution of the Church in the New Code of Canon Law*, p. 268; Coronata, *Institutiones Iuris Canonici*, I, p. 546, n. 456; Toso, *Commentaria Minora*, II, 134-135.

powers of his office to his vicar-general or any other person whom he chooses to delegate.[15] Any bishop, therefore, who incurs the penalty of excommunication,[16] interdict,[17] or suspension, is *ipso facto* prohibited from exercising his power of jurisdiction.[18] The question naturally arises: Who rules a diocese when the bishop is impeded from doing so by the presence of physical or canonical impediments? When the bishop is impeded by the presence of a physical impediment the diocese is ruled by the vicar-general, or by any other priest whom the incapacitated bishop has chosen to delegate—unless the Holy See has provided otherwise.[19] The phrase *"nisi Sancta Sedes aliter providerit"* of canon 429, § 1, implies reference to an apostolic administrator, for according to canon 312 the Holy See is wont to make such an appointment when grave and special circumstances arise.[20] Such circumstances would be present when a bishop, impaired by a lack of administrative ability, had committed his diocese to financial blunders. In this instance it would not at all be unlikely for the Holy See, in order to prevent more harm befalling the diocese, to intervene by appointing an apostolic administrator until matters had become righted.

On the other hand, in the case of the bishop who is impeded from the rule of his see through the existence of a canonical impediment, e.g., excommunication, interdict, or suspension, the situation is different. The canonically impeded bishop is incapable of transferring his jurisdiction to the vicar-general, whose jurisdiction is *ipso facto* suspended when the bishop is thus impeded.[21]

[15] Canon 371.

[16] Canons 2259, § 2; 2261; 2265.

[17] Canon 2275.

[18] Canons 2283; 2284; Coronata, *Institutiones Iuris Canonici,* I, p. 546, footnote 7.

[19] Canon 429, §1.

[20] Jaeger, *The Administration of Vacant and Quasi-Vacant Dioceses,* p. 214; Wernz—Vidal, *Ius Canonicum* (7 tom. in 8 vols., Romae: Apud Aedes Universitatis Gregorianae, 1923-1938), II, p. 753, n. 709; Cance, *Le Code de Droit Canonique,* I, p. 390, n. 381; Toso, *Commentaria Minora,* III, 77.

[21] Canon 371.

Instead, the administration of the diocese passes to the Metropolitan who must have recourse to the Holy See. In the event that the Metropolitan is under censure or fails to act, the oldest suffragan bishop shall at once have recourse to the Holy See.[22] Again, in this instance, the Holy See may deem it necessary to dispatch an apostolic administrator to the see so deprived of its bishop. Patently, then, the apostolic administrator is eligible for appointment to a see *sede plena* when the bishop is impeded from ruling his see through the presence of a physical or canonical impediment.

B) Episcopal See Vacant

An episcopal see becomes vacant when the incumbent ceases to hold the title or to be really its bishop. This may occur by death, by resignation duly accepted by the Sovereign Pontiff, by legitimate transfer, or by deprivation of office pronounced in legal form.[23]

1) Death of the resident bishop constitutes the usual manner in which a see becomes vacant.[24] Just as all other bonds are dissolved by death, so too the bond existing between a bishop and his see terminates immediately upon the death of the bishop. Consequently, then, unless the resident bishop had an auxiliary bishop with the right of succession, the see upon his death is unquestionably vacant and the ordinary procedure involving the cathedral chapter in the election of a vicar capitular must be observed,[25] unless the Holy See has provided otherwise.[26]

2) Resignation or renunciation is the free cession, motivated by the presence of a just cause, of an ecclesiastical office made

[22] Canon 429, §5.

[23] Canons 430-431; Ayrinhac, *Constitution of the Church in the New Code of Canon Law,* p. 270; Toso, *Commentaria Minora,* III, 79-80; Coronata, *Institutiones Iuris Canonici,* I, p. 549-550, nn. 459-460; Wernz-Vidal, *Ius Canonicum,* II, pp. 751-752, n. 707.

[24] Jaeger, *The Administration of Vacant and Quasi-Vacant Dioceses,* p. 79; Blat, *Commentarium Textus,* II, p. 465, n. 474; Coronata, *Institutiones Iuris Canonici,* I, p. 549, n. 459.

[25] Canons 429-444; Maroto, *Institutiones Iuris Canonici* I, p. 802, n. 675.

[26] Canons 312-318.

to, and accepted by, a competent superior.[27] Formerly a distinction was made between a renunciation and a resignation. Renunciation, according to the Apostolic Datary, was the *pura et simplex cessio beneficii,* while resignation was the *dismissio beneficii in alterius favorem.*[28] For resignation to become effective all the above mentioned conditions must be realized and verified. Accordingly, therefore, anyone possessing his mental faculties, and capable of performing a human act is adjudged competent to resign an ecclesiastical office, unless such a resignation is expressly forbidden by a special prohibition.[29] Wherefore, outside of the cases indicated in the Code, and when there is no mental debility, special prohibition, grave and unjust intimidation, deceit, substantial error, or simony, a resignation is valid but even then only when it is made in writing, or orally in the presence of two witnesses, or through a proxy by a special mandate.[30] An episcopal resignation must be submitted to the Sovereign Pontiff, as he alone is competent to accept the resignation of bishops,[31] This type of resignation or renunciation is termed "express." Renunciation may also be "tacit."[32] An actual and de-

[27] Maroto, *Institutiones Iuris Canonici,* I, p. 804, n. 678; Wernz-Vidal, *Ius Canonicum,* II, p. 325, n. 324; Jaeger, *The Administration of Vacant and Quasi-Vacant Dioceses in the United States,* pp. 80-82; Vermeersch-Creusen, *Epitome Iuris Canonici,* I, p. 252, n. 302; Coronata, *Institutiones Iuris Canonici,* I, p. 549, n. 459; Blat, *Commentarium Textus Codicis Iuris Canonici,* II, 155-160; *Cance, Le Code de Droit Canonique,* I, p. 195, n. 176.

[28] Maroto, *Institutiones Iuris Canonici,* I, p. 804, footnote 1; Wernz-Vidal, *Ius Canonicum,* II, p. 325, footnote 1.

[29] Canons 184; 186; 1484; 1485; 1486; 89; Coronata, *Institutiones Iuris Canonici,* I, p. 314, n. 262; Toso, *Commentaria Minora,* II, 151.

[30] Canons 185-186.

[31] "Romano Pontifici praeter officia reservata ut officia episcopalia . . . " —Coronata, *Institutiones Iuris Canonici,* I, p. 319, n. 264; "Admissio renuntiationis per Romanum Pontificem omnino requiritur ad valorem resignationis . . . Episcoporum etiam titularium . . . "—Wernz-Vidal, *Ius Canonicum,* II, p. 332, n. 331.

[32] Canon 188 outlines 8 instances which *ipso facto* entail a tacit resignation.

tailed analysis of each method of ceding an ecclesiastical office will not be included here, but only the salient points of each. Other points, while of sufficient importance to warrant attention, do not fall within the scope of this treatise.

3) Transfer is the canonical change motivated by a just cause of an ecclesiastical person from one office to another office and is effected by a competent superior.[33] The Sovereign Pontiff alone is the competent superior in respect to the transfer of bishops from one see to another. A transfer implicitly contains a removal from one office and the promotion to another.[34] Quite obviously the Pope is hesitant to change a bishop from one see and send him to another unless the good of the Church and the welfare of the the bishop prompts and warrants it.[35] Transfers, however, are freely enacted by the Supreme Pontiff and it does not matter whether the bishop is willing or unwilling to be transferred, or whether the reason for such action be due to his culpability or to other causes.[36] The transferred bishop must occupy his new diocese within four months after receiving the necessary notification from the Holy See.[37] At the same time as the notification is received the bishop becomes *ipso facto* the administrator of the diocese from which he is transferred, and the vicar-general loses

[33] Coronata, *Institutiones Iuris Canonici,* I, p. 321, n. 266; Maroto, *Institutiones Iuris Canonici,* I, p. 818, n. 688; Blat, *Commentarium Textus,* II, p. 161, n. 140; Wernz-Vidal, *Ius Canonicum,* II, 341; Vermeersch-Creusen, *Epitome Iuris Canonici,* I, p. 256, n. 309; Toso, *Commentaria Minora,* II, 161.

[34] Wernz-Vidal, *Ius Canonicum,* II, p. 342, n. 349; Coronata, *Institutiones Iuris Canonici,* I, p. 550, n. 460.

[35] "Quamvis Romanus Pontifex ex plenitudine suae potestatis Episcopum confirmatum aut multo magis iam consecratum etiam invitum a vinculo unionis ecclesiae cathedralis absolvere et in aliam sedem episcopalem transferre valeat, tamen in ordinaria praxi recepta translationis episcoporum sive confirmatorum sive iam consecratorum non fiunt, nisi praevio consensu Episcopi transferendi."—Wernz-Vidal, *Ius Canonicum,* II, p. 349, n. 358.

[36] Jaeger, *The Administration of Vacant and Quasi-Vacant Dioceses,* p. 83

[37] Canons 430, §3; 34, §3, n. 3.

all his jurisdiction. Jaeger in referring to this administrator puts in parentheses the name (vicar capitular). Canon 430, § 3 however says that the transferred bishop obtains, in the former diocese, the same powers and obligations as a vicar capitular. But this canon does not call him a vicar capitular. In reality, this administrator is an apostolic administrator commissioned to administer the vacant diocese until a new bishop is appointed or the Holy See rules otherwise.[38]

4) Deprivation of an office implies that a bishop is removed from his see on account of the commission of some crime and independently of his consent.[39]

The Code makes mention of several instances wherein one is deprived of his ecclesiastical office *ipso facto,* but only one instance has reference to a bishop: namely, that in which the bishop culpably neglects to be consecrated within the stipulated time of three months and allows the neglect to continue for another three months.[40]

Although it is the custom to provide a vicar capitular until the election of a new bishop in the case of a diocese that is vacant, instances may arise which evoke the appointment of apostolic administrators.

C) Existence of Special and Grave Causes

Canon 312 stipulates that the appointment of an apostolic administrator is resorted to only when there exists a grave and special cause for the deputizing of such an official. Notwithstanding this, however, the Code does not list the causes that prove

[38] Canon 315, §2, n. 2; Jaeger, *The Administration of Vacant and Quasi-Vacant Dioceses in the United States,* p. 86.

[39] Coronata, *Institutiones Iuris Canonici,* I, p. 321, n. 266; Wernz-Vidal, *Ius Canonicum,* II, p. 350, n. 360; Jaeger, *op. cit.,* pp. 82-83; Maroto, *Institutiones Iuris Canonici,* I, p. 811, n. 685.

[40] Canon 2398:- Si quis ad episcopatum promotus, contra praescriptum can. 333 intra tres menses consecrationem suscipere neglexerit, fructus non facit suos, fabricae ecclesiae cathedralis applicandos; et si postea in eadem negligentia per totidem menses perstiterit, episcopatu privatus ipso iure manet; Jaeger, *The Administration of Vacant and Quasi-Vacant Dioceses in the United States,* pp. 82-83.

sufficient for the assigning of apostolic administrators. Obviously it rests entirely with the Sovereign Pontiff to judge whether a sufficient cause exists. It would be difficult to enumerate the multiple causes which may prompt the sending of an apostolic administrator to a diocese. Most authors give causes which, they believe, are sufficient to warrant the deputizing of an apostolic administrator. These causes in most instances, are ones which have on past occasions motivated the Sovereign Pontiff to send apostolic administrators to a vacant or an impeded diocese.

Vermeersch-Creusen divide the causes into two distinct classes which correspond to the two occasions when an apostolic administrator may be appointed; namely, when the see is vacant, and when the see is impeded.

A) *Sede plena*—a) if the bishop rules poorly; b) if he is mentally ill; c) if he is impeded by the civil government.

B) *Sede vacante*—a) when grave dissensions are present in the chapter; b) when an unworthy person has been elected vicar capitular; c) when the election of a vicar capitular has been invalid; or d) when the country is engaged in politico-ecclesiastical affairs.[41]

Wernz-Vidal utilize the same classification, noting particularly that it is often the case that the resident bishop because of some inability, whether it be culpable or inculpable is deprived of the administration of his see. This deprivation may be motivated by a) inexperience; b) mental diseases; c) unjust infringement by the civil authorities who either expel the bishop from his see or curtail the exercise of his power. A vacant see, he adds, usually demands the appointment of an apostolic administrator when, a) the bishop met a violent death; b) discord was rampant among the members of the chapter on the occasion of the election of a vicar capitular; c) the vicar capitular was unworthy or incapable; d) there existed a long episcopal vacancy.[42]

Cocchi enumerates the following causes: a) violent death of

[41] *Epitome Iuris Canonici,* I, p. 333, n. 432.
[42] *Ius Canonicum,* II, p. 588, n. 557.

the bishop; b) dissent among the members of the chapter in respect to the election of a vicar capitular; c) a long vacancy of the see; d) poor health of the resident bishop; and e) lack of administrative ability on the part of the resident bishop.[43] Augustine says: "The expedient of appointing an apostolic administrator is occasionally resorted to when the financial or religious conditions of a diocese are in a precarious state."[44] "Hence," says Jaeger, "if a bishop through old age, infirmity, physical or mental debility is unable to discharge the functions of his office, or if serious financial, religious, or political difficulties arise in a diocese and cannot be controlled by the bishop, it might be expected that the Holy See shall appoint an apostolic administrator to rule the see."[45] These above mentioned authors are only a few of the many who have been examined in order to ascertain the causes they posit for the sending of apostolic administrators.[46]

Prior to the promulgation of the Code of Canon Law authors were accustomed to enumerate rather long lists of causes which prompted the appointment of an apostolic administrator, then more commonly known as the vicar apostolic. Particularly noteworthy are the lists contained in Ferraris,[47] Pellegrinus[48] and Andreucci.[49]

Even though these authors gave rather long lists of causes for deputizing an apostolic administrator, it would be quite easy to reduce them to the few which are usually mentioned by the present day commentators on the Code of Canon Law. It is

[43] *Commentarium in Codicem Iuris Canonici,* II, p. 253, n. 229.

[44] *A Commentary on Canon Law,* II, 326.

[45] *The Administration of Vacant and Quasi-Vacant Dioceses in the United States,* p. 94.

[46] Cf. Cance, *Le Code de Droit Canonique,* I, p. 305, n. 303; Woywod, *A Practical Commentary,* I, p. 114, n. 233; Ayrinhac, *Constitution of the Church in the New Code of Canon Law,* p. 132, n. 106; Beste, *Introductio in Codicem* (Collegeville, Minnesota: St. John's Abbey, 1938), p. 158; Toso, *Commentaria Minora,* II, 135.

[47] *Prompta Bibliotheca,* s.v. "Vicarius Apostolicus," n. 52.

[48] *Praxis Vicariorum,* p. 54.

[49] *Hierarchia Ecclesiastica in varias Partes Distributas,* I, 235.

important to recall that any list of causes as suggested by private authors is of necessity incomplete, in as far as the determination of these causes rests with the Sovereign Pontiff whenever he makes the appointment. It is only by way of example that these causes are enumerated by the authors.

It is impossible to set up all the reasons which may exist as certainly adequate for sending an apostolic administrator to a vacant or impeded see. This is not, one feels, the intention of the authors in enumerating the causes which prompt the appointment of an apostolic administrator but rather their purpose is to demonstrate the causes usually present when the Holy See appoints apostolic administrators. From the procedure of the Holy See in the past they have deduced reasons which are sufficiently cogent to require an apostolic administrator. New occasions will furnish new causes, and it rests exclusively with the Holy Father to determine the presence of a cause which merits the commitment of a diocese to an apostolic administrator.

Art. II—Canonical Institution of the Apostolic Administrator

Canon 313, § 1—Quilibet Administrator Apostolicus, si datus fuerit dioecesi, sede plena, canonicam administrationis possessionem init, ostendens litteras suae nominationis tum Episcopo, si sit mentis consiliisue compos et in dioecesi versetur, tum etiam Capitulo, ad normam can. 334, § 3.

A—*Sede Plena*

The present canon states that every apostolic administrator who is appointed to administer a diocese when the proper bishop is still in possession of the see (*sede plena*) takes canonical possession of the diocese by presenting his letter of appointment both 1) to the resident bishop, provided he is of sound mind and residing in the diocese,[50] and, 2) to the cathedral chapter (the diocesan consultors in the United States) according to the man-

[50] Augustine, *A Commentary on Canon Law,* II, 327-328.

ner prescribed in canon 334, § 3. The board of diocesan consultors must be established in countries or dioceses where the cathedral chapter has not been instituted.[51] In the United States there are no cathedral chapters and obviously, therefore, wherever the word "cathedral chapter" is found in the text of the code the words "board of diocesan consultors" are to be substituted.[52]

The words *"Quilibet Administrator Apostolicus"* include every type of apostolic administrator who is sent by the Sovereign Pontiff to a diocese that is *plena*: namely, the permanent as well as the temporary apostolic administrator. The mode of taking canonical possession imposed on the apostolic administrator is not a mere formality, but absolutely essential for the valid exercise of jurisdiction. Consequently, the failure to observe this canon will nullify all acts of the apostolic administrator in the same manner as the acts of the bishop are null if he fails to observe the canonical form of possession.[53] In the event that the resident bishop is not mentally well, or is hindered in any other way from receiving the letters presented by the apostolic administrator, the presentation made to the cathedral chapter, or in the United States to the board of diocesan consultors, will suffice. This manner of presentation required of the apostolic administrator is the same as the one imposed on a bishop when he takes canonical possession of the diocese to which he has been promoted.[54]

Under the provisions of canon 334, § 3, the newly appointed bishop can exercise no jurisdiction in the see to which he has been

[51] Canon 423.

[52] Klekotka, *Diocesan Consultors,* The Catholic University of America, Canon Law Studies, n. 8 (Washington, D. C.: The Catholic University of America, 1920), p. 39.

[53] "Obtento per provisionem titulo officii, sequatur oportet captio possessionis, a qua non ex natura rei, sed ex positiva valde convenienti iuris dispositione vel ipse *validus* usus iurisdictionis cum titulo officii acceptae fit dependens."—Wernz-Vidal, *Ius Canonicum,* II, p. 623, n. 597; "In hoc casu necessariae sunt ad valorem ambae praesentationes litterarum nempe capitulo et Episcopo, ita ut alterutra deficiente Administrator nullam de facto iurisdictionem consequatur."—Coronata, *Institutiones Iuris Canonici,* I, p. 458, footnote 4; Toso, *Commentaria Minora,* II, 135-136.

[54] Canon 334, § 3.

assigned until his apostolic brief or letter is presented either by himself or by a procurator to the cathedral chapter or to the board of diocesan consultors of that diocese. Of course, if the bishop has already been exercising jurisdiction as the vicar capitular (administrator) he remains in that office, but he does not attain the power of a bishop, *sede plena,* until he takes canonical possession of the diocese the same way as any other bishop by presenting his letter of appointment to the cathedral chapter or the board of diocesan consultors. The secretary of the cathedral chapter, or the chancellor of the diocese where the board of diocesan consultors exists, must be present to record the proceedings in the authentic acts of the diocese.[55]

Therefore, from the moment the apostolic administrator who is appointed to a see that is occupied fulfills the norms set down by law for taking canonical possession of the diocese to which he has been assigned he can exercise jurisdiction over both the spiritual and temporal welfare of the diocese—unless it is stipulated contrariwise in his letter of appointment. For just as a bishop can exercise jurisdiction over his diocese upon taking canonical possession, so too, analogously, the apostolic administrator can assume full administration over diocesan affairs when he has taken canonical possession.[56]

Hence any official acts, concerning the diocese, performed by the apostolic administrator prior to his canonical possession of the diocese are null. This precaution is well founded, for otherwise how can one actually determine whether a person has been legitimately assigned to rule a see unless he has a letter of appointment to substantiate his claim?[57]

[55] Klekotka, *Diocesan Consultors,* pp. 154-155; Cocchi, *Commentarium in Codicem Iuris Canonici,* II, p. 198, n. 257; Blat, *Commentarium Textus,* II, p. 349, n. 355; Canon 373 § 5.

[56] " . . . Episcopus antequam possessionem canonice ceperit nequit per se aut per alios ullo sub titulo se ingerere in regimen dioecesis: si tamen ante promotionem iam esset legitime constitutus Vicarius Capitularis, officialis aut oeconomus, haec officia etiam post promotionem retinere et exercere posset."—Wernz-Vidal,, *Ius Canonicum,* II, p. 624, n. 597.

[57] Canons 313, § 1, 334, §3; Blat, *Commentarium Textus,* II, p. 327, n.

B—*Sede Vacante*

Canon 313, § 2—Si sedes fuerit vacans, vel si Episcopus non sit mentis consiliique compos, aut in dioecesi non moretur, Administrator Apostolicus possessionem sumit ad instar Episcopi secundum cit. can. 334, § 3.

Paragraph 2 of canon 313 makes provisions for the apostolic administrator who is deputized by the Sovereign Pontiff to administer a see that is vacant, or a see whose proper bishop is not mentally well or is absent from the diocese. Such an apostolic administrator may be appointed temporarily or permanently according to the letter of appointment. In the commentary on canon 312 it has been indicated that a diocese can become vacant by the death, resignation, transfer or removal of the bishop. A see, on the other hand, becomes impeded when the proper bishop is unable to communicate with his diocese even by letter, whether this be due to imprisonment, relegation, exile, or his own physical or mental disability.[58]

In both instances, namely, when the see is vacant or impeded, the apostolic administrator takes possession of the diocese in the same manner as a newly appointed bishop that is, by presenting his letter of appointment to the cathedral chapter or the board of diocesan consultors in the presence of the secretary of the chapter, or the chancellor of the diocese, who records the proceedings in the acts of the diocese.[59] Any apostolic administrator

331; "Ou bien le diocese à encore un evêque en état de prendre part part à cette prise de possession ou bien il n'en a pas. Dans la première hypothese deux actes prealables seront necessaires pour que l'administrateur apostolique puisse exercer sa jurisdiction: 1—la presentation de ses lettres de nomination des bulles, à l'evêque lui-même; 2—la même presentation au chapitre."—Villien-Magnin, *Dictionnaire de Droit Canonique,* s.v. *"Administrateur Apostolique,"* n. 188.

[58] Canon 429, § 1.

[59] Canon 334, § 3: " . . . et quamvis hae litterae non oretenus legerentur sed oculis, sufficeret, illud tamen est rationabilius et securius, conditione subsequente omnino adhibita . . . "—Blat, *Commentarium Textus Codicis Iuris Canonici,* II, p. 349, n. 355.

who disregards this canonical mode of possession provided for in § §1 and 2 and takes charge of a diocese without presenting the necessary letter to the proper authorities becomes incapable of acquiring an office, and the chapter or the board of diocesan consultors who admitted him before exacting the presentation of his letter is *ipso facto* suspended from the right of election, presentation, or nomination *ad beneplacitum Sedis Apostolicae.*[61]

All these prescriptions relevant to canonical possession of a diocese by a bishop or apostolic administrator are not new with the Code of Canon Law, but date back to Decretal Law, wherein the minute precautions attending the canonical possession of a see were indicated:

> Iniunctae nobis debitum servitutis exposcit, ut . . . ibi praecipue reformationis accommodae remedium apponamus, ubi maius respicimus periculum imminere. Sane, quam periculosum existat, quod aliquis in officio, dignitate vel gradu fore se asserat, et pro tali etiam habeatur, nisi prius ipse quod asserit legitimis ostenderit documentis, tam ex civilibus quam ex canonicis institutis colligitur evidenter. Asserenti namque cum mandatis principis se venisse credendum non est, nisi hoc scriptis probaverit. Nec similiter creditur se asserenti legatum. Numquam enim Apostolicae Sedis moris fuit absque signatis apicibus undecumque legationem suscipere. Sed nec dicenti se delegatum sedis eiusdem creditur vel intenditur, nisi de mandato Apostolico fide doceat oculata . . . Si quis praeterea in clerum electum se dicat, si sacerdotem sese nominet, hoc scrutandum est, quia non sine periculo est in talibus communicatio indiscussa. Quod autem in illis, qui se episcopos vel superiores praelatos, aut etiam abbates, priores seu alios monasteriorum rectores, quocumque nomine censeantur, appellant, sit discussio celebris et diligens facienda, luculenter apparet, si scandala et pericula gravia, quae ipsorum parere possit communicatio indiscussa diligentius attendantur.[62]

[61] Canon 2394; Ayrinhac, *Penal Legislation in the New Code of Canon Law* (New York: Benziger Brothers, 1936), pp. 309-310.

[62] C. 1, *de electione,* I, 3, in Extravag. com.

CHAPTER 6

RIGHTS, DUTIES, AND PRIVILEGES OF THE APOSTOLIC ADMINISTRATOR

Canon 314. Iura, officia ac privilegia Administratoris desumantur ex litteris suae deputationis, vel, nisi in eisdem aliud caveatur expresse, ex praescripto canonum qui sequuntur.

ART. 1—INTRODUCTORY NOTIONS

The rights, duties, and privileges of the apostolic administrator are to be ascertained from his letter of appointment, or in the event that the letter makes no special provision, from the rules laid down in canons 315 to 318.[1] Although many of the letters employed in deputizing an apostolic administrator contain only the mere announcement of his appointment, some delineate even to the smallest detail the various rights, duties, and privileges of the particular apostolic administrator. Should the letters simply state, however, that the designated person was commissioned as apostolic administrator to a specified diocese without signifying anything further, then the appointee would have to determine his rights, duties, and privileges from the designated canons.[2] Obviously, then, it is of paramount importance to stress the necessity of examining the letter of appointment in order to discern and ascertain if it simply states the appointment, or if it contains greater faculties than those granted by the canons of the Code, or if is has curtailed some of the faculties or imposed new duties.[3] Such amplification or diminution of the faculties is

[1] Woywod, *A Practical Commentary,* I, p. 114, n. 234; Augustine, *A Commentary on Canon Law,* II, 328; Ayrinhac, *Constitution of the Church in the New Code of Canon Law,* p. 133, n. 107.

[2] Canons 315-318.

[3] "Itaque, harum litterarum dispositionibus, quae quoniam a circumstantiis et a voluntate Pontificis unice pendent, diversissimae esse possunt, relictis, de generalibus dispositionibus Codicis videamus."—Toso, *Commentaria Minora,* II, p. 328, n. 332.

oftentimes occasioned by the condition of the diocese in question. Likewise, if the person selected as the apostolic administrator is one who is endowed with only the priestly character, the Holy See may deem it advisable and advantageous to grant him the power of consecrations—a faculty usually denied to apostolic administrators who are not invested with the episcopal character. Contrariwise, the Sovereign Pontiff may find it necessary to deprive some apostolic administrators of the use of certain faculties accorded to them by the Code. Particularly is this true when the appointment is a provisionary measure, and will be of very short duration. Such variegated situations which may reflect a diversified grant of faculties to the apostolic administrator show the importance of inspecting the letter of appointment. If the letter determines nothing more than the appointment, then the faculties of the apostolic administrator are definitely determined from the canons of the Code.

Prior to the promulgation of the Code the letter of appointment alone indicated the rights, duties, and privileges of the apostolic administrator. This made it quite difficult to determine what faculties were common to the apostolic administrator, especially when hardly any two letters granted the same faculties. Consequently, because of the diversity of the faculties granted in the various letters of appointment, no general norm could be followed. Authors of the pre-Code period went so far as to say that if the letters of appointment did not deny specifically a certain faculty, then the apostolic administrator could exercise it. This line of reasoning is well founded when the law of Boniface VII is recalled:

> Is, cui procuratio seu administratio cathedralis ecclesiae plena et libera in spiritualibus et temporalibus a Sede Apostolica, cui soli hoc competit, est commissa, potest alienatione bonorum immobilium dumtaxat excepta, omnia, quae iurisdictionis episcopalis existunt, et quae potest electus exequi confirmatus, libere exercere. Illa quippe, quae ministerium consecrationis exposcunt, nisi fuerit episcopus, per alias faciat episcopus expedire." [4]

[4] C. 42, *de electione et electi potestate*, I, 6, in VI°.

This statement is substantiated by pointing out a few letters of the pre-Code appointments of apostolic administrators.

Carolum Pooten Administratorem Apostolicum Archidiocesis Antibarensis nominato

Dilecto Filio presbytero Carolo Pooten

Quum ad componenda ecclesiastica negotia in Archdiocesi Antibarensi necesse prorsus visum fuerit, administratorem apostolicum statuere, suspenso interim ac remoto ven. fratre Vincentio Battucci archiepiscopo ab exercitio Episcopalis iurisdictionis, Nos de venn. fratrum Nost. S.R.E. Cardinalium Negotiis Propagandae Fidei praepositorum consilio, te, de cujus pietate, doctrina, ac fidei catholicae promovendae studio praeclara accepta sunt testimonia in hujusmodi administratorem eligere statuimus. Te igitur, quum Episcopum Maroniensis in partibus infidelium per similes Apostolicas litteras, hoc ipso die datas . . .
administratorem apostolicum Archidioecesis Antibarensis suspenso interim ac remota ab exercitio iurisdictionis episcopalis ven. fratre Vincentio Battucci Archiepscopo, cum omnibus et singulis facultatibus quibus ipse Vincentius potiebatur, auctoritate Nostra Apostolica, hisce literis, eligimus, constituimus, et deputamus.[5]

This appointment of Charles Pooten as apostolic administrator of Antivari in Montenegro was made during the Pontificate of Gregory XVI (1831-1846). As can be readily ascertained from the examination of this letter, Bishop Pooten was granted all the faculties which the former Archbishop, Vincent Battucci, enjoyed. In view of the fact that no restriction was made on this grant, it is admitted that Bishop Pooten could issue dimissorial letters, incardinate and excardinate, confer benefices of free bestowal, as well as exercise any other right enjoyed by the Archbishop.

During the Pontificate of Pius IX (1846-1878) John Sabbioni of Spoleto died. Rather than leave the see vacant the Sovereign Pontiff appointed John Arnaldi its apostolic administrator as stated in the following letter:

[5] *Acta Gregorii Papae XVI* (4 vols., Romae: A. M. Bernasconi, 1901-1904), III, 321.

> Cum Archiepiscopalis Ecclesia Spoletana ob obitum Archiepiscopi Joannis Sabbioni bo. men. suo sit viduata pastore, SSm̃us D. N. Pius Papa IX, qui eidem olim amantissimus Antistes praefuit, eamque semper speciali benevolentia prosequutus est, Apostolica Auctoritate regendam esse statuit, donec novo pastore provideatur. Idcirco in audientia habita 29 Septembris 1852 ab infrascripto D. prosecretario hujus S. Congregationis Episcoporum et Regularium, in ejusdem Ecclesiae Spoletanae Apostolicum Administratorem in spiritualibus et temporalibus ad Sanctitatis Suae, et Apostolicae Sedis beneplacitum deputavit atque constituit R.P.D. Joannem Baptistam Arnaldi Interamnensis Ecclesiae Administratorem, cum omnibus et singulis facultatibus etiam quoad ordinationes et dimissorias pro ordinibus conferendis (excepta dumtaxat beneficiorum collatione), quibus locorum antistites juxta canonicas sanctiones fruuntur et gaudent; cum potestate deputandi idoneam personam Ecclesiasticam sibi benevisum in suum vicarium Generalem, qui in civitate Spoletana resideat. Mandavit vero Sanctitas sua ut Administrator Apostolicus, expleto suo munere, relationem ad hanc S. Congregationem transmittat, ut ad SSm̃um Patrem ea renuntietur.[6]

This letter of appointment granted to Bishop Arnaldi of Terni all the faculties usually accorded to resident bishops except the power to confer benefices of free bestowal. Incidentally, then, if the phrase, "*excepta dumtaxat beneficiorum collatione,*" had not been inserted, his faculties would have been equivalent to those of a resident bishop.

From these two examples one can deduce how important it was to read most carefully the letters of pre-Code appointment of apostolic administrators. For in these letters were granted the faculties which determined the rights, duties, and privileges of the apostolic administrator.

Since the promulgation of the Code of Canon Law a particular group of canons,[7] contain an *ex professo* treatment of the apostolic administrators. These canons obviate the former pre-Code

[6] *Analecta Iuris Pontificii,* XXIII (1884), 767-768.

[7] Canons 312-318.

necessity of enumerating the various duties, rights, and privileges of the apostolic administrator in a rather lengthy letter of appointment. All that is necessary now is the mere indication ot the appointee—and unless there be further restrictions the pertinent canons are applied, dependent upon whether the term of office be permanent or temporary, and whether the see be vacant or filled. A few examples will clarify this assertion:

1) When James Skakla, the dean of the chapter of Bautzen, was appointed apostolic administrator of the refounded diocese of Meissen, his faculties were thus expressed:

> Quousque autem haec nova dioecesis de proprio pastore provideatur, eiusdem regimen dilecto filio, Iacobo Skala, hodierno Decano capitulari, tamquam Administratori Apostolico, committimus, ipsi tribuentes facultates ac iura omnia, quae huic muneri competunt.[8]

Instead of describing his rights, duties, and privileges, as was the custom prior to the Code, the present letter says that James Skala possesses the rights and faculties commonly assigned to this office. In other words, James Skala is given the rights, duties, and privileges delineated in canons 315-318.[9]

2) When the new diocese of Lodz was erected, Cardinal Kakowski was appointed its apostolic administrator and his faculties were thus expressed:

> Quousque autem haec nova diocesis de proprio pastore provideatur, eiusdem regimen dilecto filio Nostro Alexandro, tituli Sancti Augustini, S.R.E. presbytero Cardinali Kakowski hodierno, ex dispensatione Apostolica, Archiepiscopo Varasaviensi tamquam Administratori Apostolico, committimus, ipsi tribuentes facultates ac iura omnia quae huic muneri competunt.[10]

The letter addressed to Cardinal Kakowski, the Archbishop of Warsaw, reads similarly to the one sent to James Skala. Even though Alexander Kakowski was a Cardinal, his faculties, never-

[8] *ASS*, XIII (1921), 410.
[9] Canon 315, § 2, n. 1.
[10] *ASS*, XIII (1921), 250.

theless, were only the usual ones accorded to a temporary apostolic administrator.[11]

It is not uncommon or unusual, however, for an apostolic administrator to be granted greater faculties in his letters of appointment than are provided for in the Code. Oftentimes an apostolic administrator, even though only temporarily appointed, is granted all the faculties which the previous bishop of that particular see possessed.[12]

One appointment of recent years is particulary noteworthy, for it depicts in a most unusual way the appointment of an apostolic administrator and describes his rights, duties, and privileges very minutely. This apostolic administrator was appointed to Loreto on October 11, 1935.[13]

It will not be untimely to quote this letter of appointment in its entirety and point out its salient features. For this example very clearly illustrates the canons embraced in the section devoted to the apostolic administrator.[14]

Sacra Congregatio Consistorialis
Pontificiae administrationis Laurentanae

DECRETUM

Exacto iam anno ex quo SS.mus Dominus Noster Pius Div. Prov. Pp. XI Pontificium Sanctuarium Almae Domus Lauretanae

[11] Canon 315, § 2, n. 1.

[12] "Munus autem administrandi praedictum territorium (Danzig) Sanctitas sua deferre dignata est ad nutum Sanctae Sedis Ill. ac R.R.D. Ed. O'Rourke, episcopo titulari Caneensi, ita ut is eadem potestate ibidem fruatur, quam obtinent Ordinarii in sua dioecesi."—*ASS,* XIV (1922), 312; Villien-Magnin, *Dictionnaire de Droit Canonique* s.v. "*Administrateur Apostolique,*" n. 188.

[13] *ASS,* XXVII (1936), 71-73; *Periodica de Re Canonica et Morali utili Presertim Religiosis et Missionariis* (Bruges, 1905-), XXV (1936), 15-17; Bouscaren, *The Canon Law Digest* (2 vols., and a supplement, Milwaukee: The Bruce Publishing Company, 1934-1938), II, 54, under canon 312.

[14] Father Creusen says: "Decretum in extenso exscribendum duximus quia pulcherrimum exhibet exemplum Administratoris Apostolicae quale alibi non facile invenies."—*Periodica,* XXV (1936), 17.

aedesque continentes Suae ipsius iurisdictioni tam in spiritualibus quam in temporalibus directo subiecit, feliciter expertum est haud pauca emolumenta beneficiaque obvenisse, quae inter commemoranda sunt et aucta, per Auctoritatem Pontificiam, Basilicae dignitas, et animarum bonum uberius provectum, ope Religiosorum, qui Basilicae modo deserviunt atque toti incumbunt spirituali curae et adsistentiae fidelium, praesertim peregrinorum, qui pie ac frequenter ad Sanctuarium accedunt.

Quo vero de his, quae supra memorata sunt, beneficiis ii plenius participent, qui Mariali Basilicae propiores exstant idem SS.mus Dominus Noster, apostolicae potestatis plenitudine, suppleto quatenus opus sit interesse habentium vel habere praesumentium consensu, vi praesentis Consistorialis Decreti, benigne statuit ut iurisdictio Administratoris Pontificii Basilicae Lauretanae ad territorium Lauretanae civitatis eiusque districtus, iuxta praesentes fines civiles, quod ad dioecesim Recinetensem-Lauretanam pertinet, exstendatur, totaliter suspensa proinde, durante Administratione Pontificia, super eodem territorio, iurisdictione Ordinarii Recinetensis-Lauretani.

Ipsius igitur Pontificii Administratoris erit fideles omnes, qui praefatum territorium incolunt, regere eadem quidem potestate iisdemque facultatibus ac Episcopi residentiales; quin tamen legi residentiae, quousque praesentia adiuncta perduraverint, teneatur.

Vicario autem Administrationis Pontificiae, charactere episcopali insignito, munus competat ea omnia officia implendi quae Vicarii Generalis, ad norman iuris communis, sunt propria; necnon, absente Pontificio Administratore, functiones in Basilica peragendi, quibus Ordinarius tenetur.

Ad curam insuper animarum rite moderandam Pontificius Administrator curabit paroeciarum fines in territorio, de quo agitur, circumscribendos prout bonum animarum expostulaverit, novamque ecclesiam, S. Annae Genetrici B.V.M. dicandam, apud viae ferreae stationem, sumptibus quos Ipsa Sanctitas Sua ad id elargita est, exstruendam; ad easdem vero paroecias administrandas eisdemque inserviendum, atque ad alia ecclesiastica officia persolvenda ius vocandi quos validiores reputaverit, inter sacerdotes

Capituli Lauretani, iuniores potissimus, qui a chorali servitio exonerati fuerunt.

Cum denique dioecesis Recinentensis-Lauretana ab onere curae animarum in territorio Lauretano relevata sit, cessabit a data praesentis Decreti annuum subsidium, quod Administratio Pontificia Mensae Episcopali eiusdem dioecesis hactenus erogat.

Ad haec autem exsecutioni mandanda Sanctitas Sua deputat eumdem Pontificum Administratorem, Exc. mum P.D. Franciscum Borgongini-Duca, Archiepiscopum titularem Heracleensem et Nuntium Apostolicum in Italia, ipsi tribuentes facultates ad id necessarias et opportunas etiam subdelegandi, ad effectum de quo agitur, quemlibet virum in ecclesiastica dignitate constitutum; facto onere quam primum ad hanc S. C. Consistorialem mittendi authenticum exemplar actus peractae exsecutionis. Contrariis quibuscumque non obstantibus, etiam speciali mentione dignis.

Datum Romae, ex Aedibus S. C. Consistorialis, die II Octobris 1935, in festo Maternitatis B. M. Virginis.

Fr. R. C. Card. Rossi, *a Secretis.*
V. Santoro, *Adsessor.*

Not only the Basilica, but the town of Loretto as well, was withdrawn from the jurisdiction of the Bishop of Recanati-Loreto, and placed under the Pontifical Administrator of the Basilica of Loreto, who obtained the jurisdiction of a resident bishop without the obligation of residence. The power of a vicar-general was conferred on a titular bishop, who was made a vicar to the apostolic administrator of Loreto.[15]

The letter describes in detail how the jurisdiction of the resident bishop is restricted and the jurisdiction of the apostolic administrator is extended. It is a splendid example illustrating the reason for deputizing the apostolic administrator, the various faculties and power granted to him,[16] and the suspension of the resident bishop's power.[17]

Since canon 314 deals only with the question of how the apo-

[15] Bouscaren, *The Canon Law Digest,* II, 54.
[16] Canons 314-315.
[17] Canon 316.

stolic administrator obtains his faculties, and not with their discernment, it would be superfluous at this time to analyze this letter in every particular. That the letter itself contains a most unusual appointment is attested by the following words of Father Creusen:

> Quod autem huic Administrationi Apostolicae Lauretanae omnino peculiare videtur, praeter dispensationem a lege residentiae Exc. mo Administratori, qui simul Nuntii Apostolici in Italia munere fungitur concessam, est divisio sive dimidiatio iurisdicitonis Episcopalis Recinetensis-Lauretanae, cuius una pars, in favorem Administrationis, totaliter suspenditur, altera vero manet prorsus intacta.[18]

give a detailed analysis of the rights, duties, and privileges of the permanent and the temporary apostolic administrator sent to a see that is filled or vacant.

Art. 2—The Temporary Apostolic Administrator

A—Identity with the Vicar Capitular.

Before an attempt is made to outline the various rights and duties incumbent upon the temporary apostolic administrator, it is imperative that the status of this office be initially established. The Holy See, through the laws stated in the Code of Canon Law, has amply provided for the administration of vacant and quasi-vacant dioceses. A vacant see is ordinarily committed first to the care or administration of the cathedral chapter, or, when there is no cathedral chapter, to the board of diocesan consultors.[19] Within the stipulated period of eight days this cathedral chapter, or board of diocesan consultors, must elect a vicar capitular, or administrator, to rule the vacant diocese until the Apostolic See sends a resident bishop or provides otherwise.[20] Such is the usual procedure adopted in effecting a provisionary diocesan administration in the majority of vacant diocese. Canon 431, § 1, states that in case of vacancy the government of the diocese devolves on the cathedral chapter (or on the board of diocesan consultors

[18] *Periodica,* XXV (1936), 17.
[19] Canons 423-431.
[20] Canon 432, § 1.

where there are no Chapters), unless there be appointed an apostolic administrator or the Holy See has provided otherwise.[21] Just what is the nature of the power granted to this board of administration? The answer is ascertained from the words contained in the canon which says that at the vacancy of the bishopric, the ordinary jurisdiction of the bishop in temporal and spiritual affairs devolves on the chapter or board of diocesan consultors.[23] This power is that of jurisdiction.[24] Rightly, then, the cathedral chapter or the board of diocesan consultors is known as the *Ordinarius loci—ex iuris praescripto.*[25]

The bishop in virtue of being an *Ordinarius loci* can exercise jurisdiction over his subjects, and consequently this *regimen* is known as ordinary jurisdiction.[26] This power belongs innately to the residential bishop and it adheres in his office no mater who may be the administrator of the diocese. Quite true, too, the scope of this ordinary jurisdiction is very broad and quite comprehensive for it encompasses and includes within itself all ecclesiastical matters both spiritual and temporal, comprising within its ambit the power to legislate, judge, and punish. In addition to this threefold legislative, judicial, and coercive power the bishop also possesses executive power.[27] This executive function, although not

[21] Woywod, *A Practical Commentary on the Code of Canon Law* (5 ed., 2 vols., New York: Joseph F. Wagner, 1939), I, 154.

[23] Canon 435, § 1; Woywod, *A Practical Commentary on the Code of Canon Law,* I, 157.

[24] Canon 196.

[25] Canon 198; Ergo in iure nomine *Ordinarii* intelliguntur taxative: I. Romanus Pontifex, qui dicitur Ordinarius Ordinariorum. II. Episcopus Residentialis. III. Abbas vel Praelatus nullius. IV. Apostolicus: i-Administrator, 2—Vicarius, 3—Praefectus. V. Vicarius Generalis sive i—Episcopi, sive 2—Abbatis vel Praelati nullius. VI. Is qui praedictis deficientibus interim succedunt in regimine aut A) ex iuris praescripto, ut 1. Capitulum Cathedrale, vel abbatiae seu praelatitium, vel coetus consultorum dioecesanorum, sede episcopali vel abbatiali seu praelatitia vacante, antequam eligatur Vicarius Capitularis. " . Post suam electionem Vicarius Capitularis in Dioecesi vel Abbatia sive Praelatura vacante."—Maroto, *Institutiones Iuris Canonici,* I, p. 833, n. 701.

[26] Canon 197.

[27] "Cum potestate legislativa, iudiciaria, coactiva ad normam sacrorum

mentioned in the canons, can be deduced from canon 336 as being intrinsically requisite for the effective exercise of the episcopal power. It follows as a necessary consequence of both the legislative and judicial power, and is amply insinuated in the word "coactive." [28]

The cathedral chapter and the board of diocesan consultors both possess this legislative, judicial, coercive and executive power of the bishop by virtue of canon 435, § 1. The period of rule of the cathedral chapter or of the board of diocesan consultors is, however, limited to eight days. Within that time they are compelled to elect a vicar capitular, or, where the board of diocesan consultors exists, an administartor. What power, therefore, is granted to this vicar capitular or administrator? This vicar capitular or administrator receives all the power formerly held by the cathedral chapter or the board of diocesan consultors: "In Vicario constituendo nullam sibi iurisdictionis partem capitulum retinere potest, nec gerendo muneri tempus praefinire aliasve restrictiones praestituere." [29] Eventually the power held by the cathedral chapter or by the board of diocesan consultors is handed over wholly to the vicar capitular or administrator. Obviously, then, this vicar capitular or administrator becomes the recipient of ordinary and not merely delegated episcopal jurisdiction. He becomes, in reality, the jurisdictional successor of the bishop and necessarily the *Ordinarius loci.*[30] In consequence of this power being handed

canonum erercenda."—Canon 335; Ryan says the executive function "is the ultimate stage of diocesan government to which all other functions, doctrinal and disciplinary, are directed, and without which the purpose of the bishop's power could not be attained."—*Principles of Episcopal Jurisdiction,* The Catholic University of America, Canon Law Studies, n. 120 (Washington D. C.: The Catholic University of America, 1939), p. 141.

[28] Cf. Ryan, *op. cit.,* pp. 117-144.—for a complete treatment of the powers accorded to the bishop. Cf. also Jaeger, *The Administration of Vacant and Quasi-Vacant Dioceses in the United States,* p. 170.

[29] Canon 437; Coronata, *Institutiones Iuris Canonici,* I, p. 554, n. 461; Hermes, *De Capitulo Sede Vacante vel Impedito et de Vicario Capitulari,* p. 143; Wesnz-Vidal, *Ius Canonicum,* II p. 755, n. 710.

[31] Canons 197; 198; Maroto, *Institutiones Iuris Canonici,* I, p. 833, n. 701.

over to the vicar capitular or administrator he can exercise the legislative, judicial, coercive, and executive functions proper to the episcopal office.

From this discussion one gathers and concludes that the vicar capitular or the administrator is the successor of the bishop and not his jurisdictional inferior; for he possesses the same ordinary jurisdiction that was previously held by the bishop; namely, over the spiritual and temporal welfare of the diocese, except in instances wherein the law has expressly forbidden the performance of certain acts to the vicar capitular or administrator.[32] He merits the name *Ordinarius loci* only because he is the successor of the bishop. His jurisdiction, therefore, is circumscribed by the same laws that affected the bishop. The vicar capitular or administrator enjoys legislative power in so far as he is capable of enacting laws for the whole diocese, even though they are contrary to the laws enforced by the former bishops. He must keep before his eyes and recognize a custom which has the force of common law.[33] Prudence, however, will play an important part in restraining the legislative actions of the vicar capitular or administrator. He must of course, abstain from promulgating laws which would prove inopportune and detrimental to the welfare of the diocese, and prejudicial to his successors.[34]

The vicar capitular or administrator is the ordinary judge of the diocese. He is fully competent to judge, either personally or through his delegate, all criminal and contentious causes which come within his competence and to defend in court the right of the *mensa episcopalis.* As the *Ordinarius loci* he should commit to others the function of judging criminal causes, as well as others of grave importance. This is the judicial power of the vicar capitular or administrator.[35]

[32] Canon 435, § 1; *Fontes,* n. 565; Cocchi, *Commentarium in Codicem Iuris Canonici,* II, 343; Ayrinhac, *Constitution of the Church in the New Code of Canon Law,* p. 275.

[33] Ryan, *Principles of Episcopal Jurisdiction,* p. 135.

[34] Canons 435, § 3; 436.

[35] Canon 1653, § 1; Ryan, *Principles of Episcopal Jurisdiction,* p. 40;

The coercive power of the vicar capitular or administrator follows as a supplement of the judicial power and legislative power. Certainly he who has the power to make laws, impose precepts, and judge his subjects, can inflict penalties on those who violate laws. He may decree excommunication, interdict, suspension, deprive clerics of office or depose them because of crime, and, in fine, do all things necessary for correction, right order and discipline, just as the bishop himself within the limits of his diocese and episcopal jurisdiction.[36]

Through the executive power the vicar capitular or administrator becomes the custodian of Faith and morals in the diocese. He is to exercise vigilance, and to frustrate any attempts to demoralize his flock; he has likewise the duty of caring for the spiritual needs of the people, a duty which is exercised and accomplished through the use of proper religious instructions coupled with the provision of schools where the principles of the Catholic Religion will be properly imparted to the pupils.[37]

This office enjoyed by the vicar capitular or administrator, embracing, as it does, the fourfold episcopal functions, is not conferred solely on him. But in addition to the vicar capitular or administrator this same office is held by and conferred on, 1) a transferred bishop from the time he receives authentic notification of his transfer until he takes canonical possession of his new see;[38] 2) the vicar capitular who, at the intimation of the Holy See, is appointed by the archbishop or bishop; [39] 3) the administrator who is elected by the cathedral chapter or the board of diocesan consultors to administer a quasi-vacant diocese;[40] 4) the apostolic

Jaeger, *The Administration of Vacant and Quasi-Vacant Dioceses in the United States,* p. 169.

[36] Jaeger, *The Administration of Vacant and Quasi-Vacant Dioceses in The United States,* p. 170; Ryan, *Principles of Episcopal Jurisdiction,* p. 124.

[37] Canon 336, §§ 1 and 2; Jaeger, *op. cit.,* p. 171; Ryan, *op. cit.* p. 125.

[38] Canon 430, § 3, n. 1.

[39] Canon 431, § 2.

[40] Canon 429, § 3.

administrator who is commissioned to a diocese for a stipulated period of time.[41]

In all the above enumerated instances, unless otherwise indicated, the persons recounted enjoy the same rights and duties as are incumbent on the vicar capitular or administrator. Each of them is an *Ordinarius loci,* for he takes the place of the bishop. Each, too, possesses the legislative, judicial, coercive, and executive functions of the residential bishop.[42] Special emphasis is to be placed on the fact that the apostolic administrator here mentioned is the one appointed temporarily (*ad tempus*), and not the one assigned to a diocese permanently (*in perpetuum*).

Although the exposition of these preliminary facts may not seem to be entirely relevant to the subject of the temporary apostolic administrator, yet this explanation is required particularly when one realizes that the temporary apostolic administrator acquires the same rights and duties as the vicar capitular or administrator.[43] Even though the Code places the legislation regarding the permanent apostolic administrator [44] antecedently to the laws governing the status of temporary apostolic administrator, much needless repetition will be avoided by reversing this order and treating of the temporary apostolic administrator first. Later, in the treatment of the permanent apostolic administrator, the latter's various offices, duties, and privileges will be correlated with greater facility.

Canon 315, § 1. Administrator Apostolicus . . .
§ 2. Ei ad tempus datus sit:
n. 1. Eadem iura ac officia habet, ac Vicarius capitularis, . . .

As already noted, the temporary apostolic administrator is one who is sent by the Sovereign Pontiff to rule a canonically erected diocese. Such an appointment is usually prompted by the ex-

[41] Canon 315, § 2.
[42] Canons 335; 336.
[43] Canon 315, § 2, n. 1.
[44] Canon 315, § 1.

istence of grace and special causes. This type of apostolic administrator is instituted for a certain period of time to rule a diocese either *sede plena* or *sede vacante.* Oftentimes he is assigned a diocese which he is to administer until prevalent abuses are eradicated; or until a sick bishop is sufficiently recovered to reassume active administration; or until the return of a bishop who had been summoned to Rome. Such an apostolic administrator will not, therefore, be entrusted with complete and full power. Quite appropriately, then, this temporary apostolic administrator does not acquire all the rights, duties, and privileges of a resident bishop, but is likened to a vicar capitular. For the canon definitely states that the apostolic administrator who is temporarily assigned to administer a diocese is vested with the same rights and duties as the vicar capitular.[45]

By way of amplification of this assertion of the canon, and at the same time adequately to ascertain and comprehend the various rights and duties of the temporary apostolic administrator, it is peremptory to examine the office of vicar capitular with a view to attributing his various offices and duties to the temporary apostolic administrator.

B)—*Sede Vacante Nihil Innovetur*

At the outset the law, *sede vacante nihil innovetur,*[46] is applicable to the vicar capitular and has therefore equal relevance to the temporary apostolic administrator. This law dates back to the time of the Decretals when it was stated with a slight verbal difference, "*ne sede vacante aliquid innovetur.*" [47] Just how is this clause to be interpreted? Authors previous to the Code said that this clause, *ne sede vacante aliquid innovetur, is* understood in the sense that no prejudice should be brought to bear either on the Church itself or on the successors to the episcopal see in question. Furthermore, they added, that since during a vacancy the Church lacks a legi-

[45] Canon 315, § 2, n. 1.

[46] Canon 436.

[47] C. 1, X, *ne sede vacante aliquid innovetur,* III, 9.

timate defender,[49] the performance of any acts prejudical to the Church itself stand as null and void. Reiffensteul later added that this prescription of nullity pertained exclusively to acts which brought harm or deterioration on the Church, indicating at the same time, that any meritorious acts were highly recommended and honored with full validity. This was the common notion of the clause *ne sede vacante aliquid innovetur.*[50]

Does this axiom retain the same force in the present Code of Canon Law? This is affirmatively attested by the use of practically the same words as found in the Decretal Law—*sede vacante nihil innovetur.* Then the words of Reiffensteul are potentially contained in the words of canon 435, § 3 which reads: "Vicario Capitulari et capitulo non licet agere quidpiam quod vel diocesi vel episcopalibus iuribus praeiudicium aliquod afferre possit; . . . "

Canon 6, § 2 which says, "Canones qui ius vetus ex integro referunt, veteris iuris auctoritate, atque ideo ex receptis apud probatos auctores interpretationibus, sunt aestimandi," undoubtedly shows us that canon 435, § 3, in so far as it is a restatement of the old law, must be interpreted according to the prevalent interpretation of the old authors. Obviously, then the words, *sede vacante nihil innovetur,* are interpreted in the same manner as the words, *ne sede vacante aliquid innovetur.*[51] Therefore, the vicar capitular and the temporary apostolic administrator cannot promulgate laws which would be harmful to the diocese or to the succeeding bishops. Such a statement does not, however, prohibit the performance of acts which will redound to the benefit

[49] "Unde, quia Ecclesia vacans caret legitimo defensore, merito durante vacatione status ipsius mutari non debet; adeo ut non valeant gesta in praejudicium ipsius, sed sint nulla"—Reiffensteul, *Jus Canonicum Universum* (5 vols., in 7, Parisiis, 1864-1882). lib III, ti. IX, n. 13.

[50] Op. cit., lib. III, tit. IX, nn. 13-16; Schmalzgrueber, *Ius Ecclesiasticum Universum* (5 vols., in 12, Romae, 1843-1845), lib. III, tit. IX, nn. 1-14; Hermes, *Dissertatio Historico Canonica de Capitulo et de Vicario Capitulari,* pp. 58-58

[51] Neuberger, *Canon* 6, The Catholic University of America, Canon Law Studies, n. 44 (Washington, D. C.: The Catholic University of America, 1927), pp. 70-72.

of the diocese. For, although these diocesan authorities are prohibited from placing detrimental acts, they are not in any way curtailed in the use of their powers to promulgate new laws, revoke unpleasant laws, or employ new means to produce good results to the diocese.[52]

Even the law of the Decretals addressed to the cathedral chapters presupposed that this body governed a vacant episcopal see with ordinary jurisdiction:

> Omnia, qua ex iure communi sunt in potestate ordinaria episcopi, transeunt, sede vacante, in capitulum, exceptis iis, quae in iure sunt expresse prohibita, sive speciatim, sive propter principia generalia.

The transition, however, of ordinary episopal jurisdiction to the vicar capitular is indicated in the following words:

> Sicut ad Capitulum ante deputationem Vicarii Capitularis, ita deinde ad Vicarium Capitularem transit ordinaria Episcopi iurisdictio in spiritualibus et temporalibus, exceptis iis quae in iure expresse sunt eidem prohibita.[53]

Patently in the law prior to the Code as well as in the present law the vicar capitular possessed and possesses the same ordinary jurisdiction as the resident bishops respecting the spiritual and temporal welfare of the diocese—but in both instances the clause is added, "except in those things which the Holy See has expressly prohibited." Jaeger says: "Since the office of the administrator is by its very nature, only transitory and since, furthermore, a diocese is a moral person and is regarded by the law as a minor whose rights are safeguarded, executed and defended primarily by its proper guardian, the bishop, it is but natural that the law should place certain restrictions upon those acts of the administrator which would result in an infringement upon, or a prejudice to, the rights of the diocese or the succeeding bishop."[54]

[52] Augustine, *A Commentary on Canon Law,* II, 489-490; Vermeersch-Creusen, *Epitome Iuris Canonici,* I, 385; Blat, *Commentarium Textus,* II, 471-472; Wernz-Vidal, *Ius Canonicum,* II, pp. 755-756, n. 710.

[53] Canon 435, § 1.

[54] *The Administration of Vacant and Quasi-Vacant Dioceses in the*

The law is equally applicable to the temporary apostolic administrator: namely, he is permitted to perform the ordinary jurisdiction of the bishop except in those instances wherein the Holy See provides to the contrary. Evidently, then, in view of the fact that canon 315, § 2, n. 1, confers on the temporary apostolic administrator the same rights and duties, it is only logical to hold that the same official is likewise denied all the rights and duties which are denied to the vicar capitular, unless the law provides otherwise. With these preliminary notions in mind one can now proceed to outline some of the particular rights and duties which are denied to the temporary apostolic administrator.

C—Rights Denied to the Temporary Apostolic Administrator

Approaching the subject in a negative manner, it is concluded that the temporary apostolic administrator cannot:

1) Convoke a Synod.[55] Pre-Code legislation enumerated the vicar apostolic (apostolic administrator) among those who possessed the right to convoke a Synod. Wernz outlined those who had this right, thus: I. Episcopi Residentiales etiam nondum consecrati . . . II. Vicarii Capitulares sede vacante, si a die ultimae Synodi dioecesanae ab Episcopo habitae integer annus elapsus sit. III. Vicarii generales, si mandato speciali Episcopi ad convocandum Synodum deputantur; secus ipso iure invalida sunt statuta. IV. Praelati *nullius*, si privilegio vel indulto Apostolico gaudent. V. Vicarii Apostolici, qui ad instar Episcoporum residentialium dioecesim vel vicariatum in missionibus regunt: alli attendant necesse est tenorem suarum facultatum.[56] Even the vicar capitular was expressly allowed to convoke a Synod provided he had been in office for a year.[57] Now, however, the Code denies

United States, pp. 189-190; Vermeersch-Creusen, *Epitome Iuris Canonici*, I, n. 482.

[55] Canon 357, § 1.

[56] *Ius Decretalium*, II, p. 734, n. 859.

[57] " . . . Convocare Synodum et visitare totam dioecesim, antequam elapsus sit annus ab ultima Synodo vel visitatione per Episcopum peracta."—Wernz, *Ius Decretalium*, II, p. 609, n. 795; Pellegrinus, *Praxis*

this prerogative to both the vicar capitular and the temporary apostolic administrator. This is only reasonable, too, when one considers that Synods are convoked every ten years,[58] and it is highly improbable that the vicar capitular will rule a diocese that long. On the other hand, a temporary apostolic administrator may be left in a diocese for quite a long period of time, even extending to ten years. The obvious solution for this difficulty is for the temporary apostolic administrator to petition the Holy See for permission to convoke a diocesan synod. Previously to the Code, and particularly during the early centuries of the Church, it was the custom to hold synods rather frequently, some dioceses holding them every few months. Now the law specifically says: "In singulis dioecesibus celebranda est decimo saltem quoque anno dioecesana Synodus . . . . "[59]

2) Nominate honorary canons.[60]

3) Confer perpetual benefices of free bestowal.[61]

4) Remove the chancellor or other notaries without the consent of the cathedral chapters or of the board of diocesan consultors.[63]

5) Nominate a diocesan consultor without the consent of the other consultors.[64]

Vicariorum, p. 40, n. 13—"Potest Dioecesanam Synodum congregare, elapso tamen anno ab altero Synodo ultimo loco celebrato"; cf. also Nicolius, *Iuris Utriusque Theorica Praxis* (2 vols., Romae: Iacobus Dragondelli, 1662), II, 57, n. 14; Benedict XIV, *De Synodo Dioecesana,* I, II, cap. 9, n. 6; Ferraris, *Prompta Bibliotheca,* s.v. "Vicarius Capitularis," art. II, n. 12.

58 Canon 356, § 1.

59 Canon 356, § 1.

60 Canon 406, § 1.

62 Canon 1432, § 2. "When the See is vacant in the case of "libera collatio" which belongs exclusively to the bishop, ordinary power is not invested in the vicar capitular or administrator."—Coady, *the Appointment of Pastors,* The Catholic University of America, Canon Law Studies, n. 52 (Washington, D. C.: The Catholic University of America, 1929), p. 108; this question will be discussed in a later chapter.

63 Canon 373, § 5.

64 Canon 426, § 5; Klekotka, *Diocesan Consultors,* The Catholic University of America, Canon Law Studies, n. 8 (Washington, D. C.: The Catholic University of America, 1920), p. 45, and pp. 54-55.

6) Declare parochial incumbencies of removable character to be changed and possess an irremovable status.[65]

7) Institute Religious Congregations.[66]

8) Erect pious associations, or give consent to their aggregation.[67]

9) Grant indulgences, unless the power was expressly granted to him.[68]

10) Fix a set fee to be paid priests who, for convenience sake, say Mass in a very poor church. Such a fee serves the purpose of defraying the expenses of the utensils and other appurtenances necessary for the celebration of Mass.[69]

11) Join and unite parishes with one another on an equal or subordinate basis, or join parishes with benefices which do not entail the care of souls, even though this latter union made the non-parochial benefice accessory to the parish.[70]

12) Permit or authorize exchange of benefices.[72]

13) Remove from office the *officialis, vice-officialis,*[73] defender of the bond, or the promoter of justice.[74] Should an occasion

[65] Canon 454, § 3.

[66] Canon 492, § 1.

[67] Canon 684, § 4; *AAS,* XI (1919), 353.

[68] Canon 912; Jaeger, *The Administration of Vacant and Quasi-Vacant Dioceses in the United States,* pp. 193-194; Hagedorn, *General Legislation on Indulgences,* The Catholic University of America, Canon Law Studies, n. 22 (Washington, D. C.: The Catholic University of America, 1924), p. 73.

[69] Canon 1303, §§ 2 and 3.

[71] Canon 1423, § 1.

[72] Canon 1487, § 1.

[73] Canon 1573, § 5.

[74] Canon 1590, §1; "He [The Defender of the Bond] cannot be removed by the temporarily appointed apostolic administrator, who in all things is to be considered as the vicar capitular."—Dolan, *The Defensor Vinculi,* The Catholic University of America, Canon Law Studies, n. 85 (Washington, D. C.: The Catholic University of America, 1934), p. 27; "He [The Promotor of Justice] cannot be removed by the temporarily appointed apostolic administrator, who in all things is, practically, the counterpart of the vicar capitular."—Glynn, *The Promoter of Justice,* The Catholic University of America, Canon Law Studies, n. 101 (Washington, D. C.: The Catholic University of America, 1934) p. 71.

arise wherein one of these above mentioned officials or officers becomes involved in or commits some serious crime which demands his removal from office then the temporary apostolic administrator could take steps against him by instituting a canonical trial.[75]

14) Reserve sins.[76] This vast departure from the principle which says that those who possess the ordinary jurisdiction or power to grant faculties for hearing confessions or to inflict censures enjoy the right also of reserving to themselves certain sins.

15) Alienate anything when such an act would redound to the detriment of the status of the respective diocese, or be prejudicial to the rights of succeeding bishops. Particularly is the temporary apostolic administrator forbidden to alienate the property of the *mensa episcopalis,* or of any parish or benefice which is vacant. Even in these instances it is permitted when the good of the Church demands it, and a great loss would accrue to the diocese if there were a delay until the arrival of a new bishop.[77] Augustine says: "The vicar capitular [administrator and equally well the temporary apostolic administrator] may conclude a favorable financial deal, for instance, getting money at a lower rate of interest or converting bonds into more profitable ones. For this is not prejudical to the diocese, and opportunities, especially on the money market, easily slip away."[78] The required formalities of Canon Law must be observed, and anyone guilty of alienating ecclesiastical property contrary to the prescription of canon 1532 must be fittingly punished by ecclesiastical authority in proportion to the amount alienated.[79]

[75] Roberti, *De Processibus* (2 vols., Romae: Apud Aedes Facultatis Iuridicae ad S. Appollinaris, 1926), I, 167; Jaeger, *The Administration of Vacant and Quasi-Vacant Dioceses in the United States,* p. 194.

[76] Canon 893, § 1.

[77] Jaeger, *The Administration of Vacant and Quasi-Vacant Dioceses in the United States,* p. 198.

[78] *A Commentary on Canon Law,* II, 489-490.

[79] Canon 2347.

Art. 3—The Temporary Apostolic Administrator *Sede Plena*

Canon 315, § 1. Administrator Apostolicus . . .
§ 2. Si ad tempus datus sit:
n. 1. Eadem iura ac officia habet ac Vicarius Capitularis; *sed sede plena, potest dioecesim visitare ad tramitem iuris; nec tenetur obligatone applicandae Missae pro populo, quae Episcopum gravat:*

In the preliminary part of canon 315, § 2, n. 1, the temporary apostolic administrator is accorded the same rights and duties as is the vicar capitular. In the latter part, however, the temporary apostolic administrator is granted the right of visiting the diocese, *sede plena,* according to the norms laid down by law; and he is not bound to apply the Mass for the people as the bishop is. These two clauses demand some explanation in so far as they grant to the temporary apostolic adminisrator an amplification of the powers of the vicar capitular, and relieve him of a duty incumbent upon the vicar capitular.

A)—Canonical Diocesan Visitation

Formerly the law made provisions for the vicar capitular to visit the diocese he administered provided a year had elapsed since the bishop last visited the see. The Sacred Congregation of Rites in a decree minutely outlined the way in which this duty became a part of the office of the vicar capitular:

> Certum exploratumque quum sit in unaquaque Dioecesi, elapso anno a die novissimae Visitationis peractae ab ultimo Episcopo defuncto, posse Vicarium Capitularem legitime electum hanc ipsam Visitationem per Dioecesim instituere.[80]

Then the decree further proceeded to describe the manner in

[80] S.R.C., Abellinen., 8 nov. 1843—*Decreta Authentica Congregationis Sacrorum Rituum* (6 vols., Romae: Ex Typograhia Polyglotta, 1898-1927), n. 2864; Nicolius, *Iuris Utriusque Theorica Praxis,* II, p. 57, n. 3.

which the vicar capitular is to be received, and also informs the Church in question what special privileges and prerogatives the vicar capitular enjoys. Even until a few years before the promulgation of the Code this legislation was constant, and thus enabled the vicar capitular of a certain see to visit his respective diocese after he had witnessed the passing of a year since the last canonical visitation of the see was made:

> In specie Vicarius Capitularis nequit . . . visitare totam dioecesim, antequam elapsus sit annus ab ultima . . . . visitatione per episcopum peracta.[81]

How do we know that the vicar capitular no longer possesses this right? Principally because no provision is made for it in the present Code. For the canon relevant to the canonical visitation of dioceses says: "Tenentur Episcopi obligatione visitandae quotannis dioecesi vel ex toto vel ex parte, ita ut saltem singulis quinquenniis universam vel ipsi per se vel, si fuerint legitime impediti, per Vicarium Generalem aliumve lustrent."[82] This canon even prohibits the vicar-general from canonically visiting the diocese unless he has received a special authorization from the resident bishop. Therefore, the axiom which notes that what is denied to the vicar-general is *ipso facto* denied to the vicar capitular is verified and substantiated by canon 430, § 2: "Nihilominus, excepta collatione beneficiorum aut officiorum ecclesiasticorum, omnia vim habent quae gesta sunt a Vicario Generali . . . "

In addition to the above mentioned reason, it is believed that this right is also denied to the vicar capitular by the very fact that *Canon* 315, § 2, *n.* 1, points to this right as being conferred solely on the temporary apostolic administrator, and so designates it as one of the special prerogatives of this administrator when he is appointed *sede plena.* For otherwise such a reference would have been superfluous if the vicar capitular already possessed this right. Likewise, too, since the visitation of the diocese is obligatory at least every five years there is hardly any instance existing wherein

[81] Wernz, *Ius Decretalium,* II, p. 609, n. 795.
[82] Canon 343, § 1.

the vicar capitular will rule a diocese for such a long period of time. Rome will provide for any exceptional cases.[83]

On this Canonical Diocesan Visitation the temporary apostolic administrator *sede plena* must examine into all those matters which pertain to faith and morals, the administration of the Sacraments, preaching, the observance of the feasts, divine worship, the education of youth, and ecclesiastical discipline. In fine, the same method utilized by the residential bishop in performing his diocesan visitation is to be followed by the temporary apostolic administrator *sede plena.*[84]

On these Canonical Visitations can the residential bishop interfere with the work of the temporary apostolic administrator? This query was settled at the time of the Council of Trent and has been answered many times since by various authors.[85] In no manner is the resident bishop to interfere with the canonical visitation of the diocese which is being made by the temporary apostolic administrator *sede plena.*

This power which is accorded to the temporary apostolic administrator who is appointed *sede plena,* but denied to the vicar capitular, can be exercised whenever the good of the diocese demand it; however, it is not resorted to unless a considerable length of time has transpired since the visitation was last made by the resident bishop. Thus in the words of Toso:

> In primis, sede quidem vacante, Administrator ad tempus datus, sicuti et Vicarius Capitularis canonicam dioecesis

[83] "Thus, the duties of the visiting *ad limina Apostolorum,* of the canonical visitation of the diocese, and of reporting the status of the diocese to the Holy See, certainly are not incumbent upon the administrator, especially since it is the policy of the Holy See in modern times to avoid long periods of vacancy."—Jaeger, *The Administration of Vacant and Quasi-Vacant Diocese in the United States,* p. 205.

[84] Canons 343-346.

[85] "Potest similiter visitare dioecesim, cum et ita facultas specialiter ei tribuatur. Est autem in hoc advertendum, quo si cum ipso vesitet etiam Episcopus, non potest Episcopus sese ingerere in visitatione, sed solum in exercitio Pontificalium, confirmando, vel aliquid simile faciendo, quod ad ordinem Episcopalem spectaret, si non fit ei interdictum."—Pellegrinus, *Praxis Vicariorum,* p. 57, n. 6.

> visitationem peragere non possunt: idque, ne suis forte decretis in visitatione latis, quidquam praeiudicii futuro titulari afferre videantur (cfr. can. 435, § 3). Contra, sede plena, cum hoc in casu per longum quoque tempus protrahi possit pontificia dioecesis administratio, Administratori Ap. ius et obligatio incumbit dioecesim visitandi ad tramitem iuris, deest tempore et modo a iure Episcopis residentialibus statuto.[86]

B—The *Missa pro Populo*

Under the present discipline residential bishops must apply Holy Mass for the faithful committed to their care on all Sundays, holydays of obligation, and suppressed feast days.[87] This application is likewise prescribed to the vicar capitular; "Vicarius Capitularis obligatione tenetur . . . applicandae Missae pro populo ad normam can . . . 339." [88] Ordinarily, too, this duty is incumbent on the apostolic administrator who is temporarily deputed to a diocese *sede vacante;* but not on the temporary apostolic administrator who is sent to a diocese *sede plena,* since the canon says that the temporary apostolic administrator who is administering a see *sede plena* is not obligated to offer the *Missa pro populo* for the souls committed to his care. This is an exception to the general rule that confers on the temporary apostolic administrator the same rights and duties that pertains to the vicar capitular.[89] This obligation is called negative when applied to the temporary Apostolic Administrator *sede plena.*

If the permanent apostolic administrator, the temporary apostolic administrator *sede vacante,* and the vicar capitular are obligated to the application of the *Missa pro populo,* why not also the temporary apostolic administrator who is appointed to a diocese *sede plena?* The answer is contained in the following words of the law: "Episcopus Missam pro populo diebus supra indicatis per se applicare debet; . . . " [90] These words show very plainly

[86] *Commentaria Minora,* II, 137.

[87] Canon 339.

[88] Canon 440.

[89] Canon 315, § 2, n. 1.

[90] Canon 339, § 4.

that the application of the *Missa pro populo* is an exclusive burden of the residential bishop; or in the event that the diocese is vacant, this application falls on the lawful administrator of the diocese whether he be the vicar capitular or the apostolic administrator, for they are the successors of the bishops. So imperative is the obligation that it does not even expire when the bishop is ill or otherwise incapacitated by some existing moral or physical handicap. This solemn obligation rests on the bishop who is the *episcopus proprius,* and he alone is competent to perform this task after the manner stipulated by law. The law does recognize, nevertheless, the existence of causes over which the bishop has no control: namely, a bishop is hindered by a legitimate cause which prevents him from applying on the proper day the *Missa pro populo* for his flock. In this circumstance the law allows him either to procure another person to satisfy the obligation for him, or to transfer the obligation to a day on which he can fulfill this obligation himself.[91]

If the temporary apostolic administrator *sede plena* has been assigned to a diocese where the bishop is mentally ill, and therefore incapable of offering the *Missa pro populo,* does this duty of application then devolves upon the temporary apostolic administrator? No! Not even in this instance, but here too the dictates of *Canon* 339, § 4, still retain their force. However, *ex caritate,* and not *ex iustitia,* this duty should be assumed by the temporary apostolic administrator *sede plena* for he can reimburse himself for this *officium* of offering the *Missa pro populo* by claiming a stipend which is to be taken from the *mensa episcopalis.*[92]

ART. 4—THE SECRET DIOCESAN ARCHIVES

Another right granted to the temporary apostolic administrator but denied to the vicar capitular or administrator concerns the

[91] Canon 338, § 4.

[92] Hofmeister, "Von den Apostolischen Administratorem de Diözesen und Abteien."—*Archiv für Katholisches Kirchenrecht,* Innsbruck, 1857-1861; Mainz, 1862-), CX (1930), 346; (hereafter this work will be referred to as *AKKR*).

secret diocesan archives.[93] Canon 382, § 1 states that the vicar capitular may break the seal and open the secret archives only in case of urgent necessity, and he must do so in the presence of two canons or two consultors; in their presence he may consult the documents, but he may not take them away; after the consultation, he replaces them and seals the archives in the presence of two witnesses. When the new bishop arrives in the diocese, the vicar capitular or diocesan administrator who opened the secret archives shall give the bishop an account of the reason for opening the archives.[94] In the words of the canon, therefore, the vicar capitular is allowed to open the sealed archives only *urgente necessitate,*[95] and even then he can act only under the supervision of two witneses. Any misuse of his office by fraud, embezzlement, or in the essential change of any document subjects him to an *ipso facto* excommunication *simpliciter* reserved to the Holy See.[96]

When a temporary apostolic administrator administers an episcopal see sede plena the situation is different despite the legislation handed down in canon 315, § 2, n. 1. The temporary apostolic administrator receives the same right as the resident bishop possesses in respect to the secret archives of the diocese. It is the right of the temporary apostolic administrator to open the secret archives, examine the documents, and replace them without supervision of any witnesses. This is verified in the following words:

> Episcopus vel Administrator Apostolicus, repetita altera clave, ipse solus, nemine adstante, archivum vel armarium secretum,ubi opus fuerit, aperire et inspicere potest, quod deinde utraque clavi iterum claudatur.[97]

[93] Canons 379-382.

[94] Cf. Woywod, *A Practical Commentary on the Code of Canon Law,* I, 137.

[95] Cf. Blat, *Commentarium Textus Codicis Iuris Canonici,* II, p. 471, n. 479; Coronata, *Institutiones Iuris Canonici,* I, p. 509, n. 429; Wernz-Vidal, *Ius Canonicum,* II, p. 688, n. 648.

[96] Canons 382; 435, § 3; 2405.

[97] Canon 379, § 4.

The resealing is not necessary, nor is he subject to the penalty levied against the vicar capitular for any misuse of his office or for essential changes made in the documents.[98]

Therefore, the temporary apostolic administrator enjoys the same privileges as a resident bishop over the diocesan secret archives; on the other hand, the vicar capitular or administrator must not enter or consult the secret archives except in the case of urgent necessity and even then he must follow the requirements expressed in the law. Finally, in the words of canon 381, the difference between the temporary apostolic administrator and the vicar capitular is made even more pronounced when the temporary apostolic administrator occupies a see that is vacant. In the latter case the secret archives are opened; but with the election of the vicar capitular or administrator the archives remain sealed until the arrival of the new bishop.

Art. 5—Rights of the Temporary Apostolic Administrator In Regard to Ordinations

The temporary apostolic administrators who are endowed with the episcopal dignity may, in view of their episcopal status, exercise the episcopal right of ordinations in these territories which are committed to their administration. Such power, consequently, includes the conferring of all degrees of the Sacrament of Holy Orders, in addition to the conferring of the Sacrament of Confirmation, the consecration of Churches, altars, chalices, etc. On the other hand, the temporary apostolic administrator adorned with only the priestly character does not receive by virtue of his appointment the power to confer orders, unless this faculty was bestowed in his letter of appointment. In many cases the temporary apostolic administrator has no need for this special faculty

[98] "Canon 3405, employs the term "Vicarius Capitularis." Since penalties are to be strictly interpreted, canonists hold that this penalty would not be incurred by a transferred bishop who is acting as Administrator (canon 430, § 3, n. 1), nor by an apostolic administrator (canon 431, § 1, . . . "—Jaeger, *The Administration of Vacant and Quasi-Vacant Dioceses in the United States*, p. 191, footnote n. 114.)

owing to the fact that his office continues only for a short time, and no occasions arise wherein the use of this faculty is needed. Nevertheless, if occasions do present themselves the temporary apostolic administrator can not presume this faculty but has to petition Rome for it. The Decretal law very clearly stated that the apostolic administrator was permitted or granted the power to exercise full and free administration over the spiritual and temporal welfare of the diocese, but needed episcopal consecration for acts that demanded the episcopal character.

> Is, cui procuratio seu administratio cathedralis ecclesiae plena ac libera in spiritualibus et temporalibus a Sede Apostolica, cui soli hoc competit, est commissa, potest, alienatione bonorum immobilium duntaxat excepta, omnia quae iurisdictionis episcopalis exsistunt, et quae potest electus exsequi confirmatus, libere exercere. Illa quippe, quae ministerium consecretionis exposcunt, nisi fuerit episcopus, per alios faciat episcopos expediri.[99]

Herein is expressed the law which is reiterated in *canon* 1147, § 1:

> Consecrationes nemo qui charactere episcopali careat, valide peragere potest, nisi vel iure vel apostolico indulto id ei permittatur.

The temporary Apostolic Administrator not endowed with the episcopal dignity may, like the Vicar Capitular, invite into the diocese any bishop for any consecration.[100]

The Holy See very graciously grants additional faculties to those temporary Apostolic Administrators who are adorned with only the priestly character when it deems them necessary. These faculties often extend so far as to comprise the indult to confirm, to confer the minor orders, to consecrate chalices, church bells, and so forth. These faculties were very clearly outlined when the Holy See received a question proposed by the temporary Apostolic Administrator of Brixen, Prelate Mutschlechner. He asked the Holy See if, in virtue of his appointment as Apostolic administra-

[99] C. 42, *de electione et electi potestate,* I, 6, in VI°.
[100] Canon 435, § 2.

tor, he could impart the same blessings that vicars and prefects apostolic could impart, in addition he asked if he could consecrate chalices, patens, altars, as well as confirm and give tonsure and the minor orders. The Sacred Congregation of the Consistory replied on November 29, 1928, that these faculties were not included among the faculties which ordinarily are granted to apostolic administrators who lack the episcopal character.[101] In the meantime, prior to the question of the temporary apostolic administrator, Pope Pius XI on November 23 of the same year (1928), *attentis necessitatibus istius dioecesis Brixinensis*, imparted to the temporary apostolic administrator of Brixen the right: "Impertiendi benedictiones Episcopis reservatas, consecrandi calices, patenas et altaria atque conferendi Sacramentum Confirmationis." Herein, then, is embodied the whole spirit of the law. And it only seems to be good judgment to grant to the temporary apostolic administrator *carente episcopali charactere*, more rights of consecration the longer he is in office, but these rights are granted *ex speciali gratia* by the Holy See.

Since *canon* 1147, § 1, states that consecrations cannot be validly performed by anyone except consecrated bishops, and by those who are given this faculty either by law or by an apostolic indult, the temporary apostolic administrator who is not a bishop but a priest must have a special faculty to consecrate chalices, patens, portable altars, alter stones, bells, etc. Such faculties are now included in the quinquennial faculties granted to Ordinaries. The term now used is "Ordinarii locorum" and not "episcopi" as formerly. Therefore under the term *Ordinarii locorum* the temporary apostolic administrator is included.[102] Undoubtedly the quinquennial faculties in so far as they are addressed to the *Ordinarii locorum* are granted to the temporary apostolic administrator, even though he is not endowed with the episcopal character. Therefore it is particularly important that the apostolic admin-

[101] "Quod facultates . . . enumeratae non continentur in genere intra facultates quae ordinarie conceduntur Administratoribus Apostolicis dignitate episcopali non insignitis."—*AKKR,* CX, (1930), 335.

[102] Canon 198, § 1.

istrator who is not endowed with the episcopal dignity consult the quinquennial faculties in order to ascertain what consecrations are permitted to him.[103]

Art. VI.—Privileges of the Temporary Apostolic Administrator

Canon 315, § 2, n. 2. Ad honorifica privilegia quod attinet, valeat praescriptum can. 308 . . .

After having considered the various rights and duties connected with the office of a temporary apostolic administrator, we come to an investigation of his honorary privileges. Canon 315, § 2, n. 2, simply states that with respect to the honorary privileges of the temporary apostolic administrator canon 308 is decisive. Toso says that canon 308 does not treat faculties, but only of the particular rights or honorary privileges, *"sive in sacris funtionibus peragendis sive extra."* [104] It is necessary, therefore, to investigate canon 308 in order to determine definitely the honorary privileges conferred on the temporary apostolic administrator.

> Vicars and Prefects Apostolic who are bishops are entitled to the same privileges of honor which the law gives to titular bishops. If they are not bishops, they have during their office and within their own territory the insignia and privileges of Protonotaries Apostolic *de numero participantium.*[105]

Previous to applying this canon to the temporary apostlic administrator it is deemed fitting to state at the outset that the person who is designated to assume the office of an aposolic administrator does not have to be invested with the episcopal dignity. This is quite evident from canon 312 where it is stipulated that an apostolic administrator is one who is sent by the Sovereign Pontiff. Pre-Code legislation classified apostolic administrators

[103] Jaeger, *The Administration of Vacant and Quasi-Vacant Dioceses in the United States,* 179; *canons* 66, § 2; 198, § 1.

[104] *Commentaria Minora,* II, 130.

[105] Canon 308; Cf. Woywod, *A Practical Commentary on the Code of Canon Law,* I, p. 112, n. 230.

thus: a) "alii episcopali charactere carent; b) alii vero consecrantur in Episcopum, . . . "[106] Vermeersch-Creusen say: "Administrator Apostolicus est clericus, plerumque charactere episcopali insignitus, . . ."[107] The definition offered by Vermeersch-Creusen is found also in various other authors. It reveals that according to his own will the Holy Father may appoint as an apostolic administrator either a priest or a bishop.[108] Cocchi,[109] and Coronata[110] refer to an apostolic administrator as a *prelatus*. The word prelate in ecclesiastical law denotes a cleric, either secular or regular, who has ordinary jurisdiction in the external forum.[111] Cocchi says: Huiusmodi *praelatus* generatim est alius Episcopus residentialis."[112] Coronata, on the other hand, says: "Administrator Episcopus esse potest, non autem necessario."[113]

Consequently, then, it is quite patent that a distinction must be made between the temporary apostolic administrator invested with the episcopal dignity, and the temporary apostolic administrator endowed only with the priestly character. Quite true, the case or circumstance is not infrequently present when the Sovereign Pontiff elects to deputize a priest, in preference to a bishop, to administer a vacant or quasi-vacant diocese. Such an occasion would be verified in a small diocese when the residential bishop becomes mentally incapacitated and the Holy See appoints a priest to the office of temporary apostolic administrator. Although it is true that most of the persons chosen by the Holy See to administer dioceses, as apostolic administrators, are either neighboring bishops, or titular bishops, there are found, nevertheless, instances when a priest is assigned to this office, particularly when the

[106] Bouix, *Tractatus de Curia Romana* (Parisiis: Bourget Calas & Cie., 1895), p. 646.

[107] *Epitome Iuris Canonici*, I, p. 331, n. 431.

[108] Wernz-Vidal, *Ius Canonicum*, II, p. 587, n. 557; Beste, *Introductio in Codicem*, p. 258; Ferreres, *Institutiones Canonicae*, I, p. 221, n. 615.

[109] *Commentarium in Codicem Iuris Canonici*, II, p. 158, n. 229.

[110] *Institutiones Iuris Canonici*, I, p. 457, n. 379.

[111] Canon 110.

[112] *Commentarium in Codicem Iuris Canonici*, II, 158, n. 229.

[113] *Institutiones Iuris Canonici*, I, p. 457, n. 379.

cathedral chapter has elected an unworthy vicar capitular and the Holy See has taken action by appointing the Dean of the cathedral chapter the temporary apostolic administrator.[114] Since the presence or absence of the episcopal character makes a decided difference in the honorary privileges possessed, there will be discussed here: 1) the honorary privileges of those who are invested with the episcopal dignity; and 2) the honorary privileges of those who are not endowed with the episcopal character.

A)—*Invested with the Episcopal Dignity*

Temporary apostolic administrators who are invested with the episcopal dignity are granted according to canon 308 all the honorary privileges of a titular bishop.[115] In order, then, to comprehend what is contained in this grant it is necessary to inspect canon 349, wherein are delineated the honorary privileges of a titular bishop. Canon 349 says, in effect, that residential and titular bishops, from the time they receive authentic notification of their promotion receive, in addition to other privileges mentioned in the respective titles of the Code, many of the privileges of Cardinals enumerated in canon 239. These privileges of Cardinals which are extended to the temporary apostolic administrator who is endowed with the episcopal dignity include the following:

1) He can choose for himself and the members of his household a confessor, who, if he has no jurisdiction, receives it by the very fact of being chosen, and has the power to absolve from all the reservations of the Ordinary, and from all papal reserved sins and censures with the exception of those reserved *specialissimo modo,* and those which are incurred by the relevation of a secret of the Holy Office.[116]

2) He can preach everywhere outside his proper territory with

114 *Bullarium Diplomatum et Privilegiorum Sanctorum Romanorum Taurinensis Editio,* XVI, 782.

115 Canon 348.

116 Canon 239, § 1, n. 2.

at least the presumed permission or consent of the respective ordinary.[117]

3) He can celebrate, or permit another to celebrate in his presence, one Mass on Holy Thursday and three Masses on Christmas night, provided, of course, he is not obligated to celebrate in the Cathedral.[118]

4) He can bless everywhere, with the rites prescribed by the Church, beads, rosaries, crucifixes, medals, statues and scapulars approved by the Holy See, with all the indulgences attached to these objects by the latter.[119] Pertinent to this privilege a doubt was proposed by Archbishop Hanna, formerly of San Francisco: "An liceat Episcopis communicare presbyteris suae ditionis habitualiter potestatem benediciendi rosaria, etc., de qua in canon 349, § 1, n. 1, cum applicatione indulgentiarum, observatis ritibus ab Ecclesia praescriptis." The Congregation of the Sacred Apostolic Penitentiary after giving the question mature consideration replied *"negative."* [120] A little later, in 1920, many doubts relevant to the privileges, insignia, and functions of bishops were solved.[121]

5) He can erect the Stations of the Cross in Churches and Oratories, even though the latter be private, and also in other pious places which are used for devotional purposes. On behalf of those who are prevented by infirmity or by any other reasons from making the way of the Cross, he may bless and apply to crucifixes all the indulgences granted for making the Stations.[122]

6) He can celebrate Mass on a portable altar, not only in his own

[117] Canon 239, § 1, n. 3.

[118] Canon 239, § 1, n. 4; Canon 349, § 1, n. 1.

[119] Canon 239, §1, n. 4.

[120] 18 iulii, 1919—*ASS*, XI (1919), 332; Blat, *Commentarium Textus,* II, 374; "Hanc facultatem non habet Vicarius Generalis, nec Episcopus potest eam delegare ne per modum quidem actus."—Coronata, *Institutiones Iuris Canonici,* I, 484; *AAS,* XVIII (1926), 500.

[121] *AAS,* XII (1920), 177-182; Bouscaren, *Canon Law Digest,* I, 204-208.

[122] Canon 239, § 1, n. 6.

residence, but wherever he travels. This privilege permits another Mass to be celebrated in his presence.[123]

7) He can celebrate Mass at sea, provided due precaution is observed.[124]

8) He enjoys daily the benefit of a personally privileged altar.[125]

9) He can celebrate Mass according to his own *Ordo* in any Church or oratory.[126]

10) He can gain in his own private chapel those indulgence which necessitate a visit to a Church or a public place of worship. This privilege is equally enjoyed by the members of his household.[127]

11) He can bless the people after the manner of bishops, but in the City of Rome this can be done only in Churches, pious institutions, and at gatherings of the faithful.[128]

12) He can wear all the episcopal insignia according to the prescription of the liturgical law.[129]

The episcopal insignia are the pastoral staff or crosier, the mitre, the pectoral cross,[130] the episcopal ring,[131] dalmatics and tunicella, gloves and sandals. Pope Leo XIII added to these the skull-cap of violet color.[132] The Sacred Congregation of the Sacraments declared on the 22nd of April, 1910, that even those who had been

[123] Canon 239, § 1, n. 7.

[124] Canon 239, § 1, n. 8.

[125] Canon 239, § 1, n. 10.

[126] Canon 239, § 1, n. 9.

[127] Canon 239, § 1, n. 11.

[128] Canon 239, § 1, n. 12.

[129] Canon 349, § 1, n. 2.

[130] Etiam Episcopi titulares gestare possunt publice crucem pectoralem —Coronata, *Institutiones Iuris Canonici,* I, 484, footnote 4.

[131] Fideles animo contrito devote osculantes annulum episcopalem indulgentiam quinquaginta dierum lucrantur—S.C.S. Off., Martii 1909—*AAS,* I, (1909), 277.

[132] Litt, ap. *"Praeclaro,"* 3 febr. 1888,—*Fontes,* n. 597; Vermeersch-Creusen, *Epitome Iuris Canonici,* I, p. 348, n. 461; Augustine, *A Commentary on Canon Law,* II, 377.

elected to the episcopal honor but who had not yet been consecrated could make use of the skull-cap in sacred ceremonies, except from the Preface to the Communion of the Mass.[133]

On the other hand, the temporary apostolic administrator who is a residential bishop is not permitted certain privileges which are prerogatives of residential bishops.

1) He cannot receive the income of the *Mensa episcopalis.* An exception to the rule of canon 349, § 2, n. 1, is had in the transferred bishop who temporarily retains the administration of his former see as apostolic administrator.[134] Such a transferred bishop from the moment he receives notice of his change obtains the powers of a vicar capitular over his former see.[135] He continues, however, to receive the income of the *mensa episcopalis.*[136]

2) He cannot grant indulgences of fifty days after the manner of residental bishops.

3) He cannot erect in all the Churches of the diocese the throne with a canopy.

4) He cannot have his name mentioned in the Canon of every Mass celebrated in the diocese; neither can he on the anniversary of his election have the commemoration of it made at every Mass.[137]

From this enumeration it is evident that the temporary apostolic administrator who is invested with the episcopal dignity possesses all the privileges of a titular bishop which includes, in addition to the above mentioned, many others intimated throughout the Code.[138] It is patently beyond the scope of this disserta-

[133] "Pileolo violaces uti possunt etsi non sunt consecrati, etiam in missae celebratione excepto tamen tempore a prefatione ad Communionem." —*AAS,* II, (1910), 330.

[134] Canon 315, § 2, n. 2.

[135] Canon 430, § 3, n. 1.

[136] Canons 430, § 3, n. 3; 194, § 2.

[137] Moretti, *De Sacris Functionibus* (4 vols., Taurini: Marietti, 1936-1939), II, n. 1390, *in fine.*

[138] Canons 811, § 2; 812; 914; 1401; 1770, § 2, n. 1; 2343, § 3; 2227, § 2; 1557, § 1, n. 3; 1557, § 2, n. 1; 120, § 2.

tion, however, to search out every privilege granted to the temporary apostolic administrator who is a bishop. Quite naturally there remains the necessity of examining the letter of appointment to ascertain further whether the privileges commonly granted have been augmented or curtailed.

Under this section two types of temporary apostolic administrators are included: 1) the temporary apostolic administrator appointed to rule a see that is vacant or quasi-vacant, and 2) the temporary apostolic administrator who is simultaneously a residential bishop of his own proper see and the apostolic administrator of a neighboring diocese. In both of these instances the apostolic administrators are bishops enjoying only the honorary privileges of a titular bishop.

Of the first type is the apostolic administrator who is temporarily appointed to administer a diocese. This manner of appointment was exemplified when Edward O'Rourke, the titular bishop of Canea, was appointed by the Sacred Congregation for Extraordinary Affairs as apostolic administrator to the free city of Danzig. This appointment was *ad nutum Sanctae Sedis.*[139] Bishop O'Rourke's faculties were expressed in the following words, " . . . ita ut is eadem potestate ibidem fruatur, quam obtinent Ordinarii in sua diocesi." [140] No mention, however, was made of the honorary privileges of Bishop O'Rourke. Therefore it is deduced that he enjoyed only the privileges of a titular bishop.[141]

By a decree of the Sacred Congregation of the Consistory Sigismund Waitz, the titular bishop of Cibira and auxiliary bishop of Brixen, was appointed apostolic administrator to that part of the diocese of Brixen which was located on the Austrian side. The object of this action was to afford the faithful committed to this section more opportunity to exercise their religious duties. The appointment was *ad nutum Sanctae Sedis* and his faculties were enumerated thus; " . . . cum omnibus facultatibus

[139] *AAS,* XIV (1922), 312.
[140] *Loc. cit.*
[141] Canon 349, § 1.

et officiis, quae Episcopis residentialibus in proprio territorio competunt, dimisso tamen titulo et officio Auxiliaris Episcopi Brixinensis." [142] Even though the appointment of apostolic administrator Waitz connoted all the rights and duties attached to a residential bishop, it did not, however, grant him the honorary privileges of a residential bishop. The letter of appointment mentioned faculties and duties, but made no reference to privileges. Obviously, then, his honorary privileges were provided for in canon 308, which says that those apostolic administrators who are bishops are entitled to the same privileges of honor which the law gives to titular bishops.[143]

These two examples will serve to illustrate the first type of temporary apostolic administrator who is deputized by the Sovereign Pontiff to administer a see that is vacant or quasi-vacant. Both of these apostolic administrators were given all the rights and duties of a residential bishop, which in itself was an extension of the usual rights and duties accorded to the temporary apostolic administrator by the Code.[144] Although Bishops O'Rourke and Waitz were granted all the rights and duties of residential bishops, they were denied, however, the honorary privileges of residential bishops. This is ascertained from their respective letters of appointment which fail to make any reference to these honorary privileges. Naturally, if the letters of appointment fail to indicate their privileges it is necessary to inspect the pertinent canons treating of the apostolic administrator.[145] Particularly relevant is canon 315, § 2, n. 2, which states that the honorary privileges of temporary apostolic administrators are stated in canon 308. Canon 308 states that the honorary privileges of apostolic administrators who are temporarily placed over a diocese and possess the episcopal dignity are the same as those of titular bishops.[146]

[142] *AKKR,* CVI (1926), 297-298.

[143] Woywod, *A Practical Commentary on the Code of Canon Law,* I, p. 112, n. 230.

[144] Canon 315, § 2, n. 1.

[145] Canons 315-318.

[146] Canons 348, 349, § 1, nn. 1 and 2.

The second type of temporary apostolic administrator who is endowed with the episcopal character, and who possesses the honorary privileges of a titular bishop, is the residential bishop who is appointed temporary apostolic administrator of a neighboring diocese.

The Bull "Christi Domini" issued by Pope Benedict XV on December 10, 1920, divided the archdiocese of Warsaw and created a new diocese, Lodz. In view of the fact that no immediate arrangement was made to provide the new diocese with its own bishop, the administration of Lodz was committed to Alexander Cardinal Kakowski, Archbishop of Warsaw, in the following words: "Quousque autem haec nova dioecesis de proprio pastore provideatur, eiusdem regimen dilecto filio nostro Alexandro, tituli Sancti Augustini, SR.E. Presbytero Cardinali Kakowski, hodierno, ex apostolica dispensatione, tamquam Administratori Apostolico, committimus, ipsi tribuentes facultates ac iura omnia quae huic muneri competunt."[147] From these words of appointment it can be definitely determined that Cardinal Kakowski was granted only the honorary privileges of a titular bishop over the newly created diocese of Lodz. This is gathered from the phrase *"Iura et officia quae huic muneri competunt,"* which clearly shows that he had only the *iura et officia* of a vicar capitular according to the stipulations of canon 315, § 2, n. 1, and the honorary privileges of canon 315, § 2, n. 2, coupled with canons 308 and 349, § 1, nn. 1 and 2.

John Toner, the bishop of Dunkeld, was appointed apostolic administrator to Glasgow. Although Bishop Toner enjoyed in Dunkeld all the rights, duties, and honorary privileges of a residential bishop, nevertheless, in his new capacity of apostolic administrator to Glasgow his honorary privileges in that diocese were only those of a titular bishop.[148]

On February 6, 1920 the Archbishop of Cartagena in Spain being seriously ill, the Sacred Congregation of the Consistory deemed it fitting to nominate Fernand Leynaud, the Archbishop

[147] *AAS,* XIII (1921), 249-251.
[148] *AAS,* XII (1920), 4441.

of Algiers in Africa, as temporary apostolic administrator to the Archdiocese of Cartagena.[149] This appointment made no extra provisions for the appointee, and consequently Archbishop Leynaud was assigned the duties, and enjoyed the rights of a vicar capitular, and the honorary privileges of a titular bishop as long as he administered the see of the incapacitated Archbishop of Cartagena.[150] All the above examples were chosen in preference to present day ones because they delineated more fully the duties incumbent on the appointee, while, on the other hand, examples of the present day apostolic administrator are not published in full in the *Acta Apostolicae Sedis,* and the only way of actually ascertaining what duties, privileges, etc., are granted to the present day temporary apostolic administrator would be by personal interview with the appointee, or by an examination of his letter of appointment.

In the preceding paragraph the honorary duties of the temporary apostolic administrator who is invested with the episcopal power have been explained. There is an exception to the rule which states that bishops who are made apostolic administrators receive only the honorary privileges of titular bishops. The latter part of § 2, n. 2, of canon 315 further stipulates that a bishop who is transferred to another see, but retains the administration of his former see, can claim in this former diocese also all the privileges of honor he formerly enjoyed there as residential bishop.[151] Herein is witnessed a vast departure and exception to the law respecting the honorary privileges of a temporary apostolic administrator. Thus far two possibilities have been considered; 1) the bishop (titular) who was sent to administer a vacant or quasi-vacant diocese, and 2) the resident bishop who was appointed the temporary apostolic administrator of a neighboring vacant or quasi-vacant diocese. In both of these instances, as has been explained, the respective bishops enjoyed only the

[149] *AAS,* XI (1919), 317.

[150] Canon 315, § 2, nn. 1 and 2.

[151] Cf. Woywod, *A Practical Commentary on the Code of Canon Law,* I, 115.

honorary privileges of a titular bishop unless, of course, the letter of appointment indicated otherwise. There is also a third possibility, namely; that of the former resident bishop who has been transferred to another diocese but was given the office of a temporary apostolic administrator over his former diocese. Instead of adopting the same legislation in this case as in the other two, an exception is granted and the former resident bishop is permitted to retain all his honorary privileges in his former see which he now rules as temporary apostolic administrator. Such a wide grant of honorary privileges dates back to the nineteenth centry, when in Italy a question arose as to what rights the transferred bishop possessed with regard to his former see which he retained as temporary apostolic administrator:

> Sanctissimus Dominus Noster Leo Papa XIII, attentis peculiaribus adiunctis, de speciali gratia ad beneplacitum S. Sedis valitura, benigne indulsit, ut Rmi. Episcopi Italicae Regionis, qui dimissa propria dioecesi ad aliam sive residentialem sive titularem transferuntur atque Apostolicam Administrationem temporaneam prioris dioeceseos retinent, ibidem, durante tantum eiusmodi administratione, omnibus honorificientiis, privilegiis, indultis ac facultatibus frui valeant, quae iisdem, uti propriis Episcopis Ordinariis, competebant. Contrariis non obstantibus quibuscunque. Die 25 Iunii, 1897.[152]

Leo XIII, however, stipulated that the indult was granted "'De speciali gratia ad beneplacitum Sanctae Sedis" and pertained to those bishops who were transferred to another diocese either as a residential or titular bishop, but still retained their former diocese as temporary apostolic administrator. Indeed, this was a large grant bestowing all the honorary privileges, indults and faculties which they formerly enjoyed as residential bishops. In the present Code not the entire decree as it applied to Italy is found, but only a part of it appears in the words: "Episcopo qui ad aliam sedem translatus, prioris retinet administrationem, in hac quoque omnia Episcoporum residentialium honorifica privi-

[152] *ASS*, XXX (1898), 638.

legia competunt." [153] Now, such a bishop retains in his former diocese the rights and duties of a vicar capitular,[154] but the honorary privileges of a residential bishop. Some of the honorary privileges of a residential bishop include the right to wear the mitre, to carry the crozier, to wear the cappa magna, to erect an episcopal throne and canopy in all the churches of the diocese, and to have his name mentioned in the Canon of the Mass.[155]

The three above mentioned types of temporary apostolic administrators who are invested with the episcopal dignity embrace all the possibilities contained in canon 315, § 2, n. 2.

B)—*Not Invested with the Episcopal Dignity*

The latter part of canon 308 is concerned—with those apostolic administrators who are not invested with the episcopal dignity. The relevant part of the canon says that if they (apostolic administrators) are not bishops, they have during their office and within their own territory the insignia and privileges of protonotaries apostolic *de numero participantium.*[156] Previous to the promulgation of the Code various decisions of the Roman Congregations had given to the temporary apostolic administrator the same privileges that were accorded to the vicar-general.[157]

The Code, however, has effected a great change through the instrumentality of canon 308, conceding to all non-episcopal temporary apostolic administrators the honorary privileges of the highest class of protonotary apostolic, namely, the class *de numero participantium.* Accordingly, then, they now have during their tenure of office and in their own territory the use of *pontificalia* without the crozier, the throne, the cappa magna, and the insertion of their name in the Canon of the Mass.

[153] Canon 315, § 2, n. 2.

[154] Canon 430, § 3, n. 1.

[155] Canon 349, § 2.

[156] Woywod, *A Practical Commentary on the Code of Canon Law,* I, p. 112, n. 230.

[157] "Quoad iura honorifica generatim illi Vicarii Apostolici (id est Apos. Adm.) eas tantum habent praerogativas, quibus gaudent Vicarii generales Episcoporum."—Wernz, *Ius Decretalium,* II, n. 704; *S.C.R.* 12 aug. 1684, n. 1732.

Naturally, it is important to decide just what are the more important honorary privileges of the protonotary apostolic. These privileges were very minutely outlined in the *Motu Proprio* of Pope Pius X entitled *Inter multiplices* and issued on February 21, 1905.[158] In the opening sentences of the *Motu Proprio* the Sovereign Pontiff narrates how prelates not having the episcopal power were the cause of many abuses and the occasion of infringements upon the dignity of the episcopate.[159] Pope Pius X (1903-1914) abrogated all former legislation pertaining to these prelates and declared, "Ut in posterum, Praelati Episcopis inferiores aliique, de quibus infra, qua tales, non alia insignia, privilegia, praerogativa audeant sibi vindicare, nisi quae hoc in Nostro documento, Motu Proprio dato . . . ." [160] After these prefatory remarks the various types of prelates who are inferior to bishops are considered, the *Protonotarii Apostolici de numero participantium.* It is impossible to investigate all the individual items of this *Motu Proprio* in the present study for many of them have no particular application to the temporary apostolic administrator. Consequently, only the more important sections will be considered and applied to the case in hand. Section 6 of the *Motu Proprio* forbids him always the use of a throne and crozier, as well as the cappa magna and the seventh candle. The faldstool, however, is allowed. In sacred functions he may wear the purple cassock of a prelate, sandals, a cassock with a train which is not unfolded even when he pontificates. The biretta, under which he may wear a black skull-cap, is black with a rose-colored pompon. A protonotary apostolic is permitted, at all times, to wear a ring, even in

[158] *Fontes,* III, n. 665; *Analecta Ecclesiastica,* XIII (1905), 53-59; *Ecclesiastical Review,* XXXII (1905), 612-618; XXXIII (1906), 53; Beste, *Introductio in Codicem,* pp. 260-262.

[159] "Ex quo praesertim Ponticalium usus per Decessores Nostros Romanos Pontifices aliquibus Praelatis, episcopali charactere non insignitis, concessus est, id saepe accidit, ut vel malo hominum ingenio, vel prava aut lata nimis interpretatione, ecclesiastica disciplina haud leve detrimentum ceperit, et episcopalis dignitas non parum iniuriae."—*Analecta Ecclesiastica,* ibid., 53.

[160] *Loc. cit.,* p. 54.

low Mass, and at other Church ceremonies.[161] In place of the *Dominus Vobiscum* he is never permitted to say *Pax Vobis;* neither can he impart the threefold episcopal blessing, nor say *Sit nomen Domini, et Adiutorium* before imparting his blessing to the people; but in pontifical Masses he can wear the miter and chant *Benedicat Vos.*[162] When going to the Church where he is to pontificate he is vested in the purple cassock, rochet and mantelletta, and wears the pectoral cross suspended from a cord of amaranth silk entwined with gold. Section 8 stipulates that the pectoral cross should be adorned with only one gem. He is received or may be received at the door of the Church by a master of ceremonies and two clerics. He is never allowed to bless the people as he passes through them.[163] He uses the simple white miter, but never the preciously ornamented miter.[164] Previous to the celebration of low Mass he may make the preparation and the thanksgiving in his prelatical habit, kneeling on a prie-dieu which is not draped but furnished with two purple cushions. He vests at the foot of the altar, and may be assisted by a cleric in major orders and two other ministers. He can make use of the canon, bugia, ewer, basin and towel. In the celebration of daily Mass he does not differ from other priests except that he is permitted the use of the ring and bugia. On his coat of arms he may have the purple hat with amaranth red strings each ending with six tassels on either side and disposed in three rows.[165]

The *Motu Proprio, Inter multiplices,* given by Pope Pius X in 1905 was supplemented and in part substituted by the Apostolic Constitution *Ad incrementum decoris,* dated August 15, 1934, and issued by Pope Pius XI. Evidently, it is necessary when considering the honorary privileges of an apostolic administrator who is endowed with only the priestly character to bear in mind simultaneously the *Inter multiplices* and the *Ad incrementum*

161 *"Inter multiplices"*—n. 6—*Analecta Ecclesiastica,* XIII (1905), 55.
162 *"Inter multiplices"*—n. 6.
163 *Ibid.* n. 7.
164 *Ibid.,* n. 9.
165 *Ibid.,* n. 18; Winslow, *Vicars and Prefects Apostolic,* pp. 28-30.

decoris, because the latter document has changed certain sections of the previous one.[166] Sections 41 to 52 of the Constitution *Ad incrementum decoris* are particularly important for the present study because they treat of the privileges of the protonotary apostolic. Throughout this part constant reference is made to the *Inter multiplices* demonstrating especially in which points it still is in force. Unlike the previous legislation of *Inter multiplices* the Constitution *Ad incrementum decoris* defines the material of the cassock. Furthermore, a special cassock is to be worn by the protonotary apostolic when the Holy See is vacant; namely, a black cassock made of wool, and the rochet should not be adorned with lace.[167] Indubitably, therefore, present day protonotaries apostolic are affected by those sections of the *Inter multiplices* which are not at variance with the *Ad incrementum decoris,* and from a parallel comparison, temporary apostolic administrators endowed with the priesthood enjoy only like privileges.

An exampel which illustrates this type of apostolic administrator and is found in early United States Ecclesiastical history, is believed to be worthy of note. The Sacred Congregation for the Propagation of the Faith sent a letter to Bishop Carroll of Baltimore instructing him to appoint Charles Nerinckx or another capable priest as apostolic administrator to Louisiana with the rights of an ordinary.[168] Bishop Carroll had great difficulty in persuading any of his priests to accept this post. William Du Bourg finally accepted and consented to become the apostolic administrator on August 12, 1812. Three years later the same William Du Bourg was consecrated Bishop of Louisiana. Apparently,

[166] *AAS,* XXVI (1934), 497 ss; *The Clergy Review,* VIII (1934), 417-418.

[167] *Ad incrementum decoris,* section VII—*The Clergy Review, loc. cit.*

[168] " . . . aut dilectum filium Carolum Nerinkx, de cujus zelo et virtute plurimum in Domino confidimus, aut eo forsan se imparem sentiente, alium idoneum, quem noveris, presbyterum Saecularem vel Regularem . . . " —*St. Louis Catholic Historical Review,* I (1918), 73; Sheearet, *Pontificia Americana,* The Catholic Unviersity of America, Studies in Church History, n. 15 (Washington, D. C.: The Catholic University of America, 1933), pp. 95-96.

then, from 1812 to 1815 William Du Bourg while simply endowed with the priestly character administered the territory of Louisiana. The letter addressed to him containing his faculties reads thus;

> I, the undersigned, Archbishop of Baltimore . . . delegate and send you, Very Rev. William Du Bourg, to the diocese of New Orleans in the capacity of apostolic administrator, and with the rights of an Ordinary, for so long a time as shall be the Sovereign Pontiff's and the Holy See's good pleasure.[169]

During this period, according to the prevalent customs, the temporary apostolic administrator who was not a bishop enjoyed only the honorary privileges of a vicar-general.[170] If such an appointment were effected today the honorary privileges of this temporary apostolic administrator would be definitely increased to those of a protonotary apostolic according to the Motu Proprio of Pope Pius X, and the Constitution of Pope Pius XI.

The Constitution of Pope Benedict XV, *Sollicitudo omnium ecclesiarum,* issued on June 14, 1921, conferred on James Skala, the dean of the chapter of Bautzen, the temporary apostolic administration of the reëstablished diocese of Meissen; this appointment lasted until the subsequent appointment of its first bishop Christian Schreiber. The faculties given to James Skala were expressed in the following words: *"Ipsi tribuentes facultates ac iura omnia quae huic muneri competunt."* [171] Dean Skala was invested only with the priestly character, and, therefore, had only the privileges of a protonotary apostolic as no further privileges were indicated in his letter of appointment.

On September 17, 1922, Isidore Sain, O.S.B., was appointed apostolic administrator of Fiume. This appointee was not a bishop, and since his letter of appointment did not give him any extra privileges it is deduced that he had only the honorary privileges of a Protonotary Apostolic.[172]

[169] *St. Louis Catholic Historical Review,* I (1918), 75.
[170] Wernz, *Ius Decretalium,* II, n. 704.
[171] *AAS,* XIII (1921), 409-411.
[172] *AAS,* XIV (1922), 551.

In the same year the Sacred Congregation for Extraordinary Ecclesiastical Affairs deemed it imperative to appoint an apostolic administrator, *ad nutum Sanctae Sedis,* to Upper Silesia. The Prelate appointed to this office was Augustus Hlond, a priest of the Society of St. Francis de Sales. His privileges and faculties were thus stated: " , , , cum omnibus iuribus et privilegiis tali officio adnexis." [173] These privileges accorded to Augustus Hlond, according to canon 308, were the usual ones granted to a protonotary apostolic *de numero participantium.*

In summarizing this section dealing with the honorary privileges of the temporary apostolic administrator, one may make the following three observations:

1) The temporary apostolic administrator may be endowed with the episcopal character, or he may be invested with only the priestly character.

2) The temporary apostolic administrator who is a bishop possesses, according to canons 308 and 349, § 1, nn. 1 and 2, all the honorary privileges of a titular bishop. One exception to this rule is had in the bishop who is transferred to another see but retains his former see as temporary apostolic administrator. This bishop retains all the privileges granted to him as residential bishop over his former diocese which he now rules as temporary apostolic administrator. In all other instances the episcopal apostolic administrator of a see does not enjoy the honorary privileges of a residential bishop, but is granted only the honorary privileges of a titular bishop.

3) The temporary apostolic administrator who is not a bishop but a priest is granted the honorary privileges of a protonotary apostolic, as expressed in the *Motu Proprio, Inter multiplices,* of Pope Pius X, and the Constitution, *Ad incrementum decoris,* of Pope Pius XI.

Art. VII—Transferred Bishops and Neighboring Bishops Who Are Apostolic Administrators

Sometimes it may happen that bishop who is transferred to an-

[173] *AAS,* XIV (1922), 599.

other diocese retains temporarily, as apostolic administrator, the administration of his former see. Canon 430, § 3, n. 1, alludes to this situation when it states that a transferred bishop from the moment he receives authentic notification of his transfer until he takes canonical possession of his new see loses many of the rights and duties he previously exercised over his former diocese, and has only the same rights and duties as a vicar capitular. Consequently, then, this former bishop of the diocese in question becomes a temporary apostolic administrator of the see he once governed as residential bishop. The words of the canon are: "Sed Episcopo qui, ad aliam sedem translatus, prioris retinet administrationem in hac quoque omnia Episcoporum residentialium honorificia privilegia competunt." [174] Although the transferred bishop does undergo a great diminution of his previous rights and duties in the diocese he once administered as *episcopus proprius*,[175] nevertheless, his honorary privileges remain intact, and he may exercise them at his own discretion. On the other hand, it is imperative that the transferred bishop read his letter of appointment carefully and cautiously in order to ascertain if his powers and rights and privileges have been increased or diminished. Oftentimes the Holy See recognizes the presence of circumstances which prompt either the amplifying or curtailing of the rights, duties and privileges of the temporary apostolic administrator who has been transferred to another see. But should this letter offer nothing further than the mere indication of the appointment then the legislation of the Code becomes effective, and he rules the see with the same power as a vicar capitular. Naturally, this curtailing of power is done to preserve the rights of the new bishop, and at the same time to protect the diocese from grave harm. Ob-

[174] Canon 315, § 2, n. 1.

[175] "Administrator Apostolicus in casu translationis ab una sede ad aliam Episcopus ipso iure constituitur: eius tamen potestas hoc in casu a iure dimetienda generatim erit (cf. can. 430, § 3, nn. 1-3); hoc valet solum de tempore quod intercedit a die habitae notitiae translationis, ad diem inthronizationis in novam dioecesim; tunc enim, nisi aliter a S. Sede provideatur tota potestas translati in dioecesi a qua cessat."—Coronata, *Institutiones Iuris Canonici*, I, p. 458, footnote 1.

viously the transferred bishop, if he were so disposed, could effect changes which would favor him in his new see, but the law prevents such actions. The axiom, *"Sede vacante nihil innovetur,"* is applicable.[176]

In Italy, particularly during the last two centuries, many transferred bishops, even after they assumed canonical possession of their new sees, retained the temporary administration of their former dioceses. So frequently did this occur that it became necessary to determine specifically the rights they possessed over the dioceses they administered as temporary apostolic administrators. Pope Leo XIII on June 25, 1879, stated their rights thus: "Durante tamen ejusmodi administratione omnibus honorificentiis, indultis, et facultatibus frui valeant quae iisdem, uti propriis Episcopis Ordinariis competebant." [177] A part of this decree has been incorporated into the present Code of Canon Law.[178] So wide a latitude of power is not granted to the temporary apostolic administrator in the present times; for now his rights are the same as those of a vicar capitular. All the honorary privileges, however, which he formerly had as the bishop are retained even in his capacity of temporary apostolic administrator.[179]

As has already been observed, it is not uncommon, particularly in Italy, for a residential bishop to be appointed the temporary apostolic administrator of a neighboring vacant diocese. Such a bishop is confronted with several *dubia* with respect to ruling his own see and at the same time administering the neighboring vacant see. Some of the more common difficulties are: 1) is this temporary apostolic administrator obligated to say a *Missa pro populo* for the diocese he administers, in addition to the *Missa pro populo* he must say for the faithful of his own proper see; 2) does such a bishop have two votes at the convocation of the plenary or provincial synod or council; and 3) how is such a bishop bound by the law of residence in the diocese he administers as temporary apostolic administrator.

[176] Canons 435, § 4; 436.
[177] *ASS,* XXX (1898), 638.
[178] Canon 315, § 2, n. 1.
[179] Canon 315, § 2, n. 1.

A) Relative to the *Missa pro populo*: on every bishop there is placed the obligation of applying Mass for the faithful committed to his care according to the prescriptions expressed in the law.[180] The temporary apostolic administrator, in so far as he has besides his own flock the faithful of a neighboring see which he rules as the temporary apostolic administrator, apparently incurs the two-fold obligation of being held to the *Missa pro populo* for both dioceses. Is such a bishop obligated to apply two Masses? This is not the case, for the law states: "Licet Episcopus . . . praeter propriam dioecesim, aliam vel alias in administrationem habeat, obligatione tamen satisfacit per celebrationem et applicationem unius Missae pro universo populo sibi commisso." [181] Very definitely the law obliges such a bishop merely to offer one Mass which is applied simultaneously for the faithful of both dioceses.

B) Relative to the vote at a Plenary or Provincial Council: this *dubium* is not so easily answered as the one concerning the *Missa pro populo.* Does this bishop cast two votes at a Plenary or Provincial Council? Does he vote as a representative of his own diocese and then as a representative of his temporary diocese, or does one vote constitute his total right irrespective of his representation of two dioceses? Although history has recorded occasions of which bishops attended Councils in their capacity of residential bishop of one diocese and of temporary apostolic administrator of another see, still in none of these cases has any reference been made to the number of votes these bishops cast.[182] Even the present Code of Canon Law makes no provision for such an occasion. This entire question seems to have been overlooked or simply ignored by the vast majority of commentators. When on February 15, 1919, the Sacred Congregation of the Consistory laid down definite rules respecting the holding of Councils in those localities of Italy where apostolic administrators administered

[180] Canon 339.

[181] Canon 339, § 5; Leo XIII, litt. ap. "*In Suprema,*" 10 iun. 1882:—*Fontes,* n. 585.

[182] *Collectio Lacensis, Acta et Decreta Sacrorum Conciliorum et Recentiorum* (7 vols., Friburgi Brisgoviae, 1870-1890), IV, 313, 578.

vacant sees no reference whatsoever was made to the number of votes given to such persons.[183]

Canon 20 states: "Si certa de re desit expressum praescriptum legis sive generalis sive particularis, norma sumenda est, nisi agatur de poenis applicandis, a legibus latis in similibus; . . ." This canon treats of suppletory law. Certainly there seems to be a lacuna concerning the specification of the powers of suffrage on the part of the temporary apostolic administrator of a neighboring diocese when he attends a plenary or provincial council.

Hofmeister claims that canon 164 bears a resemblance to the present question. It reads: "Etsi quis plures ob titulos ius habet ferendi nomine proprio suffragii, non potest nisi unicum ferre." This canon expressly says that even though a person may be the holder of several offices, he is, nevertheless, entitled to only one vote. By analogy, then, he applies this canon with reference to the residential bishop who is at the same time the temporary apostolic administrator of a neighboring diocese, and gives him only one vote at the plenary or provincial synod.[184] The solution as proposed by Hofmeister seems facile indeed. But despite this facile solution, there is another Canon which reads, "Qui ex diversis titulis ius patronatus obtinet tot habet in praesentatione suffragia quot titulos."[185] How is this clause to be interpreted, since it grants that he who possesses the right of patronage by many titles, shall have as many votes in the act of presentation as he has titles?[186] Godfrey says: "This prescription of the canon under discussion [1460, § 3] seems to stand in violation of canon 164, which states that although one has the right to vote by many titles, one may not cast more than one vote." However, he alleges that canon 164 refers to elections strictly so called, and from this he deduces that the two canons are not of parallel import.[187]

[183] *AAS,* XI (1919), 72 sq.

[184] *AKKR,* CX (1930), 354.

[185] Canon 1460, § 3.

[186] Godfrey, *The Right of Patronage According to the Code of Canon Law,* The Catholic University of America, Canon Law Studies, n. 21 (Washington, D. C.: The Catholic University of America, 1924), p. 84.

[187] *Op. cit.,* p. 89.

Even though Hofmeister offers this argument to supply for the *lacuna* in the law, nevertheless, it seems that there is stronger proof that the temporary apostolic administrator of a diocese who is at the same time the residential bishop of another diocese has only one vote at the Provincial or Plenary Council. For canon 287 states that "persons who are under obligation to attend a Plenary or Provincial Council, and who have a decisive vote, shall send a proxy if they are legitimately impeded from coming in person . . . The proxy, if he be one of the Fathers of the Council who has a decisive vote, shall not have a double vote; if he is not one of the Fathers of the Council, he has a consultive vote as proxy."[188] The situation encountered in canon 287 is similar to the one under discussion. In both instances the see is represented by some one other than the residential bishop. The difficulty concerns the diocese being represented by a neighboring bishop at a Provincial or Plenary Synod; canon 287 deals with the residential bishop who is incapacitated and unable personally to attend the Council and is thereby told to send a proxy, who may be the neighboring bishop or some other person according to the discretion of the bishop. If the incapacitated bishop chooses to elect a neighboring bishop to represent him, then no extra vote is granted to the representative for he already has the power to cast one vote as a residential bishop; if, on the other hand, the incapacitated bishop desires to appoint one who is not a Father of the Council, then the designated person has not a decisive vote but only a consultative vote. This analogy is not stretched too far when it is applied to our difficulty; for in reality the diocese is being represented by a Father of the Council who already has the right to one vote and does not acquire another vote because he is the representative of a neighboring diocese in the capacity of temporary apostolic administrator. It appears, then that by applying canon 20 in conjunction with canon 287, the difficulty is obviated much better than by utilizing the canon suggested by Hofmeister.

[188] Translation from Woywod, *A Practical Commentary on the Code of Canon Law,* I, p. 108, n. 220; Wernz-Vidal, *Ius Canonicum,* II, p. 570, n. 535.

C) Relative to Residence: Canon 440 states that the vicar capitular is obligated to residence in the diocese according to the norm set down in canon 339. This latter canon explains the law of residence as obligatory on resident bishops, but delineates also the times when a bishop is legitimately excused from the observance of this law. Following the prescriptions of canon 315, § 2, n. 1, the apostolic administrator is bound to the law of residence.

The Council of Trent said: "By divine precept it is enjoined on all to whom the care of souls is entrusted to know their own sheep, to offer sacrifice for them, to feed them by preaching the divine word, by the administration of the Sacraments, and by the example of all good works; likewise to have a fatherly care of the poor and other distressed persons and to apply themselves to their pastoral duties. All these offices cannot be fulfilled by those who neither watch over, nor live with their flock, but abandon it after the manner of hirelings." [189] From these two passages can be derived the seriousness of the law of residence incumbent on bishops and others who have the care of souls committed to them. How is the resident bishop who is at the same time the temporary apostolic administrator of a neighboring diocese bound by the law of residence? Apparently he violates the law because it is impossible for him to fulfill the duty of residence in both dioceses simultaneously. Such a difficulty, however, was foreseen and anticipated in the Constitution of Pope Benedict XV in his *"Boni pastoris"* of February 20, 1920. In this Constitution he handed over to the bishop of S. Severino the administration of the diocese of Treja and specified the law respecting residence thus: "Episcopum in alterutra diocesi residere poterit; officii tamen sui erit ita rem temperare, ut penes utramque, per notabile temporis spatium, iuxta rerum necessitatem, singulis annis commoretur." [190] This Constitution of Pope Benedict XV gives a practical solution to the difficulty by exacting a stay in each diocese. A similar solution was evidenced in the words of the appointment of the apos-

[189] Sess. XXIII, *de. ref.*, c. 2; Benedictus XIV, const. "Ad Universae" 3 sept. 1746—*Fontes*, n. 371.

[190] *AAS*, XII (1920), 321.

tolic administrator of Prague, "Intendit insuper, Sanctissimus Peter, ut praelaudatus Illmus ac Revmus Pater Dominus Josephus Doubrava, quo melius officium suum exequi valeat, per aliquod tempus in civitate Pragensi commorari non omittat." [191]

Art. VIII—Conditional Rights of the Temporary Apostolic Administrator

Since the above mentioned canons specifically state that certain acts are prohibited to the vicar capitular, then, *ipso facto,* they are simultaneously forbidden to the temporary apostolic administrator. On the strength of canon 315, § 2, n. 1, the same rights and duties which are accorded to the vicar capitular are similarly accorded to the temporary apostolic administrator. Obviously, too, it is only logical to deny to the temporary apostolic administrator all the rights and duties which are denied by law to the vicar capitular, unless, of course, the letter of appointment stipulates otherwise.

THE CONDITIONAL RIGHTS OF THE VICAR CAPITULAR (ADMINISTRATOR)

In addition to the ordinary faculties granted to the vicar capitular or administrator from the moment he takes canonical possession of the diocese,[192] there are others generally referred to as conditional rights, which are automatically acquired after the episcopal see has been vacant for one year. This period of one year is calculated according to the prescription of canon 34, § 3, nn. 1 and 3.[193] Nevertheless, occasions may arise when a longer vacancy is imperative, particularly when the circumstances surrounding the bishop's death require a thorough investigation, or the diocese is so far distant that the new bishop is obliged to spend much time travelling before he can reach the diocese. The additional rights conferred on the vicar capitular or administrator after the see has been vacant for a year are the following: 1) the power to grant incardination and excardination to any cleric with

[191] *AKKR,* CX (1930), 330.

[192] Canon 435.

[193] Blat, *Commentarium Textus,* II, p. 63, n. 47.

the consent of the cathedral chapter or board of diocesan consultors;[194] 2) the power to appoint incumbents—be they appointed removably or irremovably—in parishes for which the bishop can exercise his right of appointment by way of free and independent bestowal of office.[195] and 3) the power to grant dimissorial letters with the consent of the cathedral chapter or of the board of diocesan consultors.[196] These canons, amplifying, as they do, the powers of the vicar capitular or administrator, constitute a real difficulty of interpretation in connection with the temporary apostolic administrator. Does the temporary apostolic administrator acquire these rights only after he has governed the see for a year, or does he possess these rights the moment he assumes administration of the see? If the same principle is applied as was applied in the past instances, then the norm of procedure would be to predicate of the temporary apostolic administrator whatever faculties are predicted of the vicar capitular or administrator.[197] Following such a process one would almost spontaneously say that the temporary apostolic administrator acquires these rights only after the see has been vacant for a year. But this solution is not unquestionably evident. For in each of the canons wherein this extra power is granted to the vicar capitular or administrator, the phrase, *"nisi post annum a vacatione Sedis Episcopalis,"* or one similar to it, is appended to the right as a *conditio sine qua non.*[198] This episcopal vacancy must last for a year, and then, *ipso facto,* the vicar capitular or administrator acquires these new powers. It is true that all these conditions are verified in the case of the temporary apostolic administrator who is appointed *sede vacante.* He obtains, therefore, these three conditional rights after the see has been vacant for a year. But how

[194] Canon 113.

[195] Canons 455, § 2, n. 3; 1432, § 2.

[196] Canon 955, § 1; 958.

[197] Canon 315, 2, n. 1.

[198] Canon 113—nisi post annum a vacatione sedis episcopalis et cum consensu Capituli; canon 455, 2, n. 3—si sedes ab anno saltem vacaverit; canon 958—de capituli consensu Vicarius Capitularis post annum a sede vacante.

can there be a question of vacancy in the case of the temporary apostolic administrator who is appointed to rule or administer a see *sede plena?* Such an appointment does not follow upon a vacancy; in fact, no vacancy at all has taken place, because the resident bishop, although incapacitated, is still living. No provisions whatever are found in the code for the following problem. Canon 315, 2, n. 1, states that the temporary apostolic administrator has the same rights and duties as the vicar capitular. Consequently, therefore, he may exercise these rights accorded to the vicar capitular after the see has been vacant for a year.[199] But, since the see is not actually vacant may the apostolic administrator exercise these rights before the expiration of a year? Canon 315, § 2, n. 1, does not clearly attribute these rights to apostolic administrators. However, several letters of appointment do confer these rights immediately on the apostolic administrator.

Moreover, in view of the fact that the Code offers no immediate solution to the present difficulty, but may leave intact the pre-Code discipline, it is peremptory that the *dubium* be interpreted in the light of the old law. Consequently, then it is imperative to proceed along historical lines in order to indicate the background of the present legislation in each of the three cases and from this study to draw the juridically warranted conclusions.

A)—*Dimissorial Letters*

Dimissorial letters, although not defined explicitly by the Code, are generally defined by authors as the delegated faculties which are granted by an ordinary *vi suae iurisdictionis,* for the ordinations of his own subjects by other bishops[200] Dimissorial letters are absolutely necessary, as is attested in canon 958 wherein are outlined the persons competent to issue them. According to the first part of the first paragraph of canon 958 the *episcopus proprius,* and even a bishop-elect who has already taken canonical posses-

[199] Canons 113; 455, § 2, n. 3; 958.

[200] Many, *Praelectiones de Sacra Ordinatione* (Parisiis: Apud Letouzey et Ane, 1905), 150, n. 60; Wernz, *Ius Decretalium,* II, n. 29; Vermeersch-Creusen, *Epitome Iuris Canonici,* II, n. 24.

sion of his diocese, even though he has not yet been consecrated, is competent to issue dimissorial letters. Canon 958, § 1, n. 2, definitely states that the vicar-general is incompetent to issue dimissorial letters unless he has received a special mandate. Canon 958, § 1 in n. 3 is relevant to the discussion. The vicar capitular or administrator (in countries where the board of diocesan consultors replaces the cathedral chapter), can grant dimissorial letters provided two conditions are realized: 1) that the consent, and not the mere advice, of the chapter or diocesan consultors be given, and 2) that the episcopal see be vacant for a year reckoned according to canon 34, § 3, nn. 1 and 3. One exception is made in his favor viz., that he may issue dimissorial letters within the course of the year to those for whom some serious plight or perplexing predicament has been occasioned (*arctati*) by reason of a past or prospective conferment of benefice in their behalf, or also to those whose assignment to some office is so urgent that it tolerates no delay.[201]

This legislation pertaining to the vicar capitular as expressed in the Code is not new, but dates back to the origin of the cathedral chapter.[202] The Council of Trent reiterated the same legislation in the following words:

> Non liceat capitulis ecclesiarum sede vacante infra anum a die vacationis ordinandi licentiam, aut literas dimissorias . . .. concedere.[203]

Practically all the eminent canonists from the time of the Council of Trent to the publication of the Code agree in voicing the same legislation pertaining to the vicar capitular. Some of the more

[201] Moeder, *The Proper Bishop for Ordination and Dimissorial Letters,* The Catholic University of America, Canon Law Studies, n. 95 (Washington, D. C.. The Catholic University of America, 1935), pp. 84-85; Murphy, *Delinquencies and Penalties in the Administration and Reception of the Sacraments,* The Catholic University of America, Canon Law Studies, n. 17 (Washington, D. C.: The Catholic University of America, 1923), pp. 88-89.

[202] C. 3, *de temporibus ordinationum et qualitate ordinandorum,* I, 9 in VI°.

[203] Sess. VII, *de ref.,* c. 10.

distinguished who have commented on this legislation are Nicolius,[204] Pellegrinus,[205] Ferraris,[206] Riganti,[207] Wernz,[208] and Gasparri.[209]

From these sources it is quite apparent that the Code of Canon Law adopted the same legislation which was in force since the time of the Decretals namely, the right to grant dimissorial letters only after the see had been vacant for a year. In the event, however, that it was necessary for one to be ordained before the expiration of a year the advice of the cathedral chapter or of the board of diocesan consultors, was necessary.[210]

No mention is made in canon 958 of the apostolic administrator. If he is permanently appointed no difficulty arises, for then he enjoys all the prerogatives of a resident bishop; if he is temporarily instituted he enjoys the same rights as a vicar capitular and therefore, cannot issue dimissorial letters. Moeder does not expatiate on this point but merely says; " . . . he has the rights

[204] "Non potest concedere dimissorias infra annum non arctatis occasione beneficii recepti vel recipiendi."—*Lucubrationes Utriusque Iuris,* II, p. 57, n. 22.

[205] "Potest igitur Vicarius concedere litteras dimissorias ad ordines, infra annum in arctatis . . . qui non sunt arctati non potest . . . "—*Praxis Vicariorum,* s.v. "Vicarius Capitularis," nn. 2 & 3.

[206] "Post annum vero a die vacationis sedis episcopalis potest vicarius dimissorias ad ordines quibuscunque suis subditis etiam non arctatis concedere"—*Prompta Bibliotheca Canonica,* s.v. "Vicarius Capitularis," art. II, n. 6

[207] "At vero permissum non est Vicario Capitulari Litteras Dimissorias infra annum Sedis Episcopalis vacantis concedere . . . "—*Constitutiones et Ordinationes Cancellariae Apostolicae* (4 vols., in 2, Coloniae Allobrogum, 1751), vol. I, tom. II, p. 366.

[208] "In specie Vicarius capitularis nequit conferre ordines vel concedere licentiam ordinandi primo anno sedis vacantis, nisi arctatis occasione beneficii ecclesiastici recepti vel recipiendi."—*Ius Decretalium,* II, 609-610.

[209] "Ex hac lege Tridentina post annum a sede vacante viget jus commune, et ideo Vicarius capitularis potest omnibus subditis dare dimissorias."—*De Sacra Ordinatione* (2 vols., Parisiis: Delhomme et Briguet, 1893-1894), II, pp. 128-129, n. 869.

[210] Moeder, *The Proper Bishop for Ordination and Dimissorial Letters,* p. 86.

and duties of a vicar capitular or Diocesan Administrator." [211] On the other hand, the temporary apostolic administrator formerly enjoyed more rights than the Code now gives to him. It is evident that in the present connection Moeder as well as the pre-Code authors failed to consider the distinction between a temporary and a permanent apostolic administrator. Some authors even failed to insist on the distinction between a diocese that was still occupied and one that had become vacant.[212]

From the time of the Decretals of Pope Boniface VIII (1294-1303) the apostolic administrator was given the power to grant dimissorial letters, provided he was appointed by the Sovereign Pontiff:

> Huiusmodi quoque visitator, quanquam spiritualium et temporalium administrationem legitimam censeatur habere, beneficia tamen, quae ad collationem pertinent episcopi, conferre non potest, si ab alio quam a Romano Pontifice fuerit deputatus.[213]

In another place the same testimony is referred to:

> Is, cui procuratio seu administratio cathedralis ecclesiae . . . est commisa, potest . . . omnia, quae iurisdictionis episcopalis exsistunt . . . libere exercere.[214]

Undoubtedly, therefore, the apostolic administrator, regardless of whether he was temporarily or permanently installed in a diocese, was granted the power to issue dimissorial letters from the very moment of his occupation of the see.

In time, however, this legislation, although not abrogated, was tempered to such a degree that unless this favor was obtained in the letter of appointment the apostolic administrator did not have the right to grant dimissorial letters until the see had been vacant for a year. Pellegrinus goes so far as to propose the

[211] *Op. cit.*, p. 88.

[212] Cf. Ferraris, *Prompta Bibliotheca*, s.v. "Vicarius Apostolicus," n. 8; Wernz, *Ius Decretalium*, II, pp. 70-77, n. 29.

[213] C. 4, *de supplenda negligentia praelatorum*, I, 8, in VI°.

[214] C. 42, *de electione et electi potestate*, I, 6, in VI°.

question: *"An Vicarius Apostolicus possit concedere dimissorias?"* And the reply was: *"De iure posse."* [215]

Then he explains what the interpretation of *de iure* is:

> De iure autem communi canonico potest Vicarius Apostolicus dimissorias praedictas concedere, cum veniat ista facultas comprehensa in his, quae sunt jurisdictionis, non ordinis episcopalis. Stante vero hac prohibitione hodie non potest dimissorias concedere . . . Vicarius Apostolicus sede vacante potest expedire quae dirigi solent Vicariis Episcopalibus, ac dare dimissorias post annum, et infra annum arctatis . . . [216]

From the time of Pellegrinus onward (the late seventeenth century) the authors agreed that the apostolic administrator was granted *de iure* the right to issue dimissorial letters from the very moment he took canonical possession of the see. Still they were unanimous in stating that even though this power was accorded de iure to the office of apostolic administrator, it was unusual for the Holy See to give him this right in particular instances. Invariably, they said, such a grant or denial of the right to give dimissorial letters was contained in the letter of appointment.[217]

Riganti analyzed the power of the apostolic administrator to grant dimissorial letters in the following words:

> Vicarius idem Apostolicus a Papa, vel Sac. Congregatione, Sede Episcopali vacante, deputatus, nequit ad instar Vicarii Capitularis Litteras Dimissorias, nisi post annum, & infra annum arctatis solum concedere, dummodo huiusmodi facultas ei interdicta non fuerit. Et regulariter hodie facultas haec concedendi Litteras Dimissorias prohiberi solet Vicariis Apostolicis in Brevi ac Litteris respective Sac. Congregationis.[218]

[215] *Praxis Vicariorum,* p. 49, n. VII.

[216] *Ibid.,* n. IX.

[217] Andreucci, *Hierarchia Ecclesiastica,* I, 237; Nicolius, *Lucubrationes,* II, p. 49, n. 17; Ferraris, wrote, "Neque potest dimissorias ad ordines concedere, cum haec facultas illi in specie auferri soleat in brevi"—*Prompta Biblitheca,* s.v. "Vicarius Apostolicus," n. 8.

[218] *Constitutiones et Ordinationes Cancellariae Apostolicae,* Lib. II, tom. III, p. 366, n. 190-191.

Finally, Gasparri wrote:

> Haec quae diximus valent etiam de Vicario Apostolico qui a R. P. vel a S.C.C., sede vacante, deputatus est. Imo in brevi seu litteris deputationis potestas concedendi litteras dimissorias expresse reservari solent; quod si e contrario expresse conceditur, Vicarius Apostolicus eam habet intra appositos limites, sed nequit eam communicare provicario etiam in absentia e dioecesi . . .[219]

These authors clearly stated that although the apostolic administrator did enjoy the right to grant dimissorial letters *de iure,* nevertheless it was the practice to grant or deny this faculty explicitly in the letter of appointment. By way of example it may be here noted that Charles Pooten, the apostolic administrator sent to the Archdiocese of Antivari, and Raphael Terrigno, the apostolic administrator appointed to Reggio, were granted the faculty of issuing dimissorial letters.[220]

With the promulgation of the Code, and the consigning of the duties and obligations of the vicar capitular to the temporary apostolic administrator, the power of the apostolic administrator *sede vacante,* respecting the granting of dimissorial letters was explicitly decided. Hereafter the temporary apostolic administrator, *sede vcante,* may not grant dimissorial letters until the episcopal see had been vacant for a year, and the grant is further conditioned, of course, upon the consent of the cathedral chapter or of the board of diocesan consultors.[221] It is true that the Code does not make a distinction between the temporary apostolic administrator who is appointed to a see that is *sede plena,* and the one who is appointed *sede vacante.* The present writer's view, therefore, is that although the temporary administrator follows the regulations laid down, in this respect, for a vicar capitular, a distinction exists between his incumbency *sede plena* and *sede vacante.* This distinction is based specifically on the words *post annum vacationis sedis episcopalis,* which cannot be predicated of

[219] *Tractatus Canonicus de Sacra Ordinatione,* I, n. 873.

[220] *Acta Gregorii XVI* (Romae: Ex Typographia Polyglotta, 1901-1912), III, 312; *Analecta Iuris Pontificii,* XXIII (1884), 767-768.

[221] Canons 315, § 1, n. 2; 958, § 1, n. 3.

the temporary apostolic administrator of a see that is still occupied by its residential bishop. This opinion, too, seems to have some basis in pre-Code legislation, and from this legislation the conclusion is drawn: namely, that the temporary apostolic administrator, *sede plena,* has the power to grant dimissorial letters from the very moment he assumes the administration of the diocese. In substantiation of this opinion, the following is quoted from Riganti:-

> Vicario tamen Apostolico, qui fuit Episcopo deputatus, interdictum non est Sede Episcopali vacante, Litteras Dimissoriales concedere. Cum enim per obitum Episcopi, illius jurisdictio non expiret, nec Capitulum devenire possit ad electionem Vicarii Capitularis . . .[222]

From the doctrine of Riganti it can be deduced that he draws a distinction between the administrator appointed *sede vacante* (to whom he denies the power to grant dimissorial letters until the see has been vacant for a year),[223] and the apostolic administrator appointed *sede plena* (to whom he grants the power to issue dimissorial letters even after the death of the resident bishop).[224] It seems that Riganti (1661-1735) was the first author to draw this distinction. Later his opinion was quoted by Gasparri.[225] Many, under a heading entitled, "De Vicario Apostolico, sede vacante, aut quolibet administratore sedis vacantis" says:

> Potest deputari sedis vacantis administrator, non tantum a Capitulo, sed etiam a Romano Pontifice, aut in casibus a jure praevisis, a Metropolitano. Porro hi omnes prohibentur ne infra primum annum vacationis, concedant dimissorias nisi arctatis.[226]

[222] *Constitutiones et Ordinationes Cancellariae Apostolicae,* Vol. II, Tom. III, p. 366, n. 194.

[223] *Ibid.,* nn. 190-191.

[224] *Ibid.,* n. 194.

[225] "At Vicario Apostolico qui fuerat Episcopo deputatus, interdictum non est, sede episcopali vacante, litteras dimissorias concedere: cum per obitum ejus jurisdictio non expiret, nec capitulum devenire possit ad electionem Vicarii Capitularis, . . . "—*De Sacra Ordinatione,* II, n. 873.

[226] *Praelectiones de Sacra Ordinatione,* p. 155, n. 61. No reference at all is made to the vicar capitular who rules a diocese *sede plena.*

Riganti and Gasparri insisted upon making a distinction between a temporary apostolic administrator who is assigned to a see that is vacant and the one who is appointed to a see that is occupied. Both of these authors stated quite plainly that the vicar apostolic (apostolic administrator) *sede vacante* could not issue dimissorial letters until the see had been vacant for a year, unless the faculty was expressly granted to him in the letter of appointment.[227] They also stated that the apostolic administrator who is appointed to a see that is still occupied is not prohibited the use of the faculty to grant dimissorial letters even though the resident bishop dies. This doctrine naturally presupposes that the temporary apostolic administrator *sede plena* had this power to grant dimissorial letters from the beginning of his administration.

Consequently, then, it seems to the present writer that the temporary apostolic administrator who is appointed to a see that is still occupied can exercise the right to issue dimissorial letters from the very moment he assumes the administration of the diocese. Such a conclusion is not contradictory to the canons which state that the office of the temporary apostolic administrator is likened to the office of the vicar capitular in respect to his obligations and duties, and thus includes the acquisition of further conditional rights after the see has been vacant for one year.[228] This is verified in the temporary apostolic administrator who is sent to rule a see that is vacant. The temporary apostolic administrator, on the other hand who is sent to administer a see that is not vacant may from the very moment of occupation issue dimissorial letters, unless the contrary is stated in his letter of appointment.

B—*Free Bestowal of Benefices*

The right to nominate and institute pastors belongs to the bishop, except for the parishes in which the appointment is reserved to the Holy See; all contrary customs impairing this right

[227] Riganti, *op., cit.,* Lib II, Tom. III, p. 366, nn. 190-191; Gasparri, *op. cit.,* II, n. 869.

[228] Canons 315, § 1, n. 2; 958, § 1, n. 3.

of the bishop are reprobated. Those, however, who have been legitimately granted the privilege to elect or present the pastor retain that right.[229] Canon 455, § 2, nn. 1 and 3, states that when the diocese is vacant, or the bishop is prevented from exercising jurisdiction, the vicar capitular, or whoever rules the diocese, has the right to appoint pastors to parishes generally, if the see has been vacant for at least one year. The vicar capitular, in this instance, is not obliged to have the consent of the cathedral chapter or the board of diocesan consultors. Applying the principle that whatever rights and duties are granted to the vicar capitular are *ipso facto* granted to the temporary apostolic administrator, one must conclude that the temporary apostolic administrator may bestow benefices after the see has been vacant for a year. This principle is applicable to the temporary apostolic administrator when he is appointed to a vacant see, but not when he is appointed to a see that is still occupied. In the latter circumstance, the requisite lapse of the year of vacancy is not realized. Canons 455, § 1, and 1432, § 2, specify that when a diocese has been vacant for one year, the vicar capitular or administrator is fully empowered by law to confer parishes and parochial benefices of free bestowal. Furthermore it is immaterial whether the appointment to these parochial benefices connotes a removable or an irremovable incumbent in the parochial office.[230]

The above two canons express the present law pertaining to the power of the vicar capitular or administrator to confer parishes and parochial benefices. This law is new with the Code, for previous to that time the vicar capitular was denied this right even after a year of episcopal vacancy. This is attested by Decretal law:

[229] *Canon* 455, § 1; translation from Woywod, *A Practical Commentary on the Code of Canon Law,* I, p. 162, n. 329; Augustine, *A Commentary on Canon Law,* II, 522-527; Coady, *The Appointment of Pastors,* The Catholic University of America, Canon Law Studies, n. 52 (Washington, D. C.: The Catholic University of America, 1929), pp. 99-109.

[230] Jaeger, *The Administration of Vacant and Quasi-Vacant Dioceses in the United States,* p. 188; Coady, *The Appointment of Pastors,* p. 103.

> Beneficia spectantia ad collationem praelati non possunt conferri per Capitulum sede vacante.[231]

Boniface VIII in the *Liber Sextus* stated the prohibition much more clearly:

> Etsi capitulum sede vacante beneficia, quae ad collationem Episcopi pertinent, conferre non possit; praesentatos tamen a patronis potest admittere, si sint idonei, et eos instituere in beneficiis, ad quae fuerint praesentati, licet ad episcopum, si superesset, admissio et institutio huiusmodi pertineret.[232]

This rule laid down in the Decretals of Pope Boniface VIII (1294-1303) and Pope Gregory IX (1227-1241) was acknowledged by authors of the subsequent centuries up to the promulgation of the Code of Canon Law.[233] The Code of Canon Law, on the other hand, restricts the pre-Code rights of the apostlic administrator. From the time of the Decretals until the appearance of the present Code the permanent and temporary apostolic administrator if he was deputed by the Pope had the right to confer benefices of free bestowal. The Decretal law of Pope Boniface VIII (1294-1303) intimated this grant in the following words:

> Huiusmodi quoque visitator, quanquam spiritualium et temporalium administrationem legitimam censeatur habere, beneficia tamen quae ad collationem pertinent episcopi conferre non potest, si ab alio quam a Romano Pontifice fuerit deputatus.[234]

Although this specific law made no direct reference to the bestowal of benefices by the apostolic administrator, it can be inferred from the words themselves that he could. It is not interpreting

[231] C. 2, X, *ne sede vacante aliquid innovetur,* III, 9.

[232] C. 1, *de institutionibus,* III, 6, in VI°.

[233] Pellegrinus, *Praxis Vicariorum,* p. 45, n. 16; Nicolius, *Lucubrationes Utriusque Iuris,* pars secunda, p. 57, n. 22; Ferraris, *Prompta Bibliotheca,* s.v. *"Beneficium,"* art. IV, n. 72; Wernz, *Ius Decretalium,* II, p. 609, n. 795; "Quare si sedes episcopalis diutius vacet, Rom. Pontifex adeundus est, ut Vicario capitulari concedat facultatem conferendi beneficia liberae collationis"—*AKKR,* XXIII (1843), 135.

[234] C. 4, *de supplenda negligentia praelatorum,* I, 8, in VI°.

the words too widely to say that the law itself supposed this when the appointment was effected by the Sovereign Pontiff. Furthermore, the Decretal law made no distinction between the permanent and temporary apostolic administrator, or between the one sent to a vacant see and the one sent to a still occupied diocese. All that the law said was that the Visitator, unless he was appointed by the Sovereign Pontiff, could not confer benefices which pertained to the jurisdiction of the bishop. Consequently, then, the Visitator may either refer to a temporary or permanent Apostolic Administrator or to a see that was *vacans or plena*—because these appointments are conferred exclusively by the Sovereign Pontiff.[235] In general the canonists teach that when the apostolic administrator is appointed *sede plena* he can confer benefices of free bestowal, unless the letter of appointment contains the clause *"excepta collatione beneficiorum."*

The legislation from the time of the Decretals up to the promulgation of the Code gave the apostolic administartor *de iure* the right to confer benefices which were within the free bestowal of the bishop. However, with the Code this power was restricted, and unlike the former law which gave the apostolic administrator the same power as a resident bishop, the law now made a distinction between the permanent apostolic administrator,[236] and the temporary apostolic administrator.[237] Only the permanent apostolic administrator of today enjoys the same rights and honors and has the same duties as a residential bishop.[238] The temporary apostolic administrator is likened to the vicar capitular. Obviously, then, the temporary apostolic administrator who is appointed to a see acquires the right to confer benefices only after the see has been vacant for a year; and the temporary apostolic administrator who is appointed to a see that is still occupied retains his pre-Code right to confer benefices from the moment he enters upon his administration, unless, of course, this right is still re-

[235] Canon 312.
[236] Canon 315, § 1, n. 1.
[237] Canon 315, § 1, n. 2.
[238] Canon 315, § 1, 1°.

served for the resident bishop, or unless it is patently denied to the apostolic administrator in the letter of his appointment. The conclusion is based on the fact that the temporary apostolic administrator who functions *sede plena* is not to be considered as being on the mere jurisdictional level of the vicar capitular, for the non-realization of vacancy in the see leaves the two cases in distinctly different categories.

C)—*Incardination and Excardination*

The terms "incardination" and "excardination" are of rather recent origin. The former is defined as a legitimate act by which a cleric is inscribed in the service of a certain diocese and becomes subject to its local ordinary. The latter is defined as a legitimate act by which a cleric is absolutely and perpetually released from the diocese in which he has been incardinated.[239] It is recognized that any consideration of the origin, of the development and of the various modes of incardination and excardination would be an unwarranted digression in the present situation. It is not, however, irrelevant to mention that the legislation pertinent to incardination and excardination reached its greatest development with the promulgation of the Code. Prior to the present law the Council of Trent,[240] the Constitution *"Speculatores"* of Pope Innocent XII (1691-1700),[241] the Decree "A Primis,"[242] and finally a decree issued on Nov. 24, 1906,[243] successively promulgated norms affecting incardination and excardination.

Canon 112 states that the "Ordinary" is competent to grant incardination and excardination. According to *canon* 198, § 1, the term *Ordinarius loci* includes the vicar capitular and apostolic administrator. In *canon* 113, however, certain limitations and restrictions are placed on the word "Ordinary." Under the present discipline the vicar-general is forbidden to incardinate or excardinate a cleric without a special mandate; likewise the vicar capit-

239 Coronata, *Institutiones Iuris Canonici,* I, pp. 203-204, n. 173.

240 Sess. XXIII, *de ref.,* c. 16.

241 *Fontes,* n. 258, § 3.

242 *AAS,* XXXI (1898-1899), 39 ss.

243 *AAS,* XXXIX (1906), 498-499.

ular is prohibited from granting the incardination or excardination of a cleric unless the see has been vacant for a year and the consent of the cathedral chapter has been obtained. The temporary apostolic administrator (*ad tempus datus*) has the same power by law as the vicar capitular,[244] and consequently, he may incardinate or excardinate a cleric only after the see has been vacant a year and, in addition, after he has obtained the consent of the cathedral chapter or of the board of diocesan consultors.[245]

Despite the apparent facile solution induced by predicating of the temporary apostolic administrator whatever is predicted of the vicar capitular a doubt still remains. According to canon 315, § 2, n. 1, the temporary apostolic administrator acquires the same rights as a vicar capitular. Moreover in *canon* 113 a conditional right of the vicar capitular is mentioned: namely, the right to incardinate or excardinate a cleric after the see has been vacant for a year and the consent of the cathedral chapter has been obtained. This right is acquired *ipso facto* by the temporary apostolic administrator when these two conditions are verified. Unquestionably these two conditions are realized in the case of the temporary apostolic administrator *sede vacante,* but cannot be verified in the case of temporary apostolic administartor *sede plena.* In this latter case no vacancy in the see has occurred because the resident bishop, although he be incapacitated, is still living.

Even though the temporary apostolic administrator *sede plena* cannot be included in canon 113, it is difficult to ascertain his legal capacity pertinent to incardination and excardination. Unfortunately the many changes that occurred in formulating the present legislation offer no assistance in clarifying this difficulty. If one refers to the Decretal Law of Pope Boniface VIII, wherein there was granted to the visitator or administrator a full and free administration in all that pertained to the spiritual and temporal welfare of the Church,[246] it seems deducible that this grant in-

[244] *Canon* 315, § 2, *n.* 1

[245] Cf. *Canon* 34, § 3, *n.* 3, for the proper computation in determining what constitutes the lapse of a year.

[246] C. 42, *de electione et electi potestate,* I, 8, in VI°.

cluded the right to incardinate and excardinate. The Decretal Law furthermore made no distinction between a temporary or a permanent apostolic administrator, or between one who was sent to a diocese *sede plena* and one who was sent to a diocese *sede vacante*. Quite definitely the Code forbids the temporary apostolic administrator *sede vacante,* the right to incardinate or excardinate a cleric until the two conditions of canon 113 are fulfilled.[247] The basis of this denial seems to rest on the axiom *"sede vacante nihil innovetur."*[248] There is no provision made for the temporary apostolic administrator *sede plena.* Therefore he retains his pre-Code right to grant incardination and excardination. It seems plausible to say this in view of the fact that the Code has on two other occasions given the temporary apostolic administrator *sede plena* a right and a freedom from an obligation over and above those granted to the temporary apostolic administrator, *sede vacante.*[249] Neither does the axiom *"sede vacante nihil innovetur"* apply in this instance, for the see still has a resident bishop. In addition to these reasons there is the added one of canon 316, which says in effect that the bishop cannot interfere with the apostolic administrator because when he assumes the administration of the see the bishop's jurisdiction is suspended.

From these assertions it appears that the temporary apostolic administrator, *sede plena,* has, from the very moment he assumes the administration of the diocese, the right to incardinate and excardinate clerics. There is not much factual evidence available in substantiation of this assertion, not nearly as much, for example, as for the conclusions reached in the matter of giving dimissorial letters and of conferring benefices; yet the principle involved is equally applicable to all three cases.

The treatment of the conditional rights of the vicar capitular

[247] "Excardinationem et incardinationem concedere nequit Vicarius Generalis sine mandato speciali, nec Vicarius Capitularis, nisi post annum a vacatione sedis episcopalis et cum consensu Capituli."

[248] Canon 436.

[249] " . . . sed, sede plena, potest dioecesim visitare ad tramitem, iuris; nec tenetur obligatione applicandae Missae pro populo, . . ."—Canon 315, § 2, n. 1.

and their applicability to the temporary apostolic administrator, *sede vacante,* is identical. On the other hand, the temporary apostolic administrator, *sede plena,* may issue dimissorial letters, confer benefices of free bestowal, incardinate and excardinate clerics after he has assumed the administration of the see. Hofmeister practically summarizes this view, with the exception of the point that was made in the matter of incardination and excardination, with the following words:

> Fassen wir diese Ausführungen kurz zusammen, so ergibt sich, dass das bisherige Recht jedenfalls dem sede plena bestellten Apostolischen Administrator das Recht zu schrieb, Benefizien zu verleihen und Dimissorien auszustellen. Wir werden also wohl nicht fehl gehen, wenn wir dem sede plena bestellten Administrator vom Antritt seines Amtes an auch jene Rechte zuschreiben, die der Kapitelsvikar in der Regel erst nach Ablauf des Trauerjahres ausüben kann. Selbstverständlich halten wir aber den Apostolischen Administrator in diesem Falle gebunden, bei In—und Exkardination sowie bei Ausstellung vom Dimissorien die Zustimmung des Kapitels einzuholen.[250]

Art. IX.—The Election of a Vicar-General

One of the most important rights of the residential bishop is the power to choose a vicar-general for his diocese.[251] This is not solely an exclusive prerogative granted to residential bishops, for *Canon* 198, § 1, likewise confers this power on Abbots and Prelates Nullius when it enumerates as *Ordinarii locorum* the residential bishops, Abbots and Prelates nullius and their Vicars-General.[252] To these persons alone is granted the privilege of appointing a vicar-general to aid them in expediting their various tasks. From this canon, also, it is quite obvious that the vicars

[250] "Von den Apostolischen Administratorem der Diözesen und abteien" —*AKKR,* CX (1930), 348-349.

[251] Canon 366.

[252] "In iure nomine Ordinarii intelliguntur, nisi quis expresse excipiatur . . . pro suo territorio Episcopus residentialis, Abbas vel Praelatus *nullius* eorumque Vicarius Generalis, . . . "

and prefects apostolic are circumscribed by this prohibition, which consequently invalidates any attempt they make to appoint for themselves a vicar-general. Prior to the Code the vicars and prefects apostolic did enjoy this faculty.[253] Even after the promulgation of the Code many authors repeatedly asserted that the vicars and prefects apostolic still retained this pre-Code power to choose vicars-general and adduced as their reason canon 294, § 1:

> **Vicarii et Praefecti Apostolici iisdem iuribus et facultatibus in suo territorio gaudent, quae in propriis diocesibus competunt Episcopis Residentialibus, nisi quid Apostolica Sedes reservaverit.**

This canon, they said, gave the vicars and prefects apostolic the same rights and faculties enjoyed by residential bishops, which necessarily included the special prerogative of appointing a vicar-general. This doctrinal conclusion was bitterly controverted until ultimately the Holy See was compelled to make a public pronouncement respecting the ability or the inability of the vicars and prefects apostolic to elect vicars-general.[255]

The Sacred Congregation of the Propagation of the Faith declared on December 8, 1919, that the faculty of electing a vicar-general was expressly forbidden to the vicars and prefects apostolic:

> Iuxta can. 198 Codicis I. C. Vicariis et Praefectis Apostolicis ius non competit sibi eligendi Vicarium Generalem sicut fas est Episcopis Residentialibus . . . [256]

All the former preconceived notions were now officially outlawed

[253] Benedictus XIV, litt, ap. *"Ex Sublimi,"* 26 ian. 1753—*Collectanea*, n. 387; ep. encycl. *"Quam ex Sublimi,"* 8 aug. 1755—*Collectanea*, n. 396; S.C.P.F. Dec. 9, 1822—*Collectanea*, n. 777.

[255] Wernz, *Ius Decretalium*, I, p. 621, n. 804, footnote 28; *Coll. Lacen.* III, 1114; Ferraris, *Prompta Bibliotheca*, s.v. "Vicarius Generalis," n. 5; Pellegrinus, *Praxis Vicariorum*, p. 6; Andreucci, *Hierarchia Ecclesiastica*, I, 272; Nicolius, *Iuris Utriusque Theorica Praxis*, II, 49.

[256] *AAS*, XII (1920), 120;Winslow, *Vicars and Prefects Apostolic*, The Catholic University of America, Canon Law Studies, n. 24 (Washington, D. C.: The Catholic University of America, 1924), pp. 66-67.

by this proclamation of the Congregation and henceforth the right of choosing a vicar-general was recognized only for residential bishops, and for abbots and prelates who ruled over autonomous independent territories.[257]

What is the status of the apostolic administrator? Can he appoint a vicar-general, or is he restricted by the same proscription that affects vicars and prefects apostolic? At first glance the answer to the latter question seems to be in the affirmative, for canon 198, § 1, makes no allusion to the vicar-general of the apostolic administrator. Yet, on the other hand, it is an invalid and unwarranted deduction to say that since the vicars and prefects apostolic are not allowed to appoint a vicar-general, *a pari* the apostolic administrator is denied the same privilege. These two offices, despite the similarity that some authors predicate of them, are by no means parallel. It seems improper to say that what is postulated of the one must necessarily be postulated of the other. A distinction must be formulated in order adequately to comprehend the question, and a sharp line of demarcation must be drawn between the temporary apostolic administrator and the permanent apostolic administrator. The two offices are very dissimilar. Canon 315, §§ 1 and 2, in outlining the various duties and privileges of apostolic administrators, amplifies the faculties of the permanent apostolic administrator, and diminishes those of the temporary apostolic administrator. For the canon very emphatically states that the permanent apostolic administrator possesses all the rights, duties, and privileges of a residential bishop, while at the same time it is certain that the temporary apostolic administrator acquires only the same duties and rights that pertain to a vicar capitular.[258] This distinction is of paramount importance. Not to acknowledge it would be tantamount to admitting that the temporary and permanent Apostolic Administrators are of equal standing.

Although the Sacred Congregation of the Propagation of the Faith based its conclusion with reference to vicars and prefects

[257] Canon 198, § 1.
[258] Canon 315, § 1.

apostolic on the interpretation of canon 198, § 1, which makes the words, *eorumque Vicarius Generalis,* the exclusive modifiers of *Episcopus Residentialis et Abbas vel Praelatus nullius,* a like inference is not warranted with reference to apostolic administrators in general. The assumption that the latter are unauthorized to appoint vicars-general seems untenable in the light of past doctrine and practice. Was it a customary procedure for an apostolic administrator to choose a vicar-general?

Vermeersch regarded this question with a view to suggesting a practical solution.[259] In his short treatise involving the disputed question of whether the apostolic administrator can or cannot appoint a vicar-general, he says in the preface that Pirhing,[260] Leurenius[261] and Bouix[262] unhesitatingly (incunctanter) declare, that the administrator of a vacant Church could appoint a vicar-general. That this reference is not made to the vicar capitular but to the apostolic administrator is further evidenced by the following passage:

> Praeter [Episcopum] etiam qui dioecesim gubernat ut administrator durante viduitate Ecclesiae vel durante suspensione Episcopi a iurisdictione potest sibi constituere Vicarium Generalem . . . Vicarius autem ordinarius qui constituitur durante viduitate Ecclesiae non potest sibi constituere Vicarium Generalem.[263]

From this point on Vermeersch begins to formulate his own opinion respecting the power of the apostolic administrator to appoint a vicar-general. He insists primarily upon the recognition of a distinction between a temporary and a permanent apostolic administrator. After establishing this distinction he says that the temporary apostolic administrator is incapable of appointing a

[259] *"De Constitutione Vicarii Generalis vel Delegati facta ab Administratore Apostolico,"—Periodica,* XIII (1924), (15-17).

[260] *De Officio Vicarii,* I, 28.

[261] *Forum Beneficiale* (Romae, 1752), s.v. *"De Vicario Generali Episcopi,"* quaes. XXIV.

[262] *Tractatus de Iudiciis Ecclesiasticis* (2 vols., Parisiis, 1883), I, 402.

[263] Wernz, *Ius Decretalium,* II, p. 623, footnote 32.

vicar-general. This contention seems quite plausible, especially when one considers that a temporary apostolic administrator is granted only the same rights and duties the vicar capitular obtains. The above mentioned passage from Wernz precludes the capacity of the vicar capitular to select a vicar-general. Today, says Vermeersch, it is universally acknowledged that the vicar capitular or administrator does not receive the power to appoint a vicar-general.[264] In the light of this comparison, it is believed that it is quite logical to say that in view of canon 315, § 2, n. 1, the temporary apostolic administrator is unqualified to elect a vicar-general.

The reason, Vermeersch says, why a vicar and prefect apostolic are denied the power to elect a vicar-general is that by the very nature of their office they are, in reality, the deputized vicars-general of the Sovereign Pontiff in whose name they administer a section or territory that has not yet been canonically erected into a constituted diocese; whereas, the permanent apostolic administrator is likened to a residential bishop and does supply or take the bishop's place in the administering of the diocese. Therefore, disregarding the words of canon 198, § 1, he believes that the permanent apostolic administrator has the faculty of electing a vicar-general. In proof of this assertion Vermeersch calls attention to the practice of the Spanish apostolic administrators who invariably elect their own vicar-general, which prerogative they assume the moment they are appointed permanent apostolic administrators of the dioceses in question.[265] He likewise maintains that claiming for the permanent apostolic administrator the faculty of electing a vicar-general does not contradict the law of canon

[265] Periodica, *loc. cit.*

[264] Periodica, XII (1924), (16); "E certo che l'Amministratore *ad tempus* non possa perchè il codice lo equipara al Vicario Capitolare, (canon 315, § 2, n. 1), il quale, secondo l'opinione ora comunemente accettata, non può nominare il Vicario Generale."—Campagna, *Il Vicario Generale del Vescovo,* The Catholic University of America, Canon Law Studies, n. 66 (Washington, D. C.: The Catholic University of America, 1921), p. 90, footnote 14.
XIII, (1924), 17.

198, § 1, but compensates the law by denying the temporary apostolic administrator this faculty.[266] Hofmeister and Campagna offer the same arguments as Vermeersch in favor of denying the temporary apostolic administrator the power to nominate a vicar-general, but in asserting this power on the contrary, for the permanent apostolic administrator.[267]

The solution suggested by Vermeersch, and adhered to by Hofmeister and Campagna, disposes of the difficulty in a very practical manner. It is believed that the crux of the problem lies in making the distinction between a temporary and a permanent Apostolic Administrator. At the same time, we fail to ascertain the force of the opponents' argument when they offer an *a pari* argument by denying the Apostolic Administrator the power to elect a Vicar-General because this right was denied to the Vicar and Prefect Apostolic by the Sacred Congregation of the Propagation of the Faith.[268] These two offices should not be allied or parallelled because they are entirely different in respect to both purpose and stability. Even though one press the argument that formerly this right was granted to the vicar and prefect apostolic still no comparison exists. The revocation of this right did not include the same right as possessed by the permanent apostolic administrator. It is conceded that this power is lawfully denied to the temporary apostolic administrator in as much as he has

[266] "Quare non obstante c. 198, Administratori permanenter constituto facultatem nominandi Vicarium Generalem esse putamus. Accedit usus, v.g., Hispaniarum ubi plures sunt huismodi Administratores. Silentium autem c. 198 explicari potest hac ratione, quod non omnes Administratores Apostolici sed soli permanenter constituti hac potestate donentur."—*Periodica,* XII, (1924), 17.

[267] *AKKR,* CX (1930), 378; Vermeersch-Creusen, *Epitome Iuris Canonici,* I, p 332, n. 433; "Delle due opinioni, noi favoriamo quella del Vermeersch, sia perchè è più conforme alla dottrina comunemente accettata prima del codice, sia ancora perchè ci sembra armonizzare di più con lo spiritò del codice stesso."—Campagna, *Il Vicario Generale del Vescovo,* p. 90.

[268] Wernz-Vidal (*Ius Canonicum,* II, p. 674, n. 636) states: "Attento can. 198, ius constituendi Vicarium Generalem ad solos pertinet Episcopos, nec non ad abbates vel Praelatas nullius."

only the powers of a vicar capitular; but, in no way can the fact be overlooked that the permanent apostolic administrator does have the right to choose a vicar-general, a right he receives in virtue of his office which is identical with the bishop's. One could rather venture to go so far as to say that the permanent apostolic administrator is implicitly included under the term *episcopus residentialis* of canon 198, § 1.

In recapitulation it may be stated that the temporary apostolic administrator, in so far as he resembles a vicar capitular, is not allowed to elect his own vicar-general. Added to this initial reason the additional one may be suggested, namely, that the temporary apostolic administrator in as far as he temporarily represents the Sovereign Pontiff in a particular diocese, can be referred to more exactly as the deputized vicar-general of the Holy See. The permanent apostolic administrator, on the contrary, is not really fulfilling the same type of mission as the temporary apostolic administrator, but is the successor of the former resident bishop. To this permanent apostolic administrator accrue all the rights and duties of a resident bishop which naturally include the power to elect a vicar-general. Examples bear out this opinion, and already reference has been made to the practice of the Spanish permanent apostolic administrators in electing vicars-general. The letters of appointment, however, are not available for inspection. When Hofmeister quoted from such letters he was careful to acknowledge their receipt from the bishops of the dioceses in question.[269]

Art. X—The Permanent Apostolic Administrator

Canon 315, § 1—Administrator Apostolicus permanenter constitutus iisdem iuribus et honoribus fruitur, iisdemque obligationibus tenetur, ac Episcopus residentialis.

Thus far the consideration of the apostolic administrator has been limited in the main to the temporary apostolic administrator. In the remarks prefacing the treatment of canon 315 attention was

[269] *AKKR*, CX (1930), 377-379; viz., Lugano, Salerno, Cashel, Galway.

called to the advantages of first discussing the temporary apostolic administrator. In particular, emphasis was laid upon the avoidance of needless repetition which would have been otherwise necessary. Since a rather lengthy and detailed inspection of the various duties, rights, and privileges of the temporary apostolic administrator has already been made, it is felt that the treatment of the permanent apostolic administrator can be disposed of in less detailed fashion.

The permanent apostolic administrator is one who is sent by the Sovereign Pontiff to rule or administer a diocese either *sede plena* or *sede vacante.*[270] This type of an apostolic administrator is less frequently appointed than the temporary apostolic administrator. The reason is quite apparent, for it is only naural that the people and the clerics of every diocese desire their proper bishop in preference to a permanent apostolic administrator. Nevertheless, occasions have arisen in the past which made it imperative to appoint permanent apostolic administrators. Especially was this true in Italy during the nineteenth century. In that country several attempts were made by the State to suppress dioceses that had been in existence from the earliest days of the Church. The reason offered for this contemplated action was the desire to save unnecessary Church expenses. Rather than give occasion for a rift between the Church and the State the Sovereign Pontiffs found a timely solution for this difficulty by handing over the administration of these dioceses to permanent apostolic administrators. In most of these instances the permanent apostolic administrators were the neighboring bishops who, in addition to being the residential bishops of their proper dioceses, now became, simultaneously, the permanent apostolic administrators of the neighboring small dioceses.[271]

This notion of the office of the permanent apostolic administrator will be more readily understood by way of example. Of the two examples here cited the first belongs to the pre-Code period and the second pertains to our own day.

[270] Canon 312.

[271] *AAS,* XI (1919), 72.

1)—*Pre-Code*

The Apostolic Constitution of Pope Pius VII (1800-1823), *De utiliori*, of July 1818, assigned many small dioceses, as permanent apostolic administratores, to larger neighboring dioceses. This long Constitution mentions among others that the following dioceses of the two Sicilies were handed over to the neighboring bishops who administered them as permanent apostolic administrators; Acerno, Campagna, and Viesti to the Ordinaries of Salerno, Conza, and Manfredonia respectively.[272] The Constitution *De Utiliori* also suppressed the dioceses of Ostuni and Ortona. Ostuni however, was restored in 1821 with the Archbishop of Brindisi as its permanent apostolic administrator. Pope Gregory XVI (1831-1846) in his Constitution, *Ecclesiarum omnium Ecclesiarum*, of May 17, 1834, restored the diocese of Ortona and handed it over as a perpetual apostolic administrature to the Archbishop of Lanciano.[273] Very clearly and definitively this Constitution outlined the powers of the permanent apostolic administrator over the see of Ortona:

> Quique eidem Ecclesiae, civitati ac diocesi Ortonensi ut infra assignandae, illiusque clero et populo praesit, synodum convocet, ac omnia et singula iura, officia et munia episcopalia habeat, exerceatque, cum suis infrascripto capitulo . . . caeterisque fruatur pontificalibus insignis, iuribus, honoribus, praeeminentiis, gratiis, favoribus, jurisdictionibus, indultisque realibus, personalibus ac mixtis, quibus reliquarum ecclesiarum in Siciliarum regno existentium praesules . . . utuntur et gaudent.[274]

2)—*Post-Code*

The Bishopric of Treja was erected in 1816 by the Bull *Per vetustam* of Pope Pius VII (1800-1823).[275] Instead of appoint-

[272] *Bullarii Romani Continuatio* Pius VII (2 vols., Prati: In Typographia Aldina, 1850-1852), I, 1771-1776.

[273] *Acta Gregorii XVI,* (4 vols., Romae: A. M. Bernasconi, 1901-1904), I, 403.

[274] *Loc. cit.*

[275] *Continuatio Bullarii Romani Pii* VII (2 vols., Prati: In Typographia Aldina, 1850-1852), II, 1210.

ing a proper bishop for the newly erected diocese, it was instead committed to the Archbishop of Camerino who ruled it as a permanent apostolic administrator. In view of the fact that the Episcopal residence was not easily approached from the diocese of Treja, the Sacred Congregation of the Consistory transferred the administration of the see of Treja from the permanent apostolic administrator, the Archbishop of Camerino, to the bishop of San Severino, Adam Borghini, who retained the see of Treja as the temporary apostolic administrator. This statement is declared in the following words:

> Quum autem emolumento gregi sit proximum habere pastorem, visum est expedire ut parva Treiensis dioecesis, quae hucusque regebatur ab Archiepiscopo Camerinensi, longitudine et difficultate viarum ab eadem dioecesi valde distante, regenda tribueretur proximo Episcopo Sancti Severini . . . S. Congregatio Consistorialis statuit ac decrevit ut regimen dioecesis Treiensis acciperet ac retineret ad nutum S. Sedis donec aliter provideatur, Venerabilis Frater Adamus Borghini, Episcopus Sancti Severini.[276]

It is stated later, in the same decree, that the Sacred Congregation of the Consistory after due and mature deliberation decided to join the see of Treja to the diocese of San Severino as a perpetual administrature. Necessarily, then, the present bishop of the diocese of San Severino, Adam Borghini, was made in 1920 the permanent apostolic administrator of the see of Treja.[277]

The usefulness of the office of permanent apostolic adminisrator can be readily ascertained from the two illustrated examples. For in addition to alleviating the financial burdens of a diocese,

[276] *AAS*, XII (1920), 321.

[277] Nunc vero, spirituali Treiensium bono modo stabili prospicere cupientes, Nos, re mature perpensa, memoratam Treiensem dioecesim, Apostolicae potestatis plenitudine, in perpetuum coniungimus cum dioecesi Sancti Severini, ita scilicet, ut ambae iurisdictioni, regimini atque administrationi subsint unius eiusdemque Pastoris, qui proinde Episcopus Sancti Severini et Administrator Apostolicus Treiensis perpetuo nominabitur, salvis utriusque dioecesis iuribus ac privilegiis.—*AAS*, XII (1920), 321.

it also served to eliminate the necessity of suppressing dioceses of ancient origin in the Church.

Since, moreover, the permanent apostolic administrators enjoy the same rights and honors, and have the same obligations as a residential bishop, it will be unnecessary for us to delineate all these rights, duties, and honors as was the procedure when the temporary apostolic administrator was considered. The legislation favoring the permanent apostolic administrator with the same rights, duties, and obligations as the residential bishop dates back to Decretal law.[278] The decretal legislation granted the apostolic administrator who had been given the complete administration of a diocese *in spiritualibus et temporalibus* all the jurisdiction the bishop possessed; however, if the apostolic administrator was not a bishop he was obliged to call in a bishop to perform all acts of consecration. Therefore, the only restriction placed upon the power of the apostolic administrator concerned consecrations—and even these he could perform if he had the episcopal character. The same concept is found plainly restated in the present law of canon 315, § 1:

> . . . iisdem iuribus et honoribus fruitur, iisdemque obligationibus tenetur ac Episcopus residentialis.

The omission of the clause referring to the inability of the apostolic administrator to consecrate, unless he is a bishop, is justified, since invariably the permanent apostolic administrator is a bishop. Toso [279] and Wernz-Vidal [280] remark that the permanent apostolic administrator is always a bishop, and very often the neighboring bishop or Mertopolitan.

The words of canon 315, § 1, grant the permanent apostolic administrator the same power that is granted to residential bishops. The words of the canon place no restriction on his power, and

[278] C. 42, *de electione et electi potestate*, I, 6, in VI°.

[279] "Defertur autem munus huiusmodi semper clerico praedito episcopali charactere, et saepe saepius viciniori Episcopo residentiali aut Metropolitae."—*Commentaria Minora*, II, 137.

[280] " . . . solent autem ita constitui clerici episcopali charactere insigniti." —*Ius Canonicum*, II, p. 589, n. 599.

therefore it appears that one cannot restrict the scope of his power without going contrary to the words of the canon. Moreover, the permanent apostolic administrator can exercise all the rights and duties, and enjoy all the privileges which are expressly denied to the temporary apostolic administrator. The former, the very moment he enters upon his office, obtains those rights which the vicar capitular and the temporary apostolic administrator, *sede vacante,* cannot perform until the see has been vacant a year; namely, to grant incardination and excardination, to confer benefices of free bestowal, and to issue dimissorial letters.[281]

At this point it is necessary to enumerate some of the more important rights, duties and privileges of the permanent apostolic administrator.

A)—*Rights and Privileges*

1. To erect in all the Churches of the Diocese a throne with a baldachin.[282]

2. To grant indulgences of fifty days in his own territory.[283]

3. To precede in his own territory all Archbishops and Bishops, except Cardinals, Legates of the Pope, and his own Metropolitan.[284]

4. To appoint a vicar-general whenever the proper government of the diocese demands it.[285]

5. To impart the Papal Blessing with a plenary indulgence attached twice a year; namely, on Easter Sunday and on any other solemn feast he chooses.[286]

6. To decide in his diocese questions of precedence among his

[281] Canons 112, 455, 958.

[282] Canon 349, § 2, n. 3; all the privileges and rights attributed to the temporary apostolic administrator are likewise enjoyed by the permanent apostolic administrator. Canons 308; 349, § 1.

[283] Canon 348, § 2, n. 2.

[284] Canon 347.

[285] Canon 366.

[286] Canon 914.

subjects, and even in the more urgent cases among exempt persons whenever they appear in a body with others.[287]

7. To hold in his own diocese pontifical functions anywhere, even in extempt Churches. Outside the diocese he cannot make use of the miter and crozier except at least with the presumed consent of the local Ordinary and, in the case of an exempt Church, with the consent of the religious superior. The phrase *pontificalia exercere* means to perform those functions in which by the laws of the Sacred Liturgy the use of the pontifical insignia of the crozier and the miter is required.[288]

8. To be buried in the Cathedral Church.[289]

9. To inscribe his coat of arms over the door of the Cathedral Church.

10. To be named in the *preces feriales* at Lauds and Vespers, as well as in the Canon of the Mass celebrated by all priests in his diocese.

11. To grant to bishops coming from outside his diocese the permission to exercise pontifical functions, and even to permit them the use of the throne and baldachin.

12. To place a seventh candle on the altar during the celebration of pontifical Mass.

13. To bless ashes, candles, palms, and the Font without being obliged to celebrate the Mass which follows.[290]

B)—*Obligations*

1. To reside personally in his diocese.[291] The law of residence which is of grave obligation imports not only material presence in one's respective diocese, but also personal discharge of the duties involved.[292] The observance of this obligation is impossible when the

[287] Canon 106, n. 6.

[288] Canon 337, §§ 1 and 2.

[289] Canon 1205, § 2.

[290] Moretti, *De Sacris Functionibus,* I, 35-36.

[291] Canon 338.

[292] Coronata, *Institutiones Iuris Canonici,* I, p. 477, n. 396; Toso, *Com-*

permanent apostolic administrator is simultaneously a residential bishop. This problem of residence was provided for in the case of the diocese of Treja thus:

> Episcopus in alterutra dioecesi residere poterit; officii tamen sui erit ita rem temperare, ut penes utramque, per notabile temporis spatium, iuxta rerum necessitatem, singulis annis commoretur.[293]

2. To apply the *Missa pro populo,*[294] This law binds *sub gravi,* and admits no exceptions. Consequently the permanent apostolic administrator from the very day he takes canonical possession of his see incurs this obligation. The bishop who rules in addition to his own see another diocese as the permanent apostolic administrator is not obliged to offer two Masses, i.e., the *Missa pro populo* for each diocese, but one suffices for both sees.[295]

3. To make a report to the Holy See every five years about the status of his diocese.[297] This report must contain a survey of the material and spiritual state of the diocese, comprising the clergy, religious and pious institutes, and the faithful in general.

4. To make the *visitatio ad limina.*[298] On the occasion when the bishop presents his report to the Roman Pontiff he must visit the two churches of St. Peter at the Vatican and St. Paul outside of the walls, pray at the tomb of the Apostles, and inscribe his name in a book kept for this purpose in the sacristies of these Basilicas.[299]

5. To visit part of his diocese annually so as to cover the entire

mentaria Minora, II, 164; Augustine, *A Commentary on Canon Law,* II, 359; Ayrinhac, *Constitution of the Church in the New Code of Canon Law,* p. 161.

293 *AAS,* XII (1920), 321 ss.

294 Canon 339.

296 Canon 339, § 5.

297 Canon 340, § 1.

298 Canon 341.

299 Ayrinhac, *Constitution of the Church in the New Code of Canon Law,* p. 172.

diocese at least once in five years.[300] The main object of this visitation is to preserve sound and orthodox doctrine, by banishing heresy; to maintain good morals and correct disorders, to animate the people by exhortations and admonitions.[301]

6. To hold a diocesan synod at least every ten years.[302]

7. To make an inventory of the sacred furnishings, and point out distinctly those furnishings which he bought with his own money or acquired by personal donation.[303] These rights, privileges and duties are only a few of the more notable ones which attach to the office of the permanent apostolic administrator. While the matter of this entire article has been treated rather cursorily, yet nothing of importance has been omitted. In concluding the discussion of canon 315 one may well emphasize that all those acts which are forbidden to the vicar capitular and the temporary apostolic administrator can be performed by the permanent apostolic administrator,[304] and that any particular faculty granted or denied the latter may be ascertained only by a carefully investigation of the stipulations contained in the letter of appointment.

[300] Canons 343-346.

[301] Ayrinhac, *loc. cit.*

[302] Canon 356.

[303] Canon 1299.

[304] Canons 113; 152; 187; 455; 477; 686; 893; 1104; 1162; 1303; 1414; 1466; 1423; 1487; 2202; 2220; 2236; 2314; Bevilacqua, *De Episcopi seu Ordinarii Iuribus ac Obligationibus* (Romae: Pustet, 1921); Moretti, *De Sacris Functionibus,* I, 35-38.

Chapter VII

RELATION OF THE BISHOP AND THE APOSTOLIC ADMINISTRATOR

Canon 316, § 1—Si Administrator Apostolicus dioecesi, sede plena, praeficiatur, iurisdictio Episcopi eiusque Vicarii Generalis suspenditur.

When an apostolic administrator is assigned to a diocese while the resident bishop is still in possession of the see, the bishop and his vicar-general *ipso facto* lose all jurisdiction over the see; in a word, their jurisdiction is suspended. This law is absolute and neither admits exceptions nor makes distinctions. Of course, there is always the possibility that the letter appointing the apostolic administrator, *sede plena,* may stipulate that the resident bishop retains his jurisdiction. Obviously, however, this is usually not the case, for the law which prompted the simultaneous suspension of the jurisdiction of the bishop and vicar-general was occasioned by the great confusion and multiplicity of trouble that would follow if the apostolic administrator and the resident bishop exercise the same jurisdiction.[1] The reason for depriving the bishop of his jurisdiction does not necessarily imply that he has been guilty of some crime, or has in any way abused his power. It can be occasioned by no particular fault of the bishop, v.g., by old age, mental or physical sickness, or administrative incapability. On the other hand, when the bishop is at fault, excommunication, personal interdict, or suspension *ab officio* may be inflicted.[2]

[1] "Ad vitandam confusionem, si Administrator Apostolicus dioecesi praeficiatur sede plena, administratio dioecesi, paucis exceptis, ad Administratorem spectat; hinc Episcopus eiusque Vicarius Generalis caret iurisdictione quae suspensa manet."—Cocchi, *Commentarium in Codicem Iuris Canonici,* II, p. 155, n. 232; Ayrinhac, *Constitution of the Church in the New Code of Canon Law,* p. 134, n. 108; Toso, *Commentaria Minora,* II, 139.

[2] Canons 2263; 2275; 2279.

In either instance, viz., whether the reason for sending an apostolic administrator is prompted by a personal fault of the bishop, or is evoked by a defect beyond his control the result is similar, namely, the suspension not only of his own jurisdiction, but also of that of his vicar-general as well.[3] This simultaneous suspension of the jurisdiction of the bishop and of his vicar-general is found in the legal axiom:

Accessorium naturam sequi congruit principalis.[4]

No matter what the cause may be whenever the bishop loses his jurisdiction, the vicar-general likewise loses jurisdiction. This is only logical, because the jurisdiction of the Bishop and the vicar-general is one.[5] If, however, the vicar-general is also the *Officialis* he does not lose this latter office when the bishop's jurisdiction is suspended, or when the see becomes vacant.[6]

Present day commentators, except Toso,[7] dismiss canon 316, § 1, by merely paraphrasing it.[8]

The Code makes no change in the previous legislation respecting the simultaneous suspension of the jurisdiction of the bishop and of his vicar-general. This legislation has remained constant

[3] " . . . suspenditur vero suspensa Episcopali iurisdictione."—Canon 371.

[4] Reg. 42, R.J., in VI°.

[5] "Questo è un modo di suspensione di giurisdizione tutto particolare dell'ufficio del Vicario Generale, perchè egli costituisce, con suo Vescovo, un solo tribunale, una sola giuridizione."—Campagna, *Il Vicario Generale del Vescovo,* The Catholic University of America, Canon Law Studies, n. 66 (Washington, D. C.; The Catholic University of America, 1931), p. 186.

[6] Canon 1573, § 6.

[7] "Administrator Apostolicus Episcopi locum tenet. Ideoque necessario, si datus fuerit sede plena, simul ac Administrator Apostolicus possessionem cepit, omnis Episcopi, ac proinde eius Vicarii generalis (cum unum et idem sit utriusque tribunal), iurisdictio suspenditur."—*Commentaria Minora,* II, 139.

[8] Vermeersch-Creusen, *Epitome Iuris Canonici,* I, p. 333, n. 434; Blat, *Commentarium Textus,* II, p. 329, n. 334; Coronata, *Compendium Iuris Canonici,* I, p. 392, n. 690; Wernz-Vidal, *Ius Canonicum,* II, pp. 590-591, n. 560; Beste, *Introductio in Codicem,* p. 258; Cance, *Droit Canonique,* I, p. 307, n. 4; Augustine, *A Commentary on Canon Law,* II, 329; Cocchi, *Commentarium in Codicem Iuris Canonici,* II, pp. 155-156, n. 232.

throughout the centuries, and the present Canon repeats the legislation of the old law.[9] Canon 316 is the old law expressed in practically the same words, and consequently in order adequately to understand its force one must have recourse to the old law which very definitely states that once a vicar apostolic (apostolic administrator) is appointed the jurisdiction of the bishop and of his vicar-general is *ipso facto* suspended, unless something to the contrary is stated in the letter appointing the apostolic administrator.[10]

In addition to the doctrine of the above-mentioned pre-Code authors who are unanimous in asserting that when the apostolic administrator assumes the administration of a diocese *sede plena*

[9] "Nec Episcopus, dum adest Vicarius Apostolicus potest tenere Vicarium Generalem, nec alio modo sese in iurisdictionem ingerere, adeo ut nec litteras Apostolicas sibi sub nomine dignitatis directas exequi possit."—Nicolius, *Lucubrationes,* II, 49, n. VI; "Episcopus habet tantum administrationem ordinis . . . nisi fit ipsi interdicta etiam ista administratio."—Pellegrinus, *Praxis Vicariorum,* p. 55, n. VII; "Item neque potest Episcopus tenere vicarium generalem tempore, quo adest Vicarius Apostolicus, nec aliquo modo se intromittere valet in negotiis iurisdictionem tangentibus."—Ferraris, *Prompta Bibliotheca,* s.v. "Vicarius Apostolicus," n. 15; "Totum iurisdictionis exercitium spectat ad Vicarium Apostolicum, neque potest Episcopus in eam sese ullatenus intromittere cum ab omni iurisdictione et dioecesis administratione fuerit remotus. Nisi ablata etiam Episcopo fuerit administratio sacramenti Ordinis, ad ipsum pertinet ordinationes facere, . . . "—Bouix, *Tractatus de Curia Romana,* p. 659, nn. 2-3; "Vic. seu Adminis. Apostolicus, Sede plena, deputatur, efficit ut Episcopus prohibeatur ab exercenda omni iurisdictione vel saltem ab ea iurisdictionis parte, pro cuius exercitio vic. Apost. destinatus fuit."—Lega, *De Iudiciis Ecclesiasticis,* II, p. 456, n. 353; "Quodsi talis Vicarius Apostolicus deputetur, ad vitandam confusionem ordinarie totum iurisdictionis exercitium in administranda diocesi exceptis quibusdam casibus spectat ad Vicarium Apostolicum, non amplius ad Episcopum ab administratione diocesis remotum."—Wernz, *Ius Decretalium,* II, p. 471, n. 705.

[10] "Canones qui ius vetus ex integro referunt, ex veteris iuris auctoritate, atque ideo ex receptis apud probatos auctores interpretationibus sunt aestimandi."—Canon 6, § 2; Neuberger, *Canon 6, or the Relation of the Code to the Preceding Legislation,* p. 70.

the jurisdiction of both the bishop and his vicar-general is suspended, there are several pertinent decrees issued by the Sacred Congregation of Bishops and Regulars. These decrees most emphatically stated that the bishop can, in no way, interfere with the rule of the diocese when a vicar apostolic (apostolic administrator) has been appointed, and that at the same time his vicar-general loses his jurisdiction.[11]

Canon 316, § 2—Quanquam autem Administrator Apostolicus Episcopi auctoritati non subest, non debet tamen se immiscere causis Episcoporum ipsum spectantibus, neque in Vicarium eius Generalem iudicium seu processum instruere aut animadvertere ob acta praeteritae administrationis.

Although the apostolic administrator is not subject to the authority of the bishop, he should not interfere in matters concerning the bishop personally, nor should he institute a canonical trial or procedure or otherwise punish the vicar-general for acts done under the former administration of the diocese.[12] Quite evidently, therefore, unless the apostolic administrator has been assigned by the Holy See to investigate the personal affairs of the bishop, he is incompetent to initiate a trial. Furthermore the right of instituting a trial against a bishop in criminal causes belongs

[11] *Caputaquen.*, 27 mart. 1580—Bizzarri, *Collectanea*, n. 229—*Fontes*, n. 1368; "Sacra Congregatio censuit executionem litterarum Apostolicarum Episcopo, sine eius Vicario, ut proponitur directarum spectare ad Vicarium Apostolicum in vim facultatum sibi per Breve SS.mi Domini Nostri attributarum. Quinimo cum praedictus Vicarius Apostolicus iurisdictionem illam exerceat privative quoad Episcopum, iniungendus, prout tenore praesentis Decreti iniungitur eidem Episcopo, ut Vicarium generalem praedictum omnino, et statim ab officio removeat, nec per se, vel per alium in iis quae iurisdictionis etiam voluntariae existunt, in posterum quandoque sese ingerat, et certioret Sacram Congregationem de executione."—S.C. Ep. et Reg., *Naulen.*, 27 sept. 1641—*Fontes*, n. 1766.

[12] Augustine, *A Commentary on Canon Law*, II, 339; Woywod, *A Practical Commentary on the Code of Canon Law*, I, p. 115, n. 235.

exclusively to the Sovereign Pontiff.[13] Even in contentious causes the apostolic administrator cannot act unless he is delegated to do so because these trials are within the competency of the Tribunals of the Holy See.[14]

The present legislation is not new; it antedates the Code by several centuries and is the result of constant legislation for many years. Even though the apostolic administrator is appointed to a diocese and is given the same faculties as the resident bishop, he cannot in any way bring charges against the bishop or against his vicar-general without a special mandate of the Holy See.[15]

Wernz adverted to what he considered as a unique disposition of the law in that there is no demand to interpose the appeal from the sentence of the vicar apostolic (apostolic administrator) before the Roman Pontiff, but in that such an appeal could be lodged with the metropolitan:

> Illud in eiusmodi Vicariis Apostolicis singulare est, quod non obstante deputatione pontificia ab ipsorum sententiis ad metropolitam appellari possit, neque ad Romanum Pontificem appellatio interponi debeat.[16]

The unique character of this disposition of the law seems to be exaggerated by Wernz. It is true that the apostolic administrator is appointed by the Sovereign Pontiff and is a vicar of the Holy Father. Still he not like the vicar apostolic,[17] who acts in the name of the Sovereign Pontiff, and hence must be regarded in a

[13] Canon 1557, § 1, n. 3.

[14] Canon 1557, § 2, n. 1.

[15] "Quando autem Vicarius Apostolicus deputatus fuerit sede Episcopali plena, tunc etiam eamdem ferme ipse jurisdictionem habet, quam Episcopus, sed cavere debet, ne se intromittat in causis tam civilibus quam criminalibus concernentibus personam Episcopi, nisi id sibi fuerit a Curia Romana demandatum."—Andreucci, *Hierarchia Ecclesiastica,* II, 238; "Habere eamdem iurisdictionem quam habebat Episcopus."—Nicolius, *Lucubrationes,* II, p. 48, n. VI.

[16] *Ius Decretalium, II,* p. 471, n. 704; Nicolius, *Lucubrationes,* II, p. 48, n. VI

[17] Canon 292.

different capacity. As an apostolic administrator he takes the place of the bishop.[18] Toso very clearly and succinctly remarks:

> Scilicet non video, qua de causa potestas Administratoris Ap. derogare deberet superiori potestati Metropolitarum, quae et ipsa, qua talis, pontificia est.[19]

Even long previous to the Code the disposition of the law which directed that appeals from the vicar apostolic (apostolic administrator) were to be carried to the metropolitan court was given a definite explanation by the Sacred Congregation of Bishops and Regulars.

> S'è dato conto a N. S. del dubbio che V. S. haveva, se le appelationi legitime che s'interpongono a cotesto tribunale da quello di Capaccio ove hora si trova Vicario Apostolico, si deveno ricever o pur hanno da venir a questa Santa Sede immediatamente. Et Sua Santità ha ordinato che si scriva a V.S. che haveranno da andar come al Metropolitano, non obstante che il Vicario sia apostolico, perchè in somma ha la medesima autorità che gl'haveria data il vescovo se dependesse da lui.[20]

[18] "Et dum Vicarius Apostolicus Summi Pontificis vices agit, Administrator potius Episcopum supplet."—*Periodica*, XIII (1924), 16.

[19] *Commentaria Minora*, II, 139.

[20] *Salernitana*, 7 iun. 1580—*Fontes*, n. 1371.

CHAPTER VIII

PROVISIONAL ADMINISTRATION OF THE DIOCESE WHEN THE JURISDICTION OF THE APOSTOLIC ADMINISTRATOR IS IMPEDED OR CURTAILED

Canon 317.—Si impedita fuerit iurisdictio Administratoris Apostolici aut si idem Administrator defecerit, Sedes Apostolica statim moneatur: et interim, si dioecesis vacet aut Episcopus non sit sui compos, valent praescripta can. 429 seqq.; secus Episcopus dioecesim regit, nisi Sedes Apostolica aliud praestituerit.

If the jurisdiction of the apostolic administrator is impeded, or ceases, the Holy See is to be informed immediately. Meanwhile, if the diocese is vacant or the bishop is not *sui compos,* the prescripts of canon 429 along with the canons immediately following obtain force; else the bishop rules the diocese, unless the Holy See has provided otherwise.[1] The jurisdiction of an apostolic administrator can be impeded in the same way as that of a resident bishop, that is[2] by captivity or imprisonment, by relegation, by exile, or by some other personal inability.[3] The jurisdiction, therefore, of the apostolic administrator is considered to be impeded when its hindered status is occasioned by any of the foregoing causes.[4] Although these terms have already been defined in the

[1] Augustine, *A Commentary on Canon Law,* II, 330; Woywod, *A Practical Commentary on the Code of Canon Law,* I, p. 115, n. 235; Ayrinhac, *Constitution of the Church in the New Code of Canon Law,* p. 134, n. 108.

[2] Toso, *Commentaria Minora,* II, 139-140; Cocchi, *Commentarium in Codicem Iuris Canonici ad usum Scholarum,* II, p. 156, n. 233; Coronata, *Institutiones Iuris Canonici,* I, pp. 459-460, n. 383; Cance, *Le Code de Droit Canonique,* I, p. 308, n. 306; Villien-Magnin, *Dictionnaire de Droit Canonique,* s.v. "*Administrateur Apostolique,*" p. 190.

[3] Canon 429, § 1.

[4] Klekotka, *Diocesan Consultors,* p. 157; Jaeger, *The Administration of Vacant or Quasi-Vacant Dioceses in the United States,* p. 213.

treatment of an earlier canon,[5] nevertheless it is deemed timely and advantageous to reiterate the definitions particularly in view of the fact that they will help one considerably in comprehending the present canon. It has been previously stated, in the introduction to this canon, that the jurisdiction of the apostolic administrator is impeded in identically the same way as is the jurisdiction of a resident bishop; it will be necessary, therefore, to substitute the word *apostolic administrator* wherever the word *bishop* occurs in the text.[6]

1) Captivity or imprisonment of the apostolic administrator may be caused by enemies of religion, by enemies of the State, or by inimical authorities within the Church or State.

2) Relegation of the apostolic administrator is his confinement to a given town or place located outside the diocese.

3) Exile of the apostolic administrator is his banishment from his country or state.

4) Inability or incapability of the apostolic administrator may be identified with mental or physical afflictions which render him incapable of performing or exercising his jurisdictions.[7]

When anyone of these four circumstances is present then the jurisdiction of the apostolic administrator is impeded. It is expedient and imperative, moreover, that the one who succeeds the impeded apostolic administrator inform the Holy See immediately of what has occurred in the diocese and to await directions from Rome. But the present canon makes no reference as to the person upon whom devolves this duty of informing the Holy See. The statement already given in the second sentence of the present paragraph has anticipated the answer furnished by Toso.[8] Who

[5] Canon 312.

[6] Canon 429, §§ 1-5.

[7] A more complete and detailed account of how a diocese may become impeded is to be found in Jaeger, *op. cit.*, p. 213 ss.; and Klekotka, *op. cit.*, p. 157 ss.

[8] "A quo monenda [Apostolica Sedes]? Procul dubio ab eo, qui interim in dioecesis regimine succedere tenetur."—*Commentaria Minora*, II, 139.

does, in reality, administer the see when the jurisdiction of the apostolic administrator is impeded by the presence of one of the four mentioned impediments? The answer is contained in the present canon which makes a distinction between the administration of the diocese that is vacant and the diocese that is still occupied.

A) *In A Diocese That Is Vacant*

When a vacant diocese is referred to in this section it means that the see, even though an apostolic administrator has been committed to it, has no resident bishop. Such a vacancy can be caused by the death, resignation, transfer, or deprivation of the bishop's jurisdiction.[9] To such a diocese the Holy See has often sent a permanent or temporary apostolic administrator.[10] If, however, during the term of administration the apostolic administrator is impeded from exercising his jurisdiction through the presence of a physical impediment, then the diocese is ruled provisionally in the manner outlined in canon 429. When the apostolic administrator is thus hindered from administering the see committed to his care, the government of the diocese *ipso facto* falls on the vicar-general, or on any other priest delegated by the apostolic administrator, unless the Holy See has provided otherwise.[11]

At this point it is necessary to maintain again the distinction between a permanent and a temporary apostolic administrator. A permanent apostolic administrator insofar as he is likened to a resident bishop, enjoys the same rights and privileges and is held to the same duties as a resident bishop,[12] and hence he can appoint a vicar-general. A temporary apostolic administrator, insofar as he is likened to a vicar capitular, is incompetent to appoint a vicar-general unless this permission is explicitly contained in the letter of his appointment.[13] Authors are not agreed as to whether the permanent apostolic administrator can appoint a vicar-general

[9] Canon 430, § 1.

[10] Canon 312.

[11] Canon 429, § 1.

[12] Canon 315, § 1, and canon 366, § 1.

[13] Canon 315, § 2, n. 1.

or not. They are unanimous in denying this faculty to the temporary apostolic administrator. The writer, in another place discussed this question at length and concluded that the permanent apostolic administrator can appoint a vicar-general. In relation to the present canon the same doctrine is maintained.[14]

Canon 429, § 1, prescribes that if the apostolic administrator has not delegated a priest to administer the diocese, then the task of administration falls to the vicar-general. Consequently, unless the permanent apostolic administrator has appointed another priest to administer the diocese during the term of his impediment, the vicar-general will rule the see. As the see is still juridically in the hands of the permanent apostolic administrator, the vicar-general in such a case will exercise the ordinary power given to him by law,[15] and any other specific power or faculty which in addition the permanent apostolic administrator by a special mandate has chosen to delegate to him.[16] If, on the other, the permanent apostolic administrator did not appoint a vicar-general, but instead has appointed a priest to administer his diocese in the event that his own power was impeded, this priest will have only as much power as the permanent apostolic delegated to him.

The temporary apostolic administrator appointed to administer a vacant diocese is impeded from exercising his jurisdiction through exactly the same impediments as those which curtail the jurisdiction of the permanent apostolic administrator.[17] Therefore that part of canon 429, § 1, which says that, "if the bishop (in our case the temporary apostolic administrator) is in captivity, is banished, exiled, or otherwise inhabilitated, so that he cannot even by letter communicate with the people of his diocese, then the government of the diocese shall rest with the vicar-general . . . " is not applicable in those dioceses where the temporary apostolic administrator is in charge, for the temporary apostolic

[14] Cf. *supra*, pp. 219-227.

[15] Canon 366, § 1.

[16] Campagna, *Il Vicario Generale del Vescovo*, pp. 130-131.

[17] Canon 315, § 2, n. 1.

administrator is incapable of appointing a vicar-general. The latter part of canon 429, § 1, makes provisions for a priest who has been appointed by the temporary apostolic administrator, and these are applicable if the latter has designated such a person. This delegated priest receives only such faculties as the temporary apostolic administrator has delegated to him. But how is the see administered when the jurisdiction of the temporary apostolic administrator is impeded and when he has not appointed a priest to administer the see in his stead, or when the permanent apostolic administrator has not appointed a vicar-general or delegated a priest to rule the diocese provisionally? Still another situation is possible. If the permanent apostolic administrator had indeed appointed a vicar-general, but the latter has been captured, exiled, or relegated along with the bishop, who then rules the diocese? All these possibilities are provided for in canon 429, § 3, which states:

> His deficientibus, vel, uti supra dictum est, impeditis, Capitulum ecclesiae cathedralis suum Vicarium constituat, qui regimen assumat cum potestate Vicarii Capitularis.

The person thus selected by the cathedral chapter or by the board of diocesan consultors, shall, as soon as he has assumed the administration of the diocese, inform the Holy See of his election and of the existing state of diocesan affairs.[18]

An example will clarify these details. The diocese has been deprived of its resident bishop A by death. The Holy See, induced by grave reasons, deems it advantageous to appoint B as the permanent apostolic administrator to the diocese. Shortly after the permanent apostolic administrator has assumed the administration of the vacant diocese the civil authorities become very hostile toward him and eventually exile him. According to the law expressed in canon 429, § 1, the vicar-general is to administer the see, unless the permanent apostolic administrator has designated someone else. The exiled apostolic administrator, however, not

[18] Canon 429, § 4.

foreseeing that his jurisdiction would be impeded, had neither appointed a vicar-general, nor designated any particular priest to administer the diocese. In such a case the cathedral chapter or the board of diocesan consultors, has the power to elect an administrator who will administer the diocese with the rights, duties, and privileges of a vicar capitular. Just as soon as this temporary apostolic administrator assumes the administration of the diocese he is obligated to inform the Holy See (the Sacred Congregation of the Consistory) [19] of what has happened and that he has been elected by the cathedral chapter or the board of diocesan consultors to rule the diocese. The Holy See either will permit the temporary administrator to continue, or it will appoint a temporary apostolic administrator until the permanent apostolic has returned from his exile. This example can also be utilized with reference to the temporary apostolic administrator, but simultaneously it must be stressed that the temporary apostolic administrator cannot appoint a vicar-general. Speaking of canon 429, § 4, Klekotka says: "The new Code for the first time makes a provision for such a case and allows the cathedral chapter, and by consequence the diocesan consultors, to elect a temporary vicar capitular, who is to notify the Holy See as soon as possible and in the meantime will administer the vacant see with the power of a vicar capitular.[20]

Thus far only the physical causes which render an apostolic administrator incapable of exercising his jurisdiction over the see to which he has been assigned by the Sovereign Pontiff have been considered. In all these cases the apostolic administrator has retained not only his jurisdiction, but also the right to exercise it just as soon as the impediment ceases.

Canon 429, § 5, enumerates some canonical impediments. A canonical impediment hinders an apostolic administrator from discharging the functions of his office insofar as the impediment is an ecclesiastical penalty which *ipso facto* suspends his jurisdic-

[19] Canon 248.

[20] *Diocesan Consultors*, p. 158.

tion.[21] An apostolic administrator who incurs the penalty of excommunication,[22] interdict,[23] or suspension,[24] may not exercise his power of jurisdiction in the diocese to which he has been committed. Moreover, if the permanent apostolic administrator has appointed a vicar-general, he too is *ipso facto* suspended from the exercise of his jurisdiction.[25]

A situation illustrating this suspension of the lawful exercise of jurisdiction arises when the apostolic administrator who is endowed with the episcopal character consecrates another bishop without having received special permission from the Holy See.[26] When such an act is performed by the apostolic administrator his jurisdiction *ipso facto* is suspended, and if he had been permanently appointed and has a vicar-general, he also suffers a suspension of his jurisdiction. Whenever the use of the jurisdiction of the apostolic administrator is impeded by a canonical impediment the government of the diocese does not pass into the hands of the cathedral chapter or to the board of diocesan consultors; neither can the apostolic administrator in view of his suspended jurisdiction delegate another person to administer in his place. When such is the case the Code prescribes that if the apostolic administrator should have incurred excommunication, interdict, or suspension, the metropolitan—or if the metropolitan fails to act—the oldest suffragan bishop shall at once have recourse to the Holy See that proper provisions may be made.[27]

In the meantime the regular affairs of the impeded see cease until the Holy See takes cognizance of the situation and remedies it. Little delay will be caused, for in modern times the means of communication are very efficient. Jaeger makes a noteworthy

[21] Canon 2185; Jaeger, *The Administration of Vacant and Quasi-Vacant Dioceses in the United States*, p. 218.

[22] Canon 2265.

[23] Canon 2275.

[24] Canon 2283.

[25] Canon 371.

[26] Canon 2370.

[27] Canon 429, § 5.

remark when he says in effect that such a circumstance, as recounted above, will scarcely be found in practice. If a bishop, or an apostolic administrator possessing the episcopal character, is censured by a declaratory or condemnatory sentence, it is recognized that the Holy See alone has been competent to inflict this punishment.[28] Should the Holy See at such time deem any specific provision necessary, it would undoubtedly at the same time make provision for the administration of the see. Vincent Battucci, the Archbishop of Antivari, was suspended from the exercise of his jurisdiction; in the same letter Bishop Charles Pooten was appointed apostolic administrator of Antivari.[29]

It is noted further that even the penalties specified in law as *ipso facto incurrenda* require a declaratory sentence for ultimate observance, and therefore there would scarcely be an instance when the apostolic administrator would be impeded from exercising his jurisdiction.[30]

This above consideration indicates the method of procedure to be followed in those dioceses wherein the apostolic administrator's jurisdiction has been impeded through the existence of a physical or canonical impediment. Furthermore, the legislation is relevant only to those dioceses that are vacant, i. e., dioceses where the resident bishop has died, has been transferred, has resigned, or has been deprived of his see.

In addition to the jurisdiction of an apostolic administrator being impeded by the presence of physical or canonical impediment, canon 317 mentions that the same procedure is to be followed when the jurisdiction of the apostolic administrator ceases. The jurisdiction of an apostolic administrator ceases by death, resignation, transfer, or by deprivation.[31]

[28] Canons 1557; 2227, § 1; Jaeger, *The Administration of Vacant and Quasi-Vacant Dioceses in the United States,* pp. 220-221.

[29] *Acta Gregorii XVI,* III, 321.

[30] Canons 239, § 1 n. 2; 349 § 1; 2227, § 2; 2232, § 1; 2264; Klekotka, *Diocesan Consultors,* p. 161; Jaeger, *op. cit.,* p. 221; Wernz-Vidal, *Ius Canonicum,* II, p. 757, n. 706.

[31] Canon 430, § 1.

1) At the death of the apostolic administrator the administration of the diocese passes into the hands of the cathedral chapter or to the board of diocesan consultors, who must, within eight days, elect a vicar capitular or respectively a diocesan administrator to rule the diocese.[32]

2) The resignation of the apostolic administrator can not become effective until the Holy See has accepted the resignation. This is in accord with the general fundamental principle of resignation.[33] Therefore the cathedral chapter or the board of diocesan consultors, has no power until the apostolic administrator has received word that his resignation has been accepted. Even in this instance it is quite likely that at the time of the acceptance of the resignation the Holy See will appoint a new apostolic administrator or a resident bishop (since the see is vacant), and thereby make any action of the cathedral chapter or of the board of diocesan consultors unnecessary.[34]

3) Transfer of the apostolic administrator is effected in the same way as the transfer of a bishop. When a bishop has been transferred from one see to another he retains, temporarily, the administration of his former see with the same faculties as those which obtain for a vicar capitular.[35]

4) Deprivation implies the removal of the apostolic administrator from his office. Before the apostolic administrator can incur deprivation it is necessary that it be intimated to him. If the apostolic administrator was elevated to the episcopate and failed to receive episcopal consecration within six months of the announcement of his elevation then he would *ipso facto* be deprived of his office.[36]

In the cases of resignation and deprivation the Holy See will regularly make concomitant provisions for the administration of the vacant diocese. In the event that the Holy See does not pro-

[32] Canon 432, § 1.

[33] Canon 432, § 1.

[34] Klekotka, *Diocesan Consultors*, p. 160.

[35] Canon 430, § 3, n. 1.

[36] Canon 2398.

vide for the administration of the diocese, the cathedral chapter or the board of diocesan consultors administers the diocese. Until this body elects a vicar capitular or administrator it exercises the ordinary jurisdiction in the vacant diocese.[37]

B) *In A Diocese That Is Not Vacant*

Thus far the study of canon 317 has been exclusively devoted to the discussion of the apostolic administrator when his jurisdiction has been impeded or when it has ceased. When such a situation occurs while the see is vacant the diocese is administered according to the prescriptions of canons 429-444. Now the present consideration concerns itself with the apostolic administrator whose jurisdiction has been impeded or ceased—but the diocese is not vacant and the bishop is *sui compos.*

Occasions may arise when the apostolic administrator is sent to rule a diocese while its resident bishop is still alive but is hindered from exercising his jurisdiction through the presence of some incapacity or censure but is in full control of his senses. In time the jurisdiction of the apostolic administrator is impeded or ceases and the diocese is left without an administrator. Does the cathedral chapter or the board of diocesan consultors assume the administration of the see? Canon 317 explicitly states that the resident bishop will rule the diocese unless the Holy See has provided otherwise.[38]

[37] Canon 198.

[38] "Contra, si et sedes plena sit et Episcopus sui compos hic interim dioecesis regimen resumere debet."—Toso, *Commentaria Minora,* II, 140; Villien-Magnin, *Dictionnaire de Droit Canonique,* s.v. "Administrateur Apostolique," n. 190.

CHAPTER IX

CESSATION OF THE JURISDICTION OF THE APOSTOLIC ADMINISTRATOR

Canon 318, § 1—Administratoris Apostolici iurisdictio Romani Pontificis aut Episcopi obitu non cessat.

§ 2—Cessat vero cum Episcopus dioecesis vacantis possessionem legitime ceperit ad normam can. 334, § 3.

The jurisdiction of the apostolic administrator does not cease or expire at the death of the Roman Pontiff or of the resident bishop. It does cease, however, when the new bishop takes legitimate and canonical possession of the vacant diocese in the manner prescribed in canon 334, § 3.[1]

A) *Death of the Pope*

Toso in his consideration of canon 318 devotes most of his commentary or comments to the solution of the query: Why is the jurisdiction of the apostolic administrator not suspended when the Sovereign Pontiff dies?[2] In substantiation of the Code law on this point he offers the following reasons: 1) the possible detriment that could accrue to the diocese if the apostolic administrator lost his jurisdiction at the death of the Sovereign Pontiff. He mentions, in particular, the possibility of the Apostolic See remaining vacant for a long time: and 2) he asserts that the laws, decrees and precepts of the deceased pontiffs endure with all their effects, until the successor revokes them totally or partially.[3]

[1] Woywod, *A Practical Commentary on the Code of Canon Law,* I, p. 115, n. 235; Augustine, *A Commentary on Canon Law,* II, 330; Ayrinhac, *Constitution of the Church in the New Code of Canon Law,* p. 134, n. 108.

[2] *Commentari Minora,* II, 141.

[3] "Hinc cuiusque R. Pontificis leges, decreta, iussiones, per se et nisi aliud expresse cautum fuerit a iubente, vi suae legitimitatis innixa eo

Despite the cogency of these two reasons alleged by Toso in support of the retention of jurisdiction by the apostolic administrator after the death of the Sovereign Pontiff, it is believed that they are not entirely the legal background for the basis of the law. The first reason proposed by Toso—the possibility of a long delay in the election of a new Pope—is not readily conceivable in the present days. But even in the event that such a delay did occur and the apostolic administrator was *ipso facto* deprived of his jurisdiction, would not then canon 317 become effective? This canon provides for the administration of a diocese when the jurisdiction of the apostolic administrator has been impeded or when it ceases. Consequently, this initial reason offered by Toso overlooks the provision of canon 317.

The second reason advanced by Toso, namely, the perpetuity of the laws, decrees and prescripts of former Pontiffs is stronger. But the reason for this law is that the apostolic administrator enjoys ordinary jurisdiction.[4] Ordinary jurisdiction is that which is attached to an office by the law itself.[5] The scope of the ordinary jurisdiction of bishops encompasses all ecclesiastical matters, both spiritual and temporal, and includes the capacity to legislate, to judge, and to punish.[6] The apostolic administrator, in so far as he is the successor to the bishop and not his inferior, obtains the ordinary episcopal jurisdiction when he assumes the diocesan administration. Consequently he obtains full administration over the temporal welfare of the diocese, except in those affairs which are expressly excluded by the prohibition of the law. Since, then, the apostolic administrator has ordinary jurisdiction and is an *ordinarius loci,* he does not lose his power when the superior who conferred it on him dies.[7]

usque perdurant suosque omnes legitimos effectus producunt, quo ab alio R. Pontifice successore ex toto vel ex parte revocentur; ideoque et potestas inde derivata."—Toso, *Commentaria Minora,* II, 141.

[4] Canon 198, § 1.

[5] Canon 197, § 1; Cf. Kearney, *The Principles of Delegation,* p. 50.

[6] Canon 334, § 1.

[7] "Resoluto quovis modo iure Superioris a quo fuerat concessum, offi-

Canon 208 explicitly treats of the loss of ordinary jurisdiction. It says in brief: 1) The power is not lost even if the superior who has conferred the office to which that power is attached goes out of office by death, resignation, transfer or deprivation. Hence the apostolic administrator appointed by the Sovereign Pontiff does not lose his ordinary jurisdiction by a vacancy in the Holy See. 2) The ordinary jurisdiction is lost if the office itself is lost. Thus, if an apostolic administrator is recalled from office his power ceases. 3) The ordinary jurisdiction becomes quiescent if an appeal is made to a higher authority, provided the appeal is *in suspensivo* and not *in devolutivo*.[8] From this discussion, then it can be deduced that the apostolic administrator does not lose his power when the Pontiff dies, unless the office was conferred *ad beneplacitum nostrum* or *durante nostro pontificatu*, or on a like condition expressed by some similar phrase.

The notion of the continuance of the jurisdiction of the apostolic administrator is not new law introduced by the Code of Canon Law, but is found expressed in many pre-Code authors.[9] Even prior to the time of Ferraris and Pellegrinus the Sacred Congregation of Bishops and Regulars in a letter addressed to the Bishop of Lecce stated that the jurisdiction of the vicar apostolic (apostolic administrator) who was deputized by the Sovereign Pontiff did not cease when the Apostolic See became vacant.[10]

B) *Death of the Resident Bishop*

The jurisdiction of the apostolic administrator does not cease

cium ecclesiasticum non amittitur, nisi lex aliud caveat aut nisi in concessione habeatur clasula: *ad beneplacitum nostrum*, vel alia aequipollens."—Canon 183, § 2.

[8] Wernz-Vidal, *Ius Canonicum*, II, p. 366, n. 376; Blat, *Commentarium Textus*, II, p. 170, n. 157; Augustine, *A Commentary on Canon Law*, II, 190.

[9] "Vicarius Apostolicus deputatus a Papa durare solet absque controversia etiam Sede Vacante."—Ferraris, *Prompta Biblotheca*, s.v. "Vicarius Apostolicus," n. 17; Pellegrinus, *Praxis Vicariorum*, s.v. "Vicarius Apostolicus," n. 27.

[10] *Lycien.*, 17 nov. 1590—Bizzarri, *Collectanea* (Romae: Ex Typographia Polyglotta, 1885), p. 230.

when the resident bishop dies. Many times in the past the cathedral chapter, at the death of the resident bishop, even though an apostolic administrator ruled the diocese, proceeded to the election of a vicar capitular. Such action was prompted by the mistaken notion that the apostolic administrator lost his jurisdiction when the resident bishop died. The doctrine which asserted the retention of jurisdiction by the apostolic administrator is now expressed in the Code.[11]

The Sacred Congregation of Bishops and Regulars on repeated occasions emphasized the fact that the apostolic administrator did not lose his jurisdiction when the resident bishop dies.[12] Pre-Code authors were unanimous in asserting that the jurisdiction of the apostolic administrator continued even after the death of the resident bishop.[13] Another decree of the Sacred Congregation of Bishops and Regulars specifically forbade the cathedral chapter to elect a vicar capitular after the death of the resident bishop when an apostolic administrator governed the diocese.[14] Quite obviously, therefore, the present legislation as contained in canon 318, § 1, is merely a restatement of the pre-Code legislation, and it serves to illustrate the stability of the office of the apostolic administrator. In no way can the jurisdiction of the apostolic administrator be curtailed by the death of the Sovereign Pontiff who assigned him to the see, or by the death of the resident bishop to whose diocese he has been assigned. The only way his jurisdiction can cease in either of these cases is by an explicit statement to the effect in the letter of appointment. Furthermore, the Code states that in the case of vacancy the government of the diocese devolves on the cathedral chapter or on the board of diocesan consultors, unless there is an apostolic administrator or un-

[11] Canon 318, § 1.

[12] *Aquilan.,* 4 aug. 1578—Bizzarri, p. 214; *Lycien.,* 22 dec. 1628— Bizzarri, p. 248; *Aquilan.,* 4 aug. 1678—Bizzarri, pp. 276-277.

[13] "Quoties, vivo Episcopo, Vicarius Apostolicus datus sit, is adhuc mortuo Episcopo, in eodem munere continuat."—Ferraris, *Prompta Bibliotheca,* s.v. "Vicarius Apostolicus," (additiones Cassinenses), n. 24; Pellegrinus, *Praxis* Vicariorum, s.v. "Vicarius Apostolicus," n. 28.

[14] *Aprutina.,* 24 ian. 1749—Bizzarri, p. 31.

less the Holy See has ordered otherwise.[15] Thus it is specifically provided in canon 431 that when there already is an apostolic administrator, that is, in the case wherein the former bishop has been physically or mentally disabled, the jurisdiction of the apostolic administrator does not cease when the bishop dies, but continues, and the cathedral chapter or the board of diocesan consultors is incapable of electing a vicar capitular.[16]

C) *Return or Reinstatement of the Resident Bishop or the Appointment of a New Bishop*

Notwithstanding the fact that the jurisdiction of the apostolic administrator does not cease with the death of the Sovereign Pontiff or of the resident bishop, canon 318, § 2, cites an instance wherein the jurisdiction of the apostolic administrator ceases automatically. Such is the case when a new bishop has been appointed to the vacant diocese which up to the time of his appointment was ruled by an apostolic administrator. In other words, just as soon as the newly appointed bishop takes canonical possession of his see according to the norms laid down in canon 334, § 3, the jurisdiction of the apostolic administrator ceases. Cocchi says that the jurisdiction of an apostolic administrator can cease in two ways: 1) *sede vacante*—when a new bishop is appointed to the see and he takes canonical possession according to the prescript of canon 334, § 3; and 2) *sede plena*—when jurisdiction is restored to the resident bishop, or the apostolic administrator is removed from his office by the Sovereign Pontiff.[17] The distinction suggested by Cocchi is a logical one, for it is precisely in the circumstances delineated by him that the jurisdiction of the apostolic administrator ceases. When James Skala was appointed as the temporary apostolic administrator to the vacant see of Meissen the first part of his letter of appointment stated:

[15] Canon 431, § 1.

[16] Klekotka, *Diocesan Consultors,* p. 162.

[17] *Commentarium in Codicem Iuris Canonici,* II, p. 157, n. 233.

"Quousque autem haec nova dioecesis de proprio pastore provideatur." [18]

Although the Code does not consider the cessation of the jurisdiction of the apostolic administrator when the see is still occupied, nevertheless the treatment of such a case is essential in order to indicate fully the ways in which the jurisdiction of the apostolic administrator ceases. Cocchi mentions the restoration of jurisdiction to a still resident bishop as exemplifying the present case.

D)—*Canonical Causes*

The given examples do not exhaust all the possibilities whereby the jurisdiction of the apostolic administrator can cease or be recalled. Pre-Code authors usually enumerated rather long lists of causes which effected such a recall or cessation of the apostolic administrator's jurisdition. It is enough, here, to mention the more prevalent conditions under which these causes were verified:

1) If the apostolic administrator died.

2) If the apostolic administrator resigned his office.

3) If the apostolic administrator was recalled, which generally happened when:

a) the vacant Church was supplied with a new bishop.

b) the resident bishop was restored to full jurisdiction of his Church.

c) the apostolic administrator was found to be unfit.

d) the apostolic administrator neglected to guard the liberty and rights of the Church and of ecclesiastical persons.

e) the apostolic administrator was found involved in crimes.

f) the apostolic administrator was held in odium by the people and the clergy.

g) the apostolic administrator's predefined time of administration had expired.[19]

In fine, the apostolic administrator could be recalled for any cause that proved detrimental to the good of the Church and the welfare of souls committed to his care.

[18] *AAS*, XIII (1921), 410.

[19] Pellegrinus, *Praxis Vicariorum*, s.v. "Vicarius Apostolicus," n. 36; Ferraris, *Prompta Bibliotheca*, s.v. "Vicarius Apostolicus," nn. 51-52.

APPENDIX

The Salary of the Apostolic Administrator

The principle that every cleric is entitled to a decent support has not only been substantiated by tradition but also by the Pauline text, "So also the Lord ordained that they who preach the gospel, should live by the gospel." [1] This principle is similarly expressed by the canonical axiom *"Datur beneficium propter officium."* The Church since earliest times has discountenanced any attempts of her priests to support themselves through work outside the scope of their priestly duties. Every office was to be of such a nature that in the event sufficient support did not accrue from it other means were to supply the deficit. So too these principles are applicable to the office of the apostolic administrator, regardless of whether he has been assigned to administer a diocese permanently or only temporarily. Even admitting the principles which favor him, it is quite difficult to arrive at any definite conclusions regarding what will constitute a decent support. In the seven canons of the Code devoted to the apostolic administrator no reference whatsoever is made to his salary. In only a few canons of the Code does the question of decent support arise, and even then no definite norms are imposed.[2] The difficulty of establishing a scale of salaries applicable to the universal Church would be insurmountable. For one definite standard could hardly be adopted, since the varying conditions of the various countries would make the observing of it impossible. The Holy See with years of experience is naturally hesitant of creating disturbances among her flock, and consequently realizes that the question of salaries is best served according to the exigencies of each country.

One canon of the Code, however, does indicate norms to be followed in ascertaining the salary of the apostolic administrator who administers a vacant diocese:

[1] I Cor., 9:14.

[2] Canons 441; 472; 475; 1481.

> Nisi aliter fuerit legitime provisum: Vicarius Capitularis et oeconomus ius habent ad congruam retributionem, in Concilio provinciali designatam vel recepta consuetudine concedi solitam, desumendam ex reditibus mensae episcopalis aut ex aliis emolumentis.[3]

Therefore, the canon which states that the vicar capitular has the right to decent support must necessarily be predicated of the temporary apostolic administrator, who enjoys the same rights that belong to the vicar capitular.[4]

The amount of the *congrua retributio* may be determined in one of three ways: 1) By concordat; 2) by provincial council; 3) by received custom.

1) *Nisi aliter fuerit provisum.* This clause points to the case in which some agreement or stipulation has been reached by means of a concordat. Obviously this method has no application in the United States of America. But in European countries provision for the salary of the apostolic administrator is quite generally made by means of a concordat and a definite amount of salary is determined.

2) *In concilio provinciali designata.* The Code calls for the celebration of a provincial council in every ecclesiastical province at least every twenty years.[5] It is in such conciliar legislation that the question of the apostolic administrator's salary and its precise amount can receive their precise specification. The latest provincial council held in the United States was the one which was convened in Portland, Oregan, in 1932.[6] In this as in the preceding provincial councils no legislation was enacted regarding the apostolic administrator's salary or its amount. The second possible method, then, similarly has no application in this country.

3) *Vel recepta consuetudine.* It is by means of custom, the third of the possible ways for determining the amount of the

[3] Canon 441, n. 1.

[4] Canon 315, § 2, n. 1.

[5] Canon 285.

[6] *Acta et Decreta Concilii Provincialis Portlandensis in Oregon Quarti* (Portland: Sentinel Printery, 1932).

salary of the apostolic administrator, that this question is regulated in this country. Whatever amount he received custom of an ecclesiastical province designates it as the *congrua retributio,* that is the amount which stands recognized as lawful by the Code.

Canon 441, § 1, does not indicate the particular amount of salary which is to yield to the vicar capitular. It is merely stated in the canon that the salary to which the recipient is entitled must measure up to the congruous demands which the office implies. The salary is to be derived from the revenues accruing to the *mensa episcopalis* or from other emoluments.[7]

Previous to the promulgation of the Code the law did lay down certain norms in fixing the salary of the vicar apostolic (apostolic administrator) when he was appointed to a canonically erected diocese. Pellegrinus stated that the salary of the apostolic administrator was to be an amount *"scutorum ducentorum pro singulis annis."* [8] This salary was to be paid to the vicar apostolic by the resident bishop; or in the event of an episcopal vacancy the salary was to be taken from the *mensa episcopalis,* unless the brief of appointment stipuated otherwise. In addition to the two-hundred scuta an extra fifty scuta was allowed to the vicar apostolic for what is now more commonly referred to as "travelling expenses." This latter amount was to be increased or decreased according to the distance he had to travel to arrive at the

[7] "What is usually called Cathedraticum" in this country is somewhat of a misnomer. Properly the cathedraticum is a contribution made to the bishops as a recognition of his authority (canon 1504). Is amount is rather nominal. In this country, however, it is not merely a fee paid to acknowledge subjection to the bishop. It is rather a substitute for the *mensa episcopalis* and other sources of revenue which support the bishop and his curia. In order, however, to avoid unnecessary multiplication of collections our hierarchy has deemed it best to levy a tax on all parishes of the diocese for diocesan expenses."—Schaaf [?], "Cathedraticum and the Depression"—*The Ecclesiastical Review* (originally The American Ecclesiastical Review,) Philadelphia, Philadelphia, 1889)—LXXXIX (1933), 537.

[8] *Praxis Vicariorum,* 68, n. 32; Ferraris, *Prompta Bibliotheca,* s.v. "Vicarius Apostolicus," n. 31.

diocese. Furthermore, Pellegrinus states, the salary did not become effective on the day of the appointment, but on the day the vicar apostolic actually assumed his administration. And if the diocese was in a poor financial condition the vicar apostolic was to be satisfied with accepting a smaller salary than two-hundred scuta.[9] Such indefiniteness suggests that individual circumstances had to determine how the matter was to be adjusted. The pre-Code legislation further indicated the impossibility of specifying a set salary in every instance, and clearly implied that the "circumstances alter cases."

In certain instances, in the past, the Sacred Congregations have given to the vicar capitular a salary proportionate to that of the vicar-general or, to be more exact, one fourth of the bishop's income.[10] In reference to this Jaeger says: "It is the opinion, however, of many bishops in the United States, that owing to the particular conditions prevailing here, the administrator (vicar capitular) should receive more income than the vicar-general." [11] Jaeger does not cite any source in substantiation of this statement, but his observations appears well taken. Undoubtedly the vicar capitular and the apostolic administrator who are appointed to rule a vacant diocese hold a more important office and are liable to more burdensome tasks than the vicar-general. For in their hands rests the spiritual and temporal welfare of all the souls living within the territory committed to their care. Perhaps the Sacred Congregations pronouncement was prompted by the fact that invariably, in other countries, the vicar capitular was a member of the cathedral chapter or held some other office from which he received a revenue. Canon 421, § 1, n. 3, states that the vicar capitular who is simultaneously a member of the cathedral chapter receives the fruit of his prebend, but not the

[9] *Praxis Vicariorum,* p. 58, nn. 32-36; Ferraris, *Prompta Bibliotheca,* s.v "Vicarius Apostolicus," nn, 31-38; Nicolius, *Lucubrationes,* II, p. 48, n. 5; Andreucci, *Hierarchia Ecclesiastica,* I, 242; Wernz, *Ius Decretalium,* II, n. 704.

[10] S.C.C., 14 febr., 1857—*Fontes* n. 4150.

[11] *The Administration of Vacant and Quasi-Vacant Dioceses,* p. 203.

daily distribution. Patiently, then, with an income from another office the vicar capitular could be content with the same income from his office as that which is given to the vicar-general.[12]

In the United States this situation is not verified because there are no cathedral chapters. From this alone it may well be assumed that the vicar capitular or the temporary apostolic administrator is entitled to a larger salary than that of the vicar-general. Augustine advance a rather unique and exceedingly liberal opinion when he states: "the vicar capitular or administrator, therefore, is entitled to the *cathedraticum pro rata* temporis as well as to the income from dispensations." [13] This opinion is possibly applicable wherever the income of the bishop is quite small; but it is surely to be rejected when the diocese offers a lucrative cathedraticum.

On June 30, 1934, the Sacred Congregation of the Consistory enacted certain norms which were to be followed by the vicar capitular or apostolic administrator in Italy for administering the *mensa episcopalis* in a vacant see.[14] The norms in addition to directing the proper management of the *mensa episcopalis* mention that the vicar capitular or apostolic administrator should be given a decent support in an amount which is to be determined by the Congregation of Consistory according to the returns of the *mensa episcopalis.* After the salary along with the current household expenses are deducted from the total revenue accruing from the *mensa episcopalis,* the remainder is to be reserved for the new bishop.[15]

Therefore the maintenance of the temporary apostolic administrator, *sede vacante,* can be regulated very easily, for he is given the same income that yields to the vicar capitular. The salary will, of course, vary according to the different countries, and according to the different conditions that specifically obtain. Such a notion can be gleaned from the cases already noted. These peculiarities will be adjusted according to the legislation enacted

[12] Campagna, *Il Vicario Generale del Vescovo,* pp. 180-181.

[13] *A Commentary on Canon Law,* II, 493.

[14] *AAS,* XXVI (1934), 551-556.

[15] *Loc. cit.*

in each province. One exception is to be noted: When a bishop receives notification of his transfer to another see he becomes obliged to take canonical possession of his diocese within four months.[16] From the very moment he receives notification he *ipso facto* becomes the administrator of the diocese from which his is transferred, and the jurisdiction of his vicar-general ceases immediately.[17] He retains, however, all the honorary privileges of a residential bishop,[18] and receives all the income of the *mensa episcopalis.*[19] In this one case, therefore, the salary is not the one usually given to the vicar capitular. The salary of the bishop continues until he has canonically occupied his new see.

Ordinarily, then, the amount of the salary of the temporary apostolic administrator, *sede vacante,* is the same as that which is given to the vicar capitular, which, unless it is determined by a concordat, can be established by a provincial council or legitimate custom.

Endeavoring to ascertain what constitutes a decent support for the temporary apostolic administrator who has been commissioned to administer a diocese that is still occupied by its proper bishop is much more difficult. In such cases the *episcopus proprius* receives the income of the *mensa episcopalis.* From this income the bishop must support the apostolic administrator unless other provisions have been made. The Holy See will be acquainted with the financial affairs of the diocese and will take this into consideration when an apostolic administrator is appointed. Oftentimes the temporary administration can be handled by a neigh-

[16] Canon 430, § 3.

[17] Canons 315, § 2, n. 2; 430, § 3, n. 1.

[18] Canon 430, § 3, n. 2.

[19] "A certa translationis notitia Episcopus intra quatuor menses debet dioecesim *ad quam* petere eiusdemque canonicam possessionem assumere ad normam can. 333, 334 et a die captae possessionis dioecesis *a qua* plene vacat; interim vero in eadem Episcopus: Integros percipit fructus mensae episcopalis ad normam can. 194, § 2."—Canon 430, § 3, n. 3; "Reditus prioris officii translatus percipit, donec aliud occupaverit."—Canon 194, § 2.

boring bishop who will exact only the defrayal of the expenses he incurs, even though he is entitled to the same salary as a vicar capitular.

The last possibility to be considered here deals with the salary of the permanent apostolic administrator. No difficulty is encountered because he has the same rights as a residential bishop.[20] One of these rights includes decent support from the income of the *mensa episcopalis.* A resident bishop from the very day he takes canonical possession of his see enjoys the *reditus mensae episcopalis,* i.e., the income of the bishopric to which he has been assigned.[21] Therefore, from the very day the permanent apostolic administrator assumes the charge of the see to which he has been assigned he begins to enjoy, just as the resident bishop, the *reditus mensae episcopalis.* When a resident bishop is appointed as the permanent apostolic administrator of a neighboring diocese, does he receive the income of the two dioceses? This was affirmatively answered when the bishop of S. Severino was appointed the permanent apostolic administrator to the diocese of Treja:

> Insuper, hac statuta Ecclesiarum unione, decernimus ut duplicis Episcopalis mensae reditus idem Episcopus percipiat, . . . [22]

From this analysis of the question touching upon the salary of the apostolic administrator the following conclusions are drawn:

1) the amount of the *congrua retributio* can be established a) by a concordat, b) by a provincial council, or c) by custom:

2) the temporary apostolic administrator, *sede vacante,* receives the same salary as the vicar capitular;

3) in the United States the temporary apostolic administrator, *sede plena,* receives the salary which lawful and received custom determines;

4) the permanent apostolic administrator receives the same

[20] Canon 315, § 1.

[21] Canon 349, § 2, n. 1.

[22] *AAS,* XII (1920), 321.

salary and has the same care over the *mensa episcopalis* as a resident bishop.

Finally, in the light of the previous treatment of the difficult and delicate question of salaries for the apostolic administrator one can easily appreciate how impossible it is for the law to establish more than a norm of equity applicable throughout the universal Church. Too many local conditions must be considered: the country, the financial status of the diocese, the dignity and rank of the appointee, his present duties, and many other exigencies far too many to enumerate. Each province can best decide what constitutes a decent support for an apostolic administrator. The Holy See, in representing and safeguarding the universal interest of the Church, reflects its desire for the attainment of full equity in behalf of all who minister in the official name of the Church. This equity becomes realized when the furnished remuneration harmoniously corresponds to the factors involved in clerical rank and dignity.

CONCLUSIONS

1) Historically the apostolic administrator is identified in the pre-Decretal offices of the interventor, visitator, and commendator; and in the post-Decretal and pre-Code offices of the administrator, and vicar apostolic.

2) The *Sapienti Consilio* officially pronounced the title "Apostolic Administrator" as solely indicative of an official sent by the Sovereign Pontiff to administer a vacant or quasi-vacant diocese for a permanent or temporary duration. The present Code of Canon Law has retained the legislation of the *Sapienti Consilio.*

3) It is believed that the following conclusions are validly inferred from the canonical commentary:—

a) The temporary apostolic administrator, *sede plena,* from the very moment he takes canonical possession of the diocese, can issue dimissorial letters, confer parishes of free bestowal, and grant incardination and excardination. This power is not granted to the temporary apostolic administrator, *sede vacante,* until the see has been vacant for a year.

b) The permanent apostolic administrator, in so far as he has the same rights, duties, and privileges of a resident bishop, can choose a Vicar-General. The temporary apostolic administrator, on the contrary, cannot choose a vicar-general unless this power is indicated in his letter of appointment.

c) The apostolic administrator, temporary or permanent, has the same right as the resident bishop over the secret diocesan archives.

d) The salary of the temporary apostolic administrator is the same, *ceteris paribus,* as that of the vicar capitular; the permanent apostolic administrator receives the same salary as a resident bishop.

BIBLIOGRAPHY

Sources

Acta Apostolicae Sedis, Commentarium Officiale, Romae, 1909—

Acta et Decreta Sacrorum Conciliorum Recentiorum Collectio Lacensis, 7 vols., Friburgi Brisgoviae, 1870-1890.

Acta Gregorii Papae XVI, 4 vols., Romae: A. M. Bernasconi, 1901-1904.

Acta Sanctae Sedis, 41 vols., Romae, 1865-1908.

Appendix ad Bullarium Pontificum Sacrae Congregationis de Propaganda Fide, 2 vols., Romae: Typis Collegii Urbani.

Berger, E., *Les Registres D'Innocent IV,* 4 vols., Parisiis: E. Thorin, 1884-1897.

Bizzarri, Andreas, *Collectanea in Usum Secretariae Sacrae Congregationis Episcoporum et Regularium,* Romae: Ex Typographia Polyglotta, 1885.

Bullarium Benedicti Papae XIV, 12 vols., Mechliniae: P. J. Hanico, 1827.

Bullarium Diplomatum et Privilegiorum Sanctorum Romanorum Pontificum Taurinensis Editio, 25 vols., Augustae Taurinorum, 1857-1872.

Bullarium Pontificum Sacrae Congregationis de Propaganda Fide, 5 vols., Romae: Typis Collegii Urbani, 1839-1841.

Bruns, Herm., *Canones Apostolorum et Conciliorum Saeculorum IV, V, VI, VII,* 2 vols., Berolini: G. Reimeri, 1839.

Canones et Decreta Sacrosancti Oecumenici Concilii Tridentini, Lipsiae: Bernhard Tauchnitz, 1863.

Codex Iuris Canonici Pii X Pontificis Maximi iussu digestus Benedicti Papae XV auctoritate promulgatus, Romae: Typis Polyglottis Vaticanis, 1917.

Codicis Iuris Canonici Fontes cura Emi. Petri Card. Gasparri editi, 9 vols., Romae (later Civitate Vaticana): Typis Polyglottis Vaticanis, 1923-1939. (Vols. VII, VIII, IX *ed. cura et studio Emi. Iustiniani Card Serédi*).

Collectanea S. Congregationis de Propaganda Fide, 2 vols., Romae: Typographia Polyglotta S. C. de Propaganda Fide, 1907.

Collectio Lacensis, Acta et Decreta Sacrorum Conciliorum Recentiorunt, 7 vols., Friburgi Brisgoviae, 1870-1890.

Continuatio Bullarii Romani Benedicti XIV, 3 vols., in 4, Prati: In Typographia Aldina, 1854-1847.

Continuatio Bullarii Romani Clementis XIII, 3 vols., Prati: In Typographia Aldina, 1840-1845.

Continuatio Bullarii Romani Pii VI, 3 vols., Prati: In Typographia Aldina, 1847-1849.

Continuatio Bullarii Romani Pii VII, 2 vols., Prati: In Typographia Aldina, 1850-1852.

Continuatio Bullarii Romani Leonis XII, Prati: In Typographia Aldina, 1854.

Corpus Iuris Canonici, ed. Lipsiensis 2., Aemilius Ludovicus Richter—Aemilius Friedburg, 2 vols., Lipsiae, 1922.

Decreta Authentica Congregationis Sacrorum Rituum, 6 vols., Romae, 1898-1927.

De Martinis, R., *Iuris Pontificii de Propaganda Fide*, Pars Prima, 7 vols., Romae, 1888-1897.

Harduin, Jean, *Acta Conciliorum et Epistolae Decretales ac Constitutiones Summorum Pontificum*, 12 vols., Parisiis, 1715.

Jaffé, Philippus, *Regesta Pontificum Romanorum ab condita Ecclesia ad annum post Christum natum* 1198, 2 vols., in I, Berolini: Veit et Socius, 1851.

Labbeus, Philippus—Cossartius, Gabriel, *Sacrosancta Concilia ad Regiam Editionem Exacta*, 15 vols., in 16, Lutetiae Parisiorum, 1671-1672.

Leonis XIII Pontificis Maximi Acta, 22 vols., Romae: Ex Typographia Vaticana, 1881-1903.

Leonis XIII Pontificis Maximi Allocutiones, Epistolae, 6 vols., Romae, 1887-1900.

Mansi, Joannes, *Sacrorum Conciliorum Nova et Amplissima Collectio*, 53 vols., Parisiis, 1901-1927.

Migne, Jacques Paul, *Patrologiae Cursus Completus*, Series Graeca, 161 vols., Parisiis, 1856-1866.

——————, *Patrologiae Cursus Completus*, Series Latina, 221 vols., Parisiis, 1844-1864.

Mollat, G., *Jean XXII: Lettres Communes*, 15 vols., Parisiis: Albert Fontemoing, 1904-1933.

Pii VI Pont. Max. Acta Quibus Ecclesiae Catholicae Calamitatibus in Gallia Consultum est, 2 vols., in I, Romae: Marietti, 1871.

Potthast, Augustus, *Regesta Pontificum Romanorum*, 2 vols., Berolini: R. De Decker, 1874-1875.

Reference Works

Andre, Abbé, *Cours Alphabetique et Methodique de Droit Canon*, Paris, 1844.

Andre, M.-Wagner, J., *Dictionnaire de Droit Canonique*, 3 vols., and a Supplement, Paris: Hippolyte Walzer, 1901.

Andreucci Andreas, *Hierarchia Ecclesiastica in Varias Suas Partes Distributa*, 2 vols., Romae: Generosus Salomonus, 1766.

Ayrinhac, H., *Constitution of the Church in the New Code of Canon Law*, New York: Blase Benziger & Co., Inc., 1925.

———————, *Penal Legislation in the New Code of Canon Law,* New York: Benziger Brothers, 1936.

Baart, Peter, *The Roman Court,* New York: Fr. Pustet & Co., 1895.

(Bachofen) Augustine, Charles, *A Commentary on Canon Law,* vol. II, 4. ed., St. Louis: B. Herder Book Co., 1926.

Baronius, Caesar, *Annales Ecclesiastici,* 37 vols., Barri-Ducis, 1864-1883.

Benedictus XIV, *De Synodo Dioecesana,* 2 vols., Romae: Ex Typographia Sacrae Congregationis de Propaganda Fide, 1806.

Beste, Udalricus, *Introductio in Codicem,* Collegeville, Minnesota: St. John's Abbey Press, 1938.

Bingham, Joseph, *The Antiquities of the Christian Church,* 2 vols., London: Henry G. Bohn, 1850.

Blat, Albertus, *Commentarium Textus Codicis Iuris Canonici,* 6 vols., Romae: Ferrari, 1921-1927.

Bouix, Marie Dominique, *Tractatus de Curia Romana,* Parisiis: Bourget Calas & Cie., 1895.

Bouix, Marie Dominique, *Tractatus de Iudiciis Ecclesiasticis,* 2 vols., Paris, 1883.

Bouscaren, T. Lincoln, *The Canon Law Digest,* Milwaukee: The Bruce Publishing Company, vol. I (1934), vol. II (1937), Supplement (1938).

Brueck, Heinrich, *History of the Catholic Church,* 2 vols., New York, 1885,

Cappello, Felix, *De Curia Romana,* 2 vols., Romae: Fr. Pustet, 1911-1912.

Campagna, Michael, *Il Vicario Generale del Vescovo,* The Catholic University of America, Canon Law Studies, n. 66, Washington, D. C.: The Catholic University of America, 1931.

Castillo, Cayo, *Disertacion Historico-Canonica sobre la Potestad del Cabildo en Sede Vacante o Impedida del Vicario Capitular,* The Catholic University of America, Canon Law Studies, n. 4, Washington, D. C.: The Catholic University of America, 1918.

Cicognani, Amleto, *Canon Law,* Authorized English Version by J. O'Hara and F. Brennan, 2 ed., Philadelphia: The Dolphin Press, 1935.

Coady, John, *The Appointment of Pastors,* The Catholic University of America Canon Law Studies, n. 52, Washington, D. C.: The Catholic University of America, 1929.

Cocchi, Guidus, *Commentarium in Codicem Iuris Canonici,* 5 vols., in 8, Taurinorum Augustae: Marietti, 1922-1930.

Coronata, Mattheus Conte a, *Institutiones Iuris Canonici,* 5 vols., Taurini: Marietti, vols. I et II (2. ed., 1939), vol. III (1933), vol. IV (1935), vol. V (1936).

De Angelis, Philippus, *Praelectiones Iuris Canonici,* 6 vols., Romae: Ex Typographia della Pace, 1877-1878.

De Brabandere, P., *Compendium Iuris Canonici,* 2 vols., Brugis, 1866-1867.

Devoti, Ioannes, *Institutionem Canonicarum Libri IV,* 2 vols., Leodii: H. Dessain, 1860.

Dolan, John, *The Defensor Vinculi,* The Catholic University of America, Canon Law Studies, n. 85, Washington, D. C.: The Catholic University of America, 1934.

Du Cange, Carolus Du Fresne, *Glossarium Ad Scriptores Mediae et Infimae Latinitatis,* 6 vols., Parisiis: C. Osmont, 1733-1736.

Ferraris, Lucius, *Prompta Bibliotheca Canonica, Juridica, Moralis Theologica, necnon Ascetica, Polemica, Rubricistica, Historica,* 9 vols., Romae: 1885-1899.

Funk, Francis Xavier, *A Manual of Church History,* Translated from the German by P. Perciballi, 2 vols., London: Burns, Oates & Washbourne Ltd., 1931.

Gasparri, Petrus, *De Sacra Ordinatione,* 2 vols., Parisiis: Delhomme et Briguet, 1893-1894.

Glynn, John, *The Promoter of Justice,* The Catholic University of America, Canon Law Studies, n. 101, Washington, D. C.: The Catholic University of America, 1936.

Godfrey, John, *The Right of Patronage According to the Code of Canon Law,* The Catholic University of America, Canon Law Studies, n. 21, Washington, D. C.: The Catholic University of America, 1924.

Hagedorn, Francis, *General Legislation on Indulgences,* The Catholic University of America, Canon Law Studides, n. 22, Washington, D. C.: The Catholic University of America, 1924.

Hefele, Carolus—Leclercq, Henricus, *Histoire des Conciles,* 10 vols., in 19, Parisiis, 1907-1938.

Hermes, Henricus, *Dissertatio Historico-Canonica de Capitulo Sede Vacante vel Impedita et de Vicario Capitulari,* Lovanii: Valinthout Fratres, 1873.

Hilling, Nicholas, *Procedure at the Roman Curia,* New York: Joseph F. Wagner, 1907.

Jaeger, Leo Arnold, *The Administration of Vacant and Quasi-Vacant Dioceses in the United States,* The Catholic University of America, Canon Law Studies, n. 81, Washington, D. C.: The Catholic University of America, 1936.

Kearney, Raymond, *The Principles of Delegation,* The Catholic University of America, Canon Law Studies, n. 55, Washington, D. C.: The Catholic University of America, 1929.

Klekotka, Peter, *Diocesan Consultors,* The Catholic University of America, Canon Law Studies, n. 8, Washington, D. C.: The Catholic University of America, 1920.

Lega, Michael, *Praelectiones in Textum Iuris Canonici de Iudiciis Ecclesiasticis,* 4 vols., Romae: Typis Vaticanis, 1896-1901.

Leitner, Martinus, *De Curia Romana,* Ratisbonae: Fr. Pustet, 1909.

Leurenius, Petrus, *Forum Beneficiale,* Romae, 1752.

Many, S., *Praelectiones De Sacra Ordinātione,* Parisiis: Apud Letouzey et Ane, 1905.

Maroto, Philippus, *Institutiones Iuris Canonici,* 2 vols., vol. I (2. ed., Romae: Apud Commentarium Pro Religiosis, 1921), vol. II (1. ed., Madrid: Editorial del Corazion De Maria, 1919).

Martin, Michael, *The Roman Curia,* New York: Benziger Brothers, 1913.

Moeder, John, *The Proper Bishop for Ordination and Dimissorial Letters,* The Catholic University of America, Canon Law Studies, n. 95, Washington, D. C.: The Catholic University of America, 1935.

Moretti, Aloisius, *De Sacris Functionibus,* 4 vols., Taurini, Marietti, 1936-1939.

Murphy, George, *Delinquencies and Penalties in the Administration and Reception of the Sacraments,* The Catholic University of America, Canon Law Studies, n. 17, Washington, D. C.: The Catholic University of America, 1923.

Neuberger, Nicolas, *Canon* 6 *or the Relation of the Codex Iuris Canonici to the Preceding Legislation,* The Catholic University of America, Canon Law Studies, n. 44, Washington, D. C.: The Catholic University of America, 1927.

Nicolai, Franciscus, *Dissertatio Historico-Canonica De Episcopo Visitatore,* Romae: Franciscus Gonzaga, 1710.

Nicolius, Hieronymus, *Lucubrationes Utriusque Iuris Canonici et Civilis,* 2 vols., Romae: Typis Iacobi Dragdonelli, 1662.

Pellegrinus, Carolus, *Praxis Vicariorum,* Venetiis: F. Groppus, 1696.

Petra, Vincentius, *Commentaria Ad Constitutiones Apostolicas,* 5 toms. in 2 vols., Venetiis: Ex Typographia Balleoniana, 1729.

Pirhing, Ernrico, *Ius Canonicum in Quinque Libros Decretalium,* 5 vols., in 4, Dilingae: John Bencard, 1674-1678.

Reiffenstuel, Anacletus, *Ius Canonicum Universum,* 5 vols., in 7, Parisiis: 1864-1882.

Reilly, Edward, *The General Norms of Dispensation,* The Catholic University of America, Canon Law Studies, n. 119, Washington, D. C.: The Catholic University of America, 1939.

Riganti, Joannis, *Constitutiones et Ordinationes Cancellariae Apostolicae,* 4 vols., in 2, Colonia Allobrogum, 1751.

Ryan, Gerald, *Principles of Episcopal Jurisdiction,* The Catholic University of America, Canon Law Studies, n. 120., Washington, D. C.: The Catholic University of America, 1939.

Roberti, Robertus, *De Processibus,* 2 vols., Romae: Apud Aedes Facultatis Iuridicae ad S. Apollinaris, 1926.

Schmelzgrueber, Franciscus, *Ius Ecclesiasticum Universum,* 5 vols., in 12, Romae: 1843-1845.

Shea, John, *History of the Catholic Church in the United States,* 4 vols., New York, 1886-1892.

Shearer, Donald, *Pontificia Americana,* The Catholic University of America, Studies in American Church History, n. 15, Washington, D. C.: The Catholic University of America, 1933.

Tanquery, Ad., *Synopsis Theologiae Dogmaticae,* 23. ed., 3 vols., Parisiis: Desclée et Socii, 1930-1934.

Thomassinus, Ludovicus, *Vetus et Nova Ecclesiae Disciplina circa Beneficia et Beneficiarios,* 3 vols., Lucae: L. Venturini, 1728.

Toso, Albertus, *Ad Codicem Iuris Canonici Commentaria Minora,* 5 vols., Romae: Marietti, 1920-1934.

Van Hove, A., *Commentarium Lovaniense in Codicem Iuris Canonici,* vol. I, *Prolegomena,* Mechliniae: H. Dessain, 1928, Vol. II, *De Legibus Ecclesisticis,* Mechliniae: H. Dessain, 1930.

Vermeersch, A.—Creusen, J., *Epitome Iuris Canonici,* 6 ed., 3 vols., Romae: H. Dessain, 1936-1939.

Villien, A.—Magnin, E., *Dictionnaire de Droit Canonique,* Paris, 1924.

Wernz, F.—Vival, P., *Ius Canonicum,* 7 tom. in 8 vols., Romae: Apud Aedes Universitatis Gregorianiae, 1923-1938.

Wernz, Franciscus, *Ius Decretalium,* 6 vols., Romae: Ex Typographia Polyglotta, 1906-1913.

Winslow, Francis Joseph, *Vicars and Prefects Apostolic,* The Catholic University of America, Canon Law Studies, n. 24, Washington, D. C.: The Catholic University of America, 1924.

Woywod, Stanislaus, *A Practical Commentary on the Code of Canon Law,* 5. ed., 2 vols., New York: Joseph F. Wagner, 1939.

——————, *The New Canon Law,* New York: Joseph F. Wagner, 1918. Zitelli, Zephyrinus, *Apparatus Iuris Ecclesiastici,* Romae: Ex Typis Soc., Edit. Rom., 1886.

Periodicals

Analecta Juris Pontificis, Romae, 1852-1868, Paris, 1869-1891.

Analecta Ecclesiastica, Romae, 1893-1911 (a continuation of the preceding).

Archiv für katholisches Kirchenrecht, Vol. I-VI (1857-1861), Innsbruck; Vols. VI—(1862—), Mainz.

Ecclesiastical Review, The (originally *The American Ecclestiastical Review*), Philadelphia, 1889—.

Periodica de Re Canonica et Morali utili Praesertim Religiosis et Missionariis, Bruges, 1905—.

St. Louis Catholic Historical Review, 5 vols., St. Louis, 1919-1923.

ARTICLES

Creusen, J., "Annotationes," *Periodica*, XXV (1936), (15-17).

Vermeersch, A., "De Constitutione Vicarii Generalis vel delegati facta ab Administratore Apostolico,"—*Periodica*, XIII (1924), 15-17.

(Schaaf, V., ?) "Cathedraticum and the Depression," *Ecclesiastical Review*, LXXXIX (1933), 537.

Hofmeister, P., "Von den Apostolischen Administratorem der Diözesen und Abteien," *Archiv für katholisches Kirchenrecht*," CX (1930), 337-363.

ABBREVIATIONS

AAS—*Acta Apostolicae Sedis.*

AER—*American Ecclesiastical Review.*

AKKR—*Archiv für Katholisches Kirchenrecht.*

ASS—*Acta Sanctae Sedis.*

Fontes—*Codicis Iuris Canonici Fontes cura . . . Gasparri editi.*

Harduin—*Acta Conciliorum . . .*

Mansi—*Sacrorum Conciliorum Nova et Amplissima Collectio.*

MPG—*Migne, Patrologia Graeca.*

MPL—*Migne, Patrologia Latina.*

Periodica—*Periodica de Re Canonica et Morali Utili Praesertim Religiosis et Missionaris.*

BIOGRAPHICAL NOTE

Thomas Joseph McDonough was born on December 5, 1912, in Philadelphia, Pennsylvania. In September, 1928, he entered the Seminary of St. Charles Borromeo, Overbrook, Pennsylvania, where he received the degree of Bachelor of Arts in June, 1934. He was ordained to the priesthood on May 26, 1938. In September, 1938, he enrolled in the School of Canon Law at the Catholic University of America, from which he received the Baccalureate degree in Canon Law in June, 1939, and the Licentiate degree in Canon Law in June, 1940.

INDEX

CANON LAW STUDIES

1. Freriks, Rev. Celestine A., C.PP.S., J.C.D., Religious Congregations in Their External Relations, 121 pp., 1916.
2. Galliher, Rev. Daniel M., O.P., J.C.D., Canonical Elections, 117 pp., 1917.
3. Borkowski, Rev. Aurelius L., O.F.M., J.C.D., De Confraternitatibus Ecclesiasticis, 136 pp., 1918.
4. Castillo, Rev. Cayo, J.C.D., Disertacion Historico-Canonica sobre la Potestad del Cabildo en Sede Vacante o Impedida del Vicario Capitular, 99 pp., 1919 (1918).
5. Kubelbeck, Rev. William J., S.T.B., J.C.D., The Sacred Pentitentiaria and Its Relations to Faculties of Ordinaries and Priests, 129 pp., 1918.
6. Petrovits, Rev. Joseph J.C., S.T.D., J.C.D., The New Church Law On Matrimony, X-461 pp., 1919.
7. Hickey, Rev. John J., S.T.B., J.C.D., Irregularities and Simple Impediments in the New Code of Canon Law, 100 pp., 120.
8. Klekotka, Rev. Peter J., S.T.B., J.C.D., Diocesan Consultors, 179 pp., 1920.
9. Wanenmacher, Rev. Francis, J.C.D., The Evidence in Ecclesiastical Procedure Affecting the Marriage Bond, 1920 (Printed 1935).
10. Golden, Rev. Henry Francis, J.C.D., Parochial Benefices in the New Code, IV-119 pp., 1921 (Printed 1925).
11. Koudelka, Rev. Charles J., J.C.D., Pastors, Their Rights and Duties According to the New Code of Canon Law, 211 pp., 1921.
12. Melo, Rev. Antonius, O.F.M., J.C.D., De Exemptione Regularium, X-188 pp., 1921.
13. Schaaf, Rev. Valentine Theodore, O.F.M., S.T.B., J.C.D., The Cloister, X-180 pp., 1921.
14. Burke, Rev. Thomas Joseph, S.T.D., J.C.D., Competence in Ecclesiastical Tribunals, IV-117 pp., 1922.
15. Leech, Rev. George Leo, J.C.D., A Comparative Study of the Constitution, "Apostolicae Sedis" and the "Codex Juris Canonici," 179 pp., 1922.
16. Motry, Rev. Hubert Louis, S.T.D., J.C.D., Diocesan Faculties According to the Code of Canon Law, II-167 pp., 1922.
17. Murphy, Rev. George Lawrence, J.C.D., Delinquencies and Penalties in the Administration and Reception of the Sacraments, IV-121 pp., 1923.
18. O'Reilly, Rev. John Anthony, S.T.B., J.C.D., Ecclesiastical Sepulture in the New Code of Canon Law, II-129 pp., 1923.

19. Michalicka, Rev. Wenceslas Cyrill, O.S.B., J.C.D., Judicial Procedure in Dismissal of Clerical Exempt Religious, 107 pp., 1923.
20. Dargin, Rev. Edward Vincent, S.T.B., J.C.D., Reserved Cases According to the Code of Canon Law, IV-103, pp., 1924.
21. Godfrey, Rev. John A., S.T.B., J.C.D., The Right of Patronage According to the Code of Canon Law, 153 pp., 1924.
22. Hagedorn, Rev. Francis Edward, J.C.D., General Legislation on Indulgences, II-154 pp., 1924.
23. King, Rev. James Ignatius, J.C.D., The Administration of the Sacraments to Dying Non-Catholics, V-141 pp., 1924.
24. Winslow, Rev. Francis Joseph, A.F.M., J.C.D., Vicars and Prefects Apostolic, IV-149 pp., 1924.
25. Correa, Rev. Jose Servelion, S.T.L., J.C.D., La Potestad Legislativa de la Iglesia Catolica, IV-127 pp., 1925.
26. Dugan, Rev. Henry Francis, A.M., J.C.D., The Judiciary Department of the Diocesan Curia, 87 pp., 1925.
27. Keller, Rev. Charles Frederick, S.T.B., J.C.D., Mass Stipends, 167 pp., 1925.
28. Paschang, Rev. John Linus, J.C.D., The Sacramentals According to the Code of Canon Law, 129 pp., 1925.
29. Pointek, Rev. Cyrillus, O.F.M., S.T.B., J.C.D., De Indulto Exclaustrationis necnon Saecularizationis, XIII-289 pp., 1925.
30. Kearney, Rev. Richard Joseph, S.T.B., J.C.D., Sponsors at Baptism According to the Code of Canon Law, IV-127 pp., 1925.
31. Bartlett, Rev. Chester Joseph, A.M., LL.B., J.C.D., The Tenure of Parochial Property in the United States of America, V-108 pp., 1926.
32. Kilker, Rev. Adrian Jerome, J.C.D., Extreme Unction, V-425 pp., 1926.
33. McCormick, Rev. Robert Emmett, J.C.D., Confessors of Religious, VIII-266 pp., 1926.
34. Miller, Rev. Newton Thomas, J.C.D., Founded Masses According to the Code of Canon Law, VII-93 pp., 1926.
35. Roelker, Rev. Edward G., S.T.D., J.C.D., Principles of Privilege According to the Code of Canon Law, XI-166 pp., 1926.
36. Bakalarczyk, Rev. Richardus, M.I.C., J.U.D., De Novitiatu, VIII-208 pp., 1927.
37. Pizzuti, Rev. Lawrence, O.F.M., J.U.L., De Parochis Religiosis, 1927. (Not printed).
38. Bliley, Rev. Nicholas Martin, O.S.B., J.C.D., Altars According to the Code of Canon Law, XIX-132 pp., 1927.
39. Brown, Mr. Brendan Francis, A.B. LL.M., J.U.D., The Canonical Juristic Personality with Special Reference to Its Status in the United States of America, V-212 pp., 1927.

40. Cavanaugh, Rev. William Thomas, C.P., J.U.D., The Reservation of the Blessed Sacrament, VIII-101 pp., 1927.
41. Doheny, Rev. William J., C.S.C., A.B., J.U.D., Church Property: Modes of Acquisition, X-118 pp., 1927.
42. Feldhaus, Rev. Aloysius H., C.PP.S., J.C.D., Oratories, IX-141 pp., 1927.
43. Kelly, Rev. James Patrick, A.B., J.C.D., The Jurisdiction of the Simple Confessor, X-208 pp., 1927.
44. Neuberger, Rev. Nicholas J., J.C.D., Canon 6 or the Relation of the Codex Juris Canonici to the Preceding Legislation, V-95 pp., 1927.
45. O'Keefe, Rev. Gerald Michael, J.C.D., Matrimonial Dispensations, Powers of Bishops, Priests and Confessors, VIII-232 pp., 1927.
46. Quigley, Rev. Joseph A.M., A.B., J.C.B., Condemned Societies, 139 pp., 1927.
47. Zaplotnik, Rev. Johannes Leo, J.C.D., De Vicariis Foraneis, X-142 pp., 1927.
48. Duskie, Rev. John Aloysius, A.B., J.C.D., The Canonical Status of the Orientals in the United States, VIII-196 pp., 1928.
49. Hyland, Rev. Francis Edward, J.C.D., Excommunication, Its Nature, Historical Development and Effects, VIII-181 pp., 1928.
50. Reinmann, Rev. Gerald Joseph, O.M.C., J.C.D., The Third Order Secular of Saint Francis, 201 pp., 1928.
51. Schenk, Rev. Francis J., J.C.D., The Matrimonial Impediments of Mixed Religion and Disparity of Cult, XVI-318 pp., 1929.
52. Coady, Rev. John Joseph, S.T.D., J.U.D., A.M., The Appointment of Pastors, VIII-150 pp., 1929.
53. Kay, Rev. Thomas Henry, J.C.D., Competence in Matrimonial Procedure, VIII-164 pp., 1929.
54. Turner, Rev. Sidney Joseph, C.P., J.U.D., The Vow of Poverty, XLIX-217 pp., 1929.
55. Kearney, Rev. Raymond, A., A.B., S.T.D., J.C.D., The Principles, of Delegation, VII-149 pp., 1929.
56. Conran, Rev. Edward James, A.B., J.C.D., The Interdict, V-163 pp., 1930.
57. O'Neil, Rev. William H., J.C.D., Papal Rescripts of Favor, VII-218 pp., 1930.
58. Bastnagel, Rev. Clement Vincent, J.U.D., The Appointment of Parochial Adjutants and Assistants, XV-257 pp., 1930.
59. Ferry, Rev. William A., A.B., J.C.D., Stole Fees, V-135 pp., 1930.
60. Costello, Rev. John Michael, A.B., J.C.D., Domicile and Quasi-domicile, VII-201 pp., 1930.
61. Kremer, Rev. Michael Nicholas, A.B., S.T.B., J.C.D., Church Support in the United States, VI-1930.

62. Angulo, Rev. Luis, C.M., J.C.D., Legislation de la Iglesia sobre la intencion en la application de la Santa Misa, VII-104 pp., 1931.
63. Frey, Rev. Wolfgang Norbert, O.S.B., A.B., J.C.D., The Act of Religious Profession, VIII-174 pp., 1931.
64. Roberts, Rev. James Brendan, A.B., J.C.D., The Banns of Marriage, XIV-140 pp., 1931.
65. Ryder, Rev. Raymond Aloysius, A.B., J.C.D., Simony, IX-151 pp., 1931.
66. Campagna, Rev. Angelo, Ph.D., J.U.D., Il Vicario Generale del Vescovo, VII-205 pp., 1931.
67. Cox, Rev. Joseph Godfrey, A.B., J.C.D., The Administration of Seminaries, VI-124 pp., 1931.
68. Gregory, Rev. Donald J., J.U.D., The Pauline Privilege, XV-165 pp., 1931.
69. Donohue, Rev. John F., J.C.D., The Impediment of Crime, VII-110 pp., 1931.
70. Dooley, Rev. Eugene A., O.M.I., J.C.D., Church Law On Sacred Relics, IX-143 pp., 1931.
71. Orth, Rev. Raymond Clement, O.M.C., J.C.D., The Approbation of Religious Institutes, 171 pp., 1931.
72. Pernicone, Rev. Joseph M., A.B., J.C.D., The Ecclesiastical Prohibition of Books, XII-267 pp., 1932.
73. Clinton, Rev. Connell, A.B., J.C.D., The Paschal Precept, IX-108 pp., 1932.
74. Donnelly, Rev. Francis B., A.M., S.T.L., J.C.D., The Diocesan Synod, VIII-125 pp., 1932.
75. Torrente, Rev. Camilo, C.M.F., J.C.D., Las Processiones Sagradas, V-145 pp., 1932.
76. Murphy, Rev. Edwin J., C.PP.S., J.C.D., Suspension Ex Informata Conscientia, XI-122, pp., 1932.
77. Mackenzie, Rev. Eric F., A.M., S.T.L., J.C.D., The Delict of Heresy in its Commission Penalization, Absolution, VII-124 pp., 1932.
78. Lyons Rev. Avitus E., S.T.B., J.C.D., The Collegiate Tribunal of First Instance, XI-147 pp., 1932.
79. Connolly, Rev. Thomas A., J.C.D., Appeals, XI-195 pp., 1932.
80. Sangmeister, Rev. Joseph V., A.B., J.C.D., Force and Fear as Precluding Matrimonial Consent, V-211 pp., 1932.
81. Jaeger, Rev. Leo A., A.B., J.C.D., The Administration of Vacant and Quasi-vacant Episcopal Sees in the United States, IX-229 pp., 1932.
82. Rimlinger, Rev. Herbert T., J.C.D., Error Invalidating Matrimonial Consent, VII-79 pp., 1932.
83. Barrett, Rev. John D.M., S.S., J.C.D., A Comparative Study of the Third Plenary Council of Baltimore and the Code, IX-221 pp., 1932.

84. Carberry, Rev. John J., Ph.D., S.T.D., J.C.D., The Juridical Form of Marriage, X-177 pp., 1934.
85. Dolan, Rev. John L., A.B., J.C.D., The Defensor Vinculi, XII-157 pp., 1934.
86. Hannan, Rev. Jerome D., A.M., S.T.D., LL.B., J.C.D., The Canon Law of Wills, IX-517 pp., 1934.
87. Lemieux, Rev. Delisle A., A.M., J.C.D., The Sentence in Ecclesiastical Procedure, IX-131 pp., 1934.
88. O'Rourke, Rev. James J., A.B., J.C.D., Parish Registers, VII-109 pp., 1934.
89. Timlin, Rev. Bartholomew, O.F.M., A.M., J.C.D., Conditional Matrimonial Consent, X-381 pp., 1934.
90. Wahl, Rev. Francis X., A.B., J.C.D., The Matrimonial Impediments of Consanguinity and Affinity, VI-125 pp., 1934.
91. White, Rev. Robert J., A.B., LL.B., S.T.B., J.C.D., Canonical Ante-Nuptial Promises and the Civil Law, VI-152 pp., 1934.
92. Herrera, Rev. Antonio Parra, O.C.D., J.C.D., Legislation Ecclesiastica sobra el Ayuno y la Abstinencia, XI-191 pp., 1935.
93. Kennedy, Rev. Edwin J., J.C.D., The Special Matrimonial Process in Cases of Evident Nullity, X-165 pp., 1935.
94. Manning, Rev. John J., A.B., J.C.D., Presumption of Law in Matrimonial Procedure, XI-111 pp., 1935.
95. Moeder, Rev. John M., J.C.D., The Proper Bishop for Ordination and Dismissorial Letters, VII-135 pp., 1935.
96. O'Mara, Rev. William A., A.B., J.C.D., Canonical Causes For Matrimonial Dispensations, IX-155 pp., 1935.
97. Reilly, Rev. Peter, J.C.D., Residence of Pastors, IX-81 pp., 1935.
98. Smith, Rev. Mariner T., O.P., S.T.L., J.C.D., The Penal Law For Religious, VII-169 pp., 1935.
99. Whalen, Rev. Donald W., A.M., J.C.D., The Value of Testimonial Evidence in Matrimonial Procedure, XIII-297 pp., 1935.
100. Cleary, Rev. Joseph F., J.C.D., Canonical Limitations on the Alienation of Church Property, VIII-141 pp., 1936.
101. Glynn, Rev. John C., J.C.D., The Promoter of Justice, XX-337 pp., 1936.
102. Brennan, Rev. James H., S.S., A.M., S.T.B., J.C.D., The Simple Convalidation of Marriage, VI-135 pp, 1937.
103. Brunini, Rev. Joseph Bernard, J.C.D., The Clerical Obligations of Canons, 139 and 142, X-121 pp., 1937.
104. Connor, Rev. Maurice, A.B., J.C.D., The Administrative Removal of Pastors, VIII-159 pp., 1937.
105. Guilfoyle, Rev. Merlin Joseph, J.C.D., Custom, XI-144 pp., 1937.
106. Hughes, Rev. James Austin, A.B., A.M., J.C.D., Witnesses in Criminal Trials of Clerics, IX-140 pp., 1937.

107. Jansen, Rev. Raymond J., A.B., S.T.L., J.C.D., Canonical Provisions for Catechetical Instruction, VII-153 pp., 1937.

108. Kealy, Rev. John James, A.B., J.C.D,, The Introductory Libellus in Church Court Procedure, XI-121 pp., 1937.

109. McManus, Rev. James Edward, C.SS.R., J.C.D., The Administration of Temporal Goods in Religious Institutes, XVI-196 pp., 1937.

110. Moriarity, Rev. Eugene James, J.C.D., Oaths in Ecclesiastical Courts, X-115 pp., 1937.

111. Rainer, Rev. Eligius George, C.SS.R., J.C.D., Suspension of Clerics, XVII-249 pp., 1937.

112. Reilly, Rev. Thomas F., C.SS.R., J.C.D., Visitation of Religious, VI-195 pp., 1938.

113. Moriarty, Rev. Francis E., C.SS.R., J.C.D., The Extraordinary Absolution from Censures, XV-334 pp., 1938.

114. Connolly, Rev. Nicholas P., J.C.D., The Canonical Erection of Parishes, X-132 pp., 1938.

115. Donovan, Rev. James Joseph, J.C.D., The Pastor's Obligation in Prenuptial Investigation, XII-322 pp., 1938.

116. Harrigan, Rev. Robert J., M.A., S.T.B., J.C.D., The Radical Sanation of Invalid Marriages, VIII-208 pp., 1938.

117. Boffa, Rev. Conrad Humbert, J.C.D., Canonical Provisions for Catholic Schools, X-211 pp., 1939.

118. Parsons, Rev. Anscar John, O.M. Cap., J.C.D., Canonical Elections, XII-236 pp., 1939.

119. Reilly, Rev. Edward Michael, A.B., J.C.D., The General Norms of Dispensation, X-156 pp., 1939.

120. Ryan, Rev. Gerald Aloysius, A.B., J.C.D., Principles of Episcopal Jurisdiction, XII-172 pp., 1939.

121. Burton, Rev. Francis James, C.S.C., A.B., J.C.D., A Commentary on Canon 1125, X-222 pp., 1940.

122. Miaskiewicz, Rev. Francis Sigismund, J.C.D., Supplied Jurisdiction according to Canon 209, XII-340 pp., 1940.

123. Rice, Rev. Patrick William, A.B., J.C.D., Proof of Death in Prenuptial Investigation, VIII-156 pp., 1940.

124. Anglin, Rev. Thomas Francis, M.S., J.C.L., The Eucharistic Fast.

125. Coleman, Rev. John Jerome, J.C.L., The Minister of Confirmation.

126. Downs, Rev. John Emmanuel, A.B., J.C.L., The Concept of Clerical Immunity.

127. Esswein, Rev. Anthony Albert, J.C.L., Extrajudicial Penal Powers of Ecclesiastical Superiors.

128. Farrell, Rev. Benjamin Francis, M.A., S.T.L., J.C.L., The Rights and Duties of the Local Ordinary Regarding Congregations of Women Religious of Pontifical Approval.

129. Feeney, Rev. Thomas John, A.B., S.T.L., J.C.L., Restitutio in Integrum.
130. Findlay, Rev. Stephen William, O.S.B., A.B., J.C.L., Canonical Norms Governing the Deposition and Degradation of Clerics.
131. Goodwine, Rev. John, A.B., S.T.L., J.C.L., The Right of the Church to Acquire Property.
132. Heston, Rev. Edward Louis, C.S.C., Ph.D., S.T.D., J.C.L., The Alienation of Church Property in the United States .
133. Hogan, Rev. James John, S.T.L., J.C.L.,, Judicial Advocates and Procurators.
134. Kealy, Rev. Thomas M., A.B., Litt. B., J.C.L., Dowry of Women Religious.
135. Keene, Rev. Michael James, O.S.B., J.C.L., Religious Ordinaries and Canon 198.
136. Kerin, Rev. Charles A., S.S., M.A., S.T.B., J.C.L., The Privation of Christian Burial.
137. Louis, Rev. William Francis, M.A., J.C.L., Diocesan Archives.
138. McDevitt, Rev. Gilbert Joseph, A.B., J.C.L., Legitimacy and Legitimation.
139. McDonough, Rev. Thomas Joseph, A.B., J.C.L., Apostolic Administrators.
140. Meier, Rev. Carl Anthony, A.B., J.C.L., Penal Administrative Procedure Against Negligent Pastors.
141. Schmidt, Rev. John Rogg, A.B., J.C.L., The Principles of Authentic Interpretation in Canon 17 of the Code of Canon Law.
142. Slafkosky, Rev. Andrew Leonard, A.B., J.C.L., The Canonical Episcopal Visitation of the Diocese.
143. Swoboda, Rev. Innocent Robert, O.F.M., J.C.L., Ignorance in Relation to the Imputability of Delicts.
144. Dubé, Rev. Arthur Joseph, A.B., J.C.L., The General Principles for the Reckoning of Time in Canon Law.
145. McBride, Rev. James T., A.B., J.C.L., Incardination and Excardination of Seculars.

www.ingramcontent.com/pod-product-compliance
Lightning Source LLC
LaVergne TN
LVHW050245080826
844660LV00012B/598

* 9 7 8 0 8 1 3 2 2 3 2 8 5 *